New Casebooks

aunder

GEORGE ORWELL Edited by Bryan Loughrey and Graham Holderness
SHELLEY: *Frankenstein* Edited by Fred Botting
STOKER: *Dracula* Edited by Glennis Byron
WOOLF: *Mrs Dalloway* and *To the Lighthouse* Edited by Su Reid

(continued overleaf)

DRAMA

BECKETT: *Waiting for Godot* and *Endgame* Edited by Steven Connor
APHRA BEHN Edited by Janet Todd
REVENGE TRAGEDY Edited by Stevie Simkin
SHAKESPEARE: *Antony and Cleopatra* Edited by John Drakakis
SHAKESPEARE: *Hamlet* Edited by Martin Coyle
SHAKESPEARE: *Julius Caesar* Edited by Richard Wilson
SHAKESPEARE: *King Lear* Edited by Kiernan Ryan
SHAKESPEARE: *Macbeth* Edited by Alan Sinfield
SHAKESPEARE: *The Merchant of Venice* Edited by Martin Coyle
SHAKESPEARE: *A Midsummer Night's Dream* Edited by Richard Dutton
SHAKESPEARE: *Much Ado About Nothing* and *The Taming of the Shrew*
  Edited by Marion Wynne-Davies
SHAKESPEARE: *Romeo and Juliet* Edited by R. S. White
SHAKESPEARE: *The Tempest* Edited by R. S. White
SHAKESPEARE: *Twelfth Night* Edited by R. S. White
SHAKESPEARE, FEMINISM AND GENDER: Edited by Kate Chedgzoy
SHAKESPEARE ON FILM Edited by Robert Shaughnessy
SHAKESPEARE IN PERFORMANCE Edited by Robert Shaughnessy
SHAKESPEARE'S HISTORY PLAYS Edited by Graham Holderness
SHAKESPEARE'S PROBLEM PLAYS Edited by Simon Barker
SHAKESPEARE'S ROMANCES Edited by Alison Thorne
SHAKESPEARE'S TRAGEDIES Edited by Susan Zimmerman
JOHN WEBSTER: *The Duchess of Malfi* Edited by Dympna Callaghan

GENERAL THEMES

FEMINIST THEATRE AND THEORY Edited by Helene Keyssar
POST-COLONIAL LITERATURES Edited by Michael Parker and Roger Starkey

---

New Casebooks Series
Series Standing Order
ISBN 0–333–71702–3 hardcover
ISBN 0–333–69345–0 paperback
(outside North America only)

You can receive future titles in this series as they are published by placing a standing order. Please contact your bookseller or, in case of difficulty, write to us at the address below with your name and address, the title of the series and the ISBN quoted above.

Customer Services Department, Macmillan Distribution Ltd
Houndmills, Basingstoke, Hampshire RG21 6XS, England

New Casebooks

ANGELA CARTER

New Casebooks

ANGELA CARTER

EDITED BY ALISON EASTON

palgrave
macmillan

First published in Great Britain 2000 by
MACMILLAN PRESS LTD
Houndmills, Basingstoke, Hampshire RG21 6XS and London
Companies and representatives throughout the world

A catalogue record for this book is available from the British
Library.

ISBN 978-0-333-69216-5

First published in the United States of America 2000 by
ST. MARTIN'S PRESS, INC.,
Scholarly and Reference Division,
175 Fifth Avenue, New York, N.Y. 10010

ISBN 0–312–23140–7 (cloth)

Library of Congress Cataloging-in-Publication Data

Angela Carter / edited by Alison Easton.
p.   cm. -- (New casebooks)
Includes bibliographical references and index.
ISBN 0–312–23140–7
1. Carter, Angela, 1940---Criticism and interpretation. 2. Women
and literature--England--History--20th century. I. Easton, Alison,
1943. II. Series.

PR6053.A73 Z525 2000
823'.914--dc21   99-059760

Logging, pulping and manufacturing processes are
expected to conform to the environmental regulations
of the country of origin.

Printed and bound in Great Britain by
CPI Antony Rowe, Chippenham and Eastbourne

Contents

Acknowledgements

The editor and publishers wish to thank the following for permission to use copyright material:

Christina Britzolakis, for 'Angela Carter's Fetishism', *Textual Practice*, 9:3 (1995), 459–75, by permission of Routledge; Heather Johnson, for 'Textualizing the Double-gendered Body: Forms of the Grotesque in *The Passion of New Eve*', *Review of Contemporary Fiction*, 14:3 (1994), 43–8, by permission of the author; Sally Keenan, for 'Angela Carter's *The Sadeian Woman*: Feminism as Treason', in *The Infernal Desires of Angela Carter: Fiction, Femininity, Feminism*, ed. Joseph Bristow and Trev Lynn Broughton, Longman (1997), pp. 132–48, by permission of Addison-Wesley Longman Ltd; Merja Makinen, for 'Angela Carter's *The Bloody Chamber* and the Decolonization of Feminine Sexuality', *Feminist Review*, 42 (Autumn, 1992), 2–15, by permission of the author; Jill Matus, for 'Blonde, Black and Hottentot Venus: Context and Critique in Angela Carter's *Black Venus*', *Studies in Shorter Fiction*, 28 (1991), 467–76. Copyright © 1991 by Newberry College, by permission of Studies in Shorter Fiction; Gerardine Meaney, for material from *(Un)Like Subjects: Women, Theory, Fiction* (1993), pp. 78–80, 84–100, 120, by permission of Routledge; Sally Robinson, for material from *Engendering the Subject: Gender and Self-Representation in Contemporary Women's Fiction* (1991), pp. 77–9, 97–108, 111–17. Copyright © 1991 State University of New York, by permission of State University of New York Press; Mary Russo, for material from *The Female Grotesque: Risk, Excess, and Modernity* (1994), pp. 159–62, 164–81, by permission of Routledge, Inc.; Kate Webb, for 'Seriously Funny: *Wise Children*', in *Flesh and the Mirror: Essays in the Art of Angela Carter*, ed. Lorna Sage, Virago (1994), pp. 279–307, by permission of the author; Jean Wyatt, for 'The Violence of Gendering: Castration Images in Angela Carter's *The Magic Toyshop, The Passion of New Eve*, and "Peter and the Wolf"', *Women's Studies*, 25:6 (1996), 549–570, by permission of Gordon and Breach Publishers.

Every effort has been made to trace the copyright holders but if any have been inadvertently overlooked the publishers will be pleased to make the necessary arrangement at the first opportunity.

General Editors' Preface

The purpose of this series of New Casebooks is to reveal some of the ways in which contemporary criticism has changed our understanding of commonly studied texts and writers and, indeed, of the nature of criticism itself. Central to the series is a concern with modern critical theory and its effect on current approaches to the study of literature. Each New Casebook editor has been asked to select a sequence of essays which will introduce the reader to the new critical approaches to the text or texts being discussed in the volume and also illuminate the rich interchange between critical theory and critical practice that characterises so much current writing about literature.

In this focus on modern critical thinking and practice New Casebooks aim not only to inform but also to stimulate, with volumes seeking to reflect both the controversy and the excitement of current criticism. Because much of this criticism is difficult and often employs an unfamiliar critical language, editors have been asked to give the reader as much help as they feel is appropriate, but without simplifying the essays or the issues they raise. Again, editors have been asked to supply a list of further reading which will enable readers to follow up issues raised by the essays in the volume.

The project of New Casebooks, then, is to bring together in an illuminating way those critics who best illustrate the ways in which contemporary criticism has established new methods of analysing texts and who have reinvigorated the important debate about how we 'read' literature. The hope is, of course, that New Casebooks will not only open up this debate to a wider audience, but will also encourage students to extend their own ideas, and think afresh about their responses to the texts they are studying.

John Peck and Martin Coyle
University of Wales, Cardiff

Introduction: Reading Angela Carter

ALISON EASTON

I

> It seems to me that the times *shine through* certain writers, so that
> we think they see more clearly than we do, whereas in reality they
> are making *us* see more clearly. ...
>   Otherwise, I like to write about writers who give me pleasure.
> Pleasure has always had a bad press in Britain. I'm all for pleasure,
> too. I wish there was more of it around. I also like to argue.[1]

Angela Carter's readers know well the pleasures her own writings
give: delight in invention still grounded in recognisable reality; the
sensuousness and shocks of the experiences described; the exuber-
antly decorative linguistic surface; the exhilaration in crossing a line
into the unspoken or forbidden; the perfectly hit target of her
dissent; her learned wit and ribald laughter (no decorous English
gentlewoman, this); and finally, relief from terrors faced and survived through a saving irony.

But, as Carter adds, 'I also like to argue'. More pointedly, she
declared, 'All art is political and so is mine. I want readers to understand what it is that I *mean* by my stories.'[2] This does not
imply that she wrote agitprop, urging a particular course of
action: although she says she experimented once or twice with this
kind of didactic writing, she found that 'the process was not en-
joyable' and the genre unsuited to her.[3] Instead, she needed to

redefine the word 'moralist' before it could be a possible description of her work:

> I tend to be a bit mistrustful of the word, moral. ... If morals are to do with the way people behave, then I do think the novel has a moral function. But the moral function should not be hortatory in any way – telling people how to behave. I would see it as a moral compunction to explicate and to find out about things. I suppose I would regard curiosity as a moral function.[4]

To 'argue', in Carter's view, is thus to explore rather than persuade, and exploring ideas, she says, is 'the same thing as telling stories since, for me, a narrative is an argument stated in fictional terms'.[5]

There is, then, no fixed political agenda in Carter's writings; indeed, in the absence of any explicit position, a few of Carter's earliest commentators concluded that her work was apolitical. Noting the playfulness of her work, characteristic of postmodern writing of the 1970s and 80s, they thought her deconstruction of patriarchy's and imperialism's dominant narratives implied the impossibility of any meaning. But Carter came to reject as 'frivolous' the notion that books were only about books, arguing instead that postmodernists were 'sort of tap-dancing on the edge of the abyss'.[6]

Carter, instead, identified herself as a feminist, and saw her writing and life as informed by feminist principles. This is stated most clearly in her autobiographical 1983 'Notes from the Front Line', though the essay also shows why she found it hard to pin down the specifics of this in purely autobiographical terms: 'It's been amazingly difficult,' she concludes, 'trying to sort out how I feel that feminism has affected my work, because that is really saying how it has affected my life and I don't really know that because I live my life, I don't examine it. ... What I *really* like doing is writing fiction and trying to work things out *that* way.'[7] Again, in a later essay she characteristically hesitates about making the following statement (but none the less makes it):

> my life has been most significantly shaped by my gender. ... I spent a good many years being told what I ought to think, and how I ought to behave, and how I ought to write, even, because I was a woman and men thought they had the right to tell me how to feel, but then I stopped listening to them and tried to figure it out for myself but they didn't stop talking, oh, dear no. So I started answering back.[8]

Carter's explorations of gender must, however, be understood in the context of the many different, contested positions that feminism has taken over the past thirty years. Her writings exist in 'contrapuntal relationship' with feminism's constantly evolving and internally conflicted history, never simply representing any one position and never quite in step with anyone – and, as we shall see, this got her into trouble with some readers.[9] True, we can say that she was typical of one strand of British feminism in her concern for the material conditions of women's lives – she remained all her life a socialist, aware of class and rejecting capitalism – but unlike many writers with similar views she chose forms of the fantastical rather than realism as the medium for most of her explorations. Furthermore, she was heterosexual and deeply concerned with understanding sexual conflict between men and women – a difficult perspective to adopt, as Elaine Jordan points out,[10] at a time when sections of feminism were looking instead for new understandings of woman-to-woman relationships, lesbianism and queer identities.[11]

In consequence, while it was mostly feminist critics who first identified Carter as one of Britain's most significant contemporary writers, they did not always find in her works what they wanted politically, or arguably they sometimes found what they liked and needed only by rather simplifying the meaning of her texts. Feminists have been Carter's best and most engaged readers (and this New Casebook's selection is entirely feminist, though of several persuasions), but they have also been her most uneasy and baffled. As Jordan has argued in her influential series of essays, Carter is the more daring and consequently the more disturbing and challenging in taking an idiosyncratic line in feminism's incessant internal and external debates, and she contributes vitally to the feminist project of knowledge and change for that very reason.[12]

Carter frustrates those readers who would like an up-beat feminist story. She offers no clearly visualised utopian vision, no simple narrative of liberation. She makes no recourse to 'Nature' or to 'sex' as spaces of salvation since she cannot see either of these lying wholly outside history and society's constructions. So many of her fictions end with something less than the redefined 'love' with which in *The Sadeian Woman* she sought in a mere sentence and concluding quotation to oppose the savage sexual paradigms of Western society analysed in the rest of that study.[13] We may be drawn to the optimism about women's future expressed by Fevvers, the winged trapeze artist in *Nights at the Circus,* but as her surrogate mother comments: '"It's going to be more complicated than that. ... You improve your analysis, girl, and *then* we'll discuss it."'[14]

Behind the texts are the inequalities of patriarchal capitalism, what Carter calls an 'advanced, industrialized, post-imperialist country in decline'.[15] The long period of Conservative rule in Britain through the 1980s and much of the 1990s was very hard for those with politics like Carter's, and it continues to be a matter of critical debate, as we shall see, just how Carter could balance her scepticism with hope, and her fantastical writings with history's determinations. As Clare Hanson notes, her vision of how power operated in the social order is akin to Foucault's: the omnipresent power structures constitute 'a machine in which everyone is caught, those who exercise power just as much as those over whom it is exercised'.[16]

Feminist readers should therefore beware of turning her stories into anything comfortingly resembling the 'consolatory fictions' she so deplored in certain forms of feminism.[17] Identifying cosily with her characters will only land the reader in difficulty, contradiction or irresolution.[18] Instead, Carter's texts make considerable demands on us. Lorna Sage describes Carter's expectations thus: 'Her narrative utopia – her idea of an idyll for the writer – is a dialogue with the reader, a sort of deconstructive communion.'[19] Her readers can argue back; you don't have to share all her views (I don't) to appreciate them. It is the speculative thrust of her work, her daring, often mischievous 'what if ...?', which is paramount.

This speculative fiction has other consequences for writer and reader. Each fiction was a new project:

> I feel myself challenged by the world. I enjoy writing fiction, and I set myself a number of tasks each time I write a story or start to plan a long piece of fiction. I also ask myself a number of questions, but it's like answering questions in an exam: there are no right answers. There is a selection of answers which could all be adequate to some degree, there are no answers which are unequivocally correct.[20]

So there can be no one paradigm for all her work, no ready-made key. Asked in interviews about the meaning of her 1960s works, she points out how long ago they were written and that she has changed.[21] This is not to say that her works should be read in isolation from one another. Quite the contrary – the reader gains immensely from reading more than a single Carter fiction, and for this reason I hope that readers of this Casebook will read widely in the volume, not only to sample different critical approaches but also to situate the texts you know in the contexts of works less frequently read.

Carter's ideal reader is, then, one who will read the works on several levels, and read more than once: 'As a medievalist', Carter explains, 'I was trained to read books as having many layers.' But she adds a rider to this: 'But it does seem a bit of an imposition to say to readers that if you read this book you have got to be thinking all the time; so it's there only if you want it. From *The Magic Toyshop* onwards I've tried to keep an entertaining surface to the novels, so that you don't have to read them as a system of signification if you don't want to.'[22]

Two things we might note here. First, Carter does not, I think, assume an opposition between politics and pleasure. However, the relation between them is, as we shall see later in this volume, the subject of critical debate about her writings where some commentators have seen the pleasures of the text as possibly complicit with the power structures of a late-capitalist patriarchal society (more on this presently). Second, the density of reference in her texts (Carter was formidably well-read) is something with which we may need help. She uses her reading, what she calls 'a common body of knowledge, a folklore of the intelligentsia',[23] in often playful, inventive or directly interrogatory and resistant ways. We could do with far more academic studies identifying her source material and exploring the uses to which she put it, and we may yet see annotated editions of her work. There are class issues, too, in this great range of high and popular Western culture in her work, which are taken up explicitly in her last novel, *Wise Children*.[24]

II

What, then, have Carter's academic readers made of her work? We have a comparatively short critical history to consider, since apart from many newspaper and magazine reviews there was only a handful of studies before the late 1980s. At that point discussion increased in volume and debates began to crystallise. By the time this Casebook was being prepared in 1997–8 there were about 130 studies published, though nearly all of them are essay-length or shorter, and many on a single tale or novel. Books undertaking the essential task of exploring the range of her work comprehensively are a recent development: by 1998 there were four monographs by Lorna Sage (1994), Sarah Gamble (1997), Linden Peach (1998), and Aidan Day (1998), and two excellent collections of essays by divers hands, edited by Lorna Sage (1994) and by Joseph Bristow and Trev Lynn Broughton (1997). All these books can be strongly recommended.[25]

Approximately ten years' work (preceded by those few pioneers) is not a long time to establish a field of study. Inevitably, the author who liked to argue has provoked a deal of argument. Furthermore, the relationship between critics and contemporary writing is bound to be intimate, compelling and tricky. Possibly we need to be particularly wary where text and reader seem very close, particularly in the case of any academic critic who seems to find it easy to map certain theories onto Carter's fictions: critics sometimes praise Carter for 'anticipating' a certain theorist, or write confidently about 'using' certain theoretical ideas to 'explicate' her work, thereby raising questions about the status of theory and its relation to the literary text.

There are difficulties attendant on what Christina Britzolakis criticises as this 'celebratory symbiosis of fiction and theory'.[26] A glance at the bibliography Carter appends to *The Sadeian Woman* (1979) quickly shows us the issue at stake. Her philosophical re-search for this book bears a definite resemblance to the mental landscape of literary critics of the 1990s in its list of major European theoretical thinkers: Adorno, Barthes, Bataille, Fanon, Foucault, Klein and Lacan, all listed in Carter's bibliography, were not the standard fare of many literary critics in the 1970s, but they are now. Other thinkers whom Carter was reading at this time include Benjamin, Gramsci and Lévi-Strauss, as well as some major European philosophers of the past including standard figures such as Freud and Marx. Bakhtin remains the exception – someone she read only after critics had pointed out connections with *Nights at the Circus*.[27] As Lorna Sage remarks, 'She needed to *theorise* in order to feel in charge, and to cheer herself up, and that has left its mark marvellously on this 1970s fiction, which is full of ideas, *armed* with them.'[28]

However, what we are looking at here is not a matter of these theorists' direct 'influence' on Carter's writings, but rather an inventive, playful, sometimes critical and resisting use of these ideas in a fictional medium. There is no easy fit between text and theory. Ideas of carnival or maternity or identity as performance all undergo scrutiny as the fiction imagines beyond the theoretical positions. Carter (unlike certain literary critics) does not treat these ideas reverentially as Truth; after all, many of these theorists are responding to the same historical situation and cultural moment as Carter. Useful and revelatory as their theories of subjectivity or patriarchy may be, these, too, are historically produced discourses, and cannot be employed simply to confirm the validity or value of Carter's visions. We might, as one critic suggests, just as usefully use Carter to explicate the theorists.[29] Carter declared war on the myths of Western culture, and we need to be careful not to create new grand narratives out of favoured theorists.

This dialogical relationship with the theorists of Western society thus creates an intriguing and stimulating situation for academic criticism of Carter's work. It impacts, too, on a Casebook series like this one which aims to organise its material in relation to critical approaches. So, when material for this critical anthology on Carter was selected, preference was given to those studies where there is some dialogue between literary and critical texts which puts *both* texts and theories under discussion, rather than where theory is used as a key which could unlock the literary text.

But criticism of Carter's writing makes its highly contentious start with feminist questions of a more obviously political nature. Given that issues of sexuality, violence and the representation of women dominated 1970s and 80s feminist debates generally (for example, the campaigns against pornography), it is not surprising that *The Bloody Chamber* and *The Sadeian Woman* were the early focus for discussions of Carter's work (and for that reason this Casebook opens with analyses of these texts which also usefully review how earlier critics had responded). Both works are revisions/rereadings of culturally significant texts – fairy tales and the writings of the Marquis de Sade. Early, untroubled praise of Carter's recasting of patriarchal texts (a well-defined interest among feminist literary scholars in the late 1970s and early 80s)[30] was quickly followed by critics – interestingly both her would-be admirers and her convinced detractors – who argued that, in spite of Carter's deconstructive and transformative agenda, she had ended up by reproducing, rather than successfully revising, the oppression and perversities of patriarchal sexual relations which construct and are constructed by these narratives and representations of sexual roles.[31] Others went further in arguing that reactionary forms can never be revised, and that they are an all-powerful straitjacket restraining the would-be revolutionary from any movement for change.[32] These critics ask whether Carter had been caught up in the scenarios of sexual violence, or, even worse, had validated in *The Sadeian Woman* the arch pornographer of Western culture. Had Carter's outrageous daring in playing with pitch left her with dirty hands?

So central to Carter's *oeuvre* is the deconstruction and rewriting of the master narratives of the Western world (as she described it, 'putting of new wine in old bottles and, in some cases old wine in new bottles'[33]), that these issues continue in some shape or form through commentaries on other writings: if there is no space that is absolutely 'outside' existing social and cultural power structures, then what position on what margin might one occupy instead, what political agency is available to women to effect change, and in what sense can one call Carter 'dangerous' or 'subversive'; what strategies, both by the writer and her characters, can be deployed to disrupt gender identities and the economic systems to which they are tied; in particular, how do mimicry, masquerade, parody and carnival (all in some sense 'rewriting') operate; who are Carter's readers, in what differing ways do they relate to the texts and what complexities does the pervasive textual irony create for the reading process?

Both Merja Makinen's and Sally Keenan's essays (essays 1 and 2 in this volume) address those early worries about Carter's possible complicity with supposedly unalterable, all-powerful patriarchal structures. Makinen cuts through some of the critical tangle by analysing the complexities and subtleties of a *multilayered*, historically specific reading process in *The Bloody Chamber and Other Stories* which should prevent readers from identifying uncritically with the volume's heroines. Redefining the beasts in the text as aspects of the female drive for pleasure further undermines any tendency to read the book simply as the conflict between men and women. Instead, Makinen emphasises irony as Carter's prime strategy (redefined here as a simultaneous rejection and reappropriation of discourses under consideration). Makinen also suggests that meanings are produced through interactions between all ten stories rather than in separate stories. This, she argues, opens up the text to a deliberately disturbing variety of forms of female heterosexuality rather than producing uncomplicated scenarios of total liberation. In Makinen's hands *The Bloody Chamber* remains an uncomfortable book, but a knowing, rational one.

It is useful to read Sally Keenan's essay on *The Sadeian Woman* alongside Makinen's piece. Keenan also does not want to underestimate Carter's challenges both to patriarchal structures and to certain feminist positions (indeed, *The Sadeian Woman* has been a prime target for her detractors), and, like Makinen, Keenan is interested in how the text has been and can be read. She assists in the understanding of this often underread/misread and maligned work by approaching it historically, showing the feminist contexts in which it was produced and received.[34] This fits well with Carter's own determination within the text to take sexual relations out of the domain of 'nature', and restore their historically changing social and economic contexts: 'our flesh arrives to us out of history, like everything else does'.[35] With its analysis of forms of sexuality in Western society, *The Sadeian Woman* is essential reading for the student of Carter's work, both for the issues it wrestles with and its presentational strategies: using Sade as her starting point Carter intends to jolt her readers out of customary modes of thinking. Keenan's other contribution is to give the text the close and meticulously careful reading it requires, unravelling what Carter says from what she does not say, catching her nuances and paradoxes without skirting the murkier corners of her argument, and showing how typically Carter as a feminist ran headfirst into important issues but at a tangent to the paths adopted by other feminists of the period.

III

Not surprisingly, given the centrality of sexuality in Carter's work, psychoanalytic interpretations abound in academic studies of her writing, especially feminist reconsiderations of various psychoanalytic explanations of gender construction and gender relations. The next three essays in this Casebook, by Jean Wyatt, Sally Robinson, and Gerardine Meaney are all in their different ways concerned with gendered subjectivities (especially female, but also male) – that is, poststructuralist theories, which have replaced traditional liberal humanist notions of the self-generating individual with the idea of subjectivity as the experience of the subject within the social matrix and constituted by discourse, ideology and the symbolic order.

Carter herself, as previously discussed, was well versed in Freudian and post-Freudian theories, but was critical, sceptical and to an extent dismissive of certain psychoanalytic master (and indeed mistress) narratives which have been used to legitimise either patriarchal structures, identities and myths or some feminist counterpositions. These three critics trace how Carter 'writes back' against such narratives and discourses; they also play Carter's texts against other major philosophical positions. Though primarily focused on the psychic world, these studies are no less concerned with the political than the other contributors' pieces in this volume. They ask how these dominant structures are disrupted in Carter's texts, what counter-narratives may evolve, how one might rethink female and male subjectivities. In the face of the postmodern dismissal of traditional notions of identity and what Lacan diagnosed as cultural 'castration' (see Robinson and Meaney on the former and Wyatt's essay for an account of the latter), these critics ask questions about political agency and about access to language and to history, that realm where social change is effected and from which most women have traditionally been exiled.

Jean Wyatt's account (essay 3) of Freud's ideas of female and male sexuality, especially the psychological and cultural significance he gave to what he deemed women's anatomical lack (that is, no penis), makes clear Carter's target in three of her fictions. Wyatt shows why the tender detailed description of the wolf girl's genitalia in 'Peter and the Wolf' triumphs as a 'vision of real difference' in contradistinction to Freud, 'springing the subject free from established categories of thought'.[36] This standing outside to look in at cultural systems continues in *The Passion of New Eve* and *The Magic Toyshop*. Wyatt works with Lacan's extension of Freudian 'castration' as the fate of *both* the male and female child as they enter the social order (though the male commonly conceals this). This idea is shown to underpin the world of *The Passion of New Eve*, though it is worth asking whether Carter is querying rather than affirming these ideas by including a sense of the absurdity, pathos and possibilities of the novel's castrated male protagonists and by showing us their subjectivities. Carter's parodic rehearsal of Freud continues with the adolescent girl in *The Magic Toyshop*, described in suffocating detail within the phallocentric discourses and practices that Freud both identifies and validates. Carter emphasises the violence such ideas invoke but also treats them in self-consciously exaggerated descriptions which distance the reader to some extent (the 'raping' swan is terrifying but in Finn's hands surely rendered ludicrous).

Heroes and Villains is another of Carter's stories interrogating how an adolescent girl comes to assume 'feminine' roles. Freud's thinking on sexuality and woman still lurks, though in parodic form, in this novel's futuristic world, but Gerardine Meaney (essay 4) focuses more on what happens in Carter's hands to Lacanian perspectives on subjectivity and to the French feminist Irigaray's notions of an alternative female imaginary (that is, conscious and unconscious images and fantasies that partly include material from infantile, pre-verbal experience of an imagined unity and control). Meaney investigates female subjectivity by reading the novel in a mutually illuminating critique alongside another French feminist, Kristeva, whose essays on maternity and ideas about language, women's responses to their exile from history (another form of castration) and the female imaginary have all been very important to feminine theorising.

Our understanding of how Carter's 'speculative fiction' inhabits important margins is aided by Kristeva's complex ideas on what Meaney calls the 'anachronic' (the place where historical time is intersected disruptively by other forms of time) and her insistence that the semiotic (rhythmic patterns surviving from the pre-linguistic phase of one's development) exists only in dialectical relation with the symbolic (the order of culture and language). Meaney's theorising of women's space/time asks questions of agency and social change, and demonstrates how problematic this novel makes the French feminist subversive alliance of the feminine and the unconscious by creating male characters who figure female desire. Neither these nor other feminist ideas about the pre-oedipal as a wonderful maternal space outside the symbolic order remained unscathed in this novel.

Sally Robinson's poststructuralist study (essay 5) sets up another dialogue between current theorists and Carter's texts in order to put certain theoretical 'truths' into crisis – in this case Derrida's deconstruction, in *Spurs*, of phallocentric authority through a reworked narrative of sexual difference and Irigaray's response to his work. Robinson argues that it is important for feminism to resist some (but not all) of postmodernism's tendencies to dissolve all categories. Instead, her book is concerned with the possibility of working towards new theories and practices of speaking, writing and acting subjects, thereby displacing gender as essence (that is, the universalist notion of 'Woman') without transcending gender.

In the section of Robinson's study reprinted in this Casebook, she demonstrates Carter's parody in *The Infernal Desire Machines of Doctor Hoffman* of both liberal humanist and postmodern ways of de/constructing the subject and his/her world. Again the master narratives of masculine desire are written afresh: a man's subjectivity is mimicked in order to describe the fictions of his sexuality and the power structures to which these belong, including empire and colonialism. Carter's performances of parody and masquerade do not simply repeat or reaffirm those discourses of domination and subordination (that old worry of some of Carter's critics). Instead, the reader-positions of voyeurism and narcissism are disrupted by metafictional strategies (where the text draws attention to itself), thus subverting the mechanisms of identification with the characters and positioning the reader 'outside'.

IV

The next three essays in this Casebook, by Heather Johnson, Mary Russo and Jill Matus (essays 6, 7 and 8), continue the exploration of subjectivity and representation, moving the discussion from the analysis of gender norms and the binaries of patriarchal sexuality towards different narratives, in particular exploring the female body in the figure of the grotesque. In doing this they are less concerned with an individual, psychic model of specularity and more with the social relations of spectacle and performance and with questions of how liberating such masquerades might be. For Carter gender was a relation of power, and such power relations (not only those of patriarchy but of racism, capitalism and empire) 'do not simply go away when they are deconstructed'; as Russo contends, psychoanalytic models are never sufficient answer to the constraints of gender.[37] These three critics draw on various aspects of Bakhtin's work – his ideas about the grotesque, dialogic relations, and carnival (which temporarily reverses hierarchies) – though in each case the critics have needed to add the categories of gender and/or race to Bakhtin's original theorising. The work of two other analysts of power – Foucault and Benjamin – also assists these explorations of political, social and economic relations, and both are concerned with history. Carter's texts are viewed as occupying historically specific situations which demand close examination. As Meaney points out, there is a 'recurrent conflict' in Carter's writings 'between resistance to history as the agent of determinism and the desire for access to history as the arena of change'.[38]

Heather Johnson's essay (essay 6) takes up Bakhtin's notion of the post-Romantic grotesque – a transgressive body which meets hostility, alienation, inhumanity and exile. To this she adds Russo's idea of the Female Grotesque which is doubly marginalised because of gender, and Kristeva's category of the abject (that which traumatically disturbs identity and system, and must be expelled), and, briefly, Foucault on questions of sexual status. This enables her to trace the shifting values of the grotesque in *The Passion of New Eve* from its deforming parody of gender norms in all their constructiveness, to possible sites of pleasure beyond those gender boundaries and finally beyond history also.

Mary Russo's concern (essay 7) is with the grotesque as a process through which differently gendered bodies are deployed in provocative, new and possibly transformative ways. Hers is a historical materialist reading of spectacle, masquerade and carnival, reflecting the condition of late capitalism and its modes of production. Like some other commentators in this Casebook, Russo is cautious about alternatives: she sees Carter intervening in utopian narratives of progress, but suggests none the less the possibility of new political aggregates and dialogues – 'provisional, uncomfortable, even conflictual, coalitions of bodies'.[39]

Jeanne Duval, Baudelaire's EuroAfrican mistress and the central figure in Carter's 'Black Venus', had historically been constructed as another grotesque body by various powerful discourses – 'a network of associations from nineteenth-century comparative anthropology, physiology and anatomy, as well as from art and literature, in which blackness, primitive sexuality, prostitution and disease are closely linked'.[40] In establishing Carter's historical sense in her rewriting of Duval's life, Jill Matus (essay 8) also demonstrates her refusal of essentialism, of human nature as given and unchanging. Carter's sense of 'difference' and the power differentials involved in race and class as well as gender also offers a fresh take on that old 'problem' of her demythologising and rewriting. Matus employs perspectives provided by postcolonial theory as well as Bakhtin's 'dialogic interchange' to explore Carter's situation as a white author having to find a position from which to give this silenced person speech without assuming any authority to tell the 'real story'.[41]

V

This question of Carter's position is also central to the essays that follow Matus's piece in this volume, though they take different critical perspectives. The first time Lorna Sage interviewed Carter (in 1977), she asked her where she felt she belonged – a good question for a writer whose work at the time 'prowl[ed] around on the fringes of the proper English novel like dream-monsters'. On that occasion Carter answered in terms of the problematics of region, nation and class in relation to her family, 'this peculiar rootless, upward, downward, sideways socially mobile family, living in twilight zones': 'I always felt foreign'. But, as we have seen, Carter's position is more complicated than that of the simple outsider. Carter herself suggests her more culturally involved and historically determined position in that first interview: 'I do actually believe that everybody is the product of their environment, and you get the seeds of how you transcend your environment from the environment itself.'[42]

As Sage, one of the earliest and most insightful of Carter's commentators, argues, Carter's fiction 'unravels the romance of exclusion' (a romance embraced both by the pursuit of otherness in the 1960s and by 1970s feminist formulations of the woman writer as a virtuous subversive). Sage points out that '[t]he world of outsiders is not, for her, either so securely marginal, or so confined as that. Carter's novels and stories start with more sophisticated assumptions, in a setting where the structures of power (literary or otherwise) are a lot less obvious.'[43] Sage quotes Foucault to describe how power is figured in Carter's texts: 'power is everywhere; not because it embraces everything, but because it comes from everywhere'. Sage goes on, 'For Foucault there is no big binary opposition between (for example) "law" and "revolt"; but rather "a plurality of resistances ... resistances that are possible, necessary, improbable; others that are spontaneous, savage, solitary, concerted, rampant or violent; still others that are quick to compromise, interested, or sacrificial.'[44]

Christina Britzolakis and Kate Webb have different answers to this question of where Carter's works belong, and so recast those critical debates of the previous decade. Both take up Freud's accounts of libido, sexual identity and the family, but, following Benjamin, they do this in materialist and historicised contexts informed by Marx and, in Webb's case, Foucault, and take on issues of social class. (If there is one important aspect of Carter's writings too little considered by critics in the past twenty years, it is class, though it informs much of her work directly and indirectly.) Theatricality, spectacle and their associated tropes continue in these final two essays to be a focus for the discussion of identity and political challenge.

Christina Britzolakis starts her argument (essay 9) by questioning recent interest in reading Carter's writings in relation to Judith Butler's ideas of gender as performance.[45] She asks whether this idea of staging femininity is regressive rather than liberating. Britzolakis then reads Carter's relationship to global consumerist culture in terms of fetishism, taking her cue from Benjamin, who linked Marx's idea of commodity fetishism with Freud's fetish as a memorial of the male castration complex. She sees in Carter's work evidence of her succumbing to the dangerous attractions of what she meant rather to attack, thus taking a different view of this situation from Merja Makinen. Britzolakis is disturbed by what she regards as Carter's verbal fetishism – clearly a different view of language from Bakhtin's politically charged dialogic interchange (see Matus's essay). This is a less ironic Carter – for example, in Britzolakis's reading it is the author who fetishises the heroine, rather than the male protagonist from whose perspective she is described. Furthermore, Britzolakis's view must also leave open the question whether Carter, who had also read Benjamin ('I'm an admirer of Walter Benjamin'),[46] understands and shares his analysis rather than simply exemplifies the cultural situation he diagnosed.

Kate Webb's exploration of *Wise Children* (essay 10) suggests another possible route through the ambivalences and tensions identified by Britzolakis. While never denying the persistence of dualistic structures of power (figured here as the legitimate and the illegitimate), Webb avoids any simple celebration of otherness, noting that such might imply a valorisation of the system which produces the outsiders. Instead, she highlights the plurality and hybridity of British culture in the novel (particularly in terms of class, though race is another element). This plurality is not a post-modernist deletion of value but an insistence on contradiction and difference. Historically these have always existed underneath the traditional myth of order, and continue to coexist and negotiate with the powerful. This produces a politically complex position which offers a notion of the subject who is neither wholly outside nor wholly determined by the social order: Dora instead 'manages to both have her cake and eat it'[47] – to revel in her 'illegitimacy' and yet show she is part of a multiculture, which includes the world of the father. Bakhtinian carnival and masquerade are treated with wariness for what they might do to women, and yet with a sense of imagined possibilities. Where Britzolakis diagnoses verbal fetishism and impersonation, Webb argues that *Wise Children* employs an eclectic range of styles, from all levels of culture, that are used resourcefully in Bakhtinian dialogue.

And as for future possibilities among studies of Carter's work, the next decade will no doubt see many new things. My 'wish list' includes far more thorough work placing Carter and her writings in fully historicised and localised contexts as befits an author who insisted that 'everything' comes out of history (this would, for example, include her constructions of the Sixties, of Japan and of the 'British', as well as her take on a number of twentieth-century philosophers); studies of how class is present in her work; studies that set up a detailed and extended dialogue between Carter's writings and first, Foucault, and second, Benjamin, and perhaps third, Adorno ('I've learnt a lot from him');[48] and much, much more on her poetics – close textual work on her sources and her multilayered meanings, the intricacies of tone and structure. Indeed, it is highly probable that the second edition of this New Casebook may look very different.

NOTES

I would like to thank both Jo Sadler and Martin Coyle for the invaluable help they gave me in preparing this volume.

1. Angela Carter, *Expletives Deleted: Selected Writings* (London, 1992), p. 4.

2. See this volume, p. 214

3. See Helen Cagney Watts, 'An Interview With Angela Carter', *Bête Noire*, 8 (August 1985), 163.

4. Angela Carter in interview, in John Haffenden, *Novelists in Interview* (London: 1985), p. 96.

5. Carter, *Come Unto These Yellow Sands: Four Radio Plays* (Newcastle-Upon-Tyne, 1985), p. 13.

6. Kerryn Goldsworthy, 'Interview: Angela Carter', *Meanjin*, 44:1 (March 1985), 5. See also Haffenden, *Novelists in Interview*, p. 79.

7. Carter, 'Notes from the Front Line', in *Gender and Writing*, ed. Michelene Wandor (London, 1985), p. 77.

8. Carter, *Expletives Deleted*, p. 5.

9. See Joseph Bristow and Trev Lynn Broughton (eds), 'Introduction', *The Infernal Desires of Angela Carter: Fiction, Femininity, Feminism* (London, 1997), p. 19. See also Elaine Jordan, 'The Dangerous Edge', in *Flesh and the Mirror: Essays on the Art of Angela Carter*, ed. Lorna Sage (London, 1994), pp. 189–215.

10. Jordan, 'The Dangers of Angela Carter', in *New Feminist Discourses: Critical Essays on Theories and Texts*, ed. Isobel Armstrong (London, 1992), p. 128; see also Jordan, 'Enthralment: Angela Carter's Speculative Fictions', in *Plotting Change: Contemporary Women's Fictions*, ed. Linda Anderson (London, 1990), pp. 19–40.

11. Critics with lesbian concerns continue to find less than they would like in Carter's work. See Paulina Palmer, 'From "Coded Mannequin" to Bird Woman: Angela Carter's Magic Flight', in *Women Reading Women's Writing* (Brighton, 1987), pp. 179–205; and Patricia Dunker, 'Queer Gothic: Angela Carter and the Lost Narratives of Sexual Subversion', *Critical Survey*, 8:1 (1996), 58–68.

12. See notes 9 and 10 above; also Jordan, 'Down the Road, or History Rehearsed', in *Postmodernism and the Re-Reading of Modernity*, ed. Peter Hulme and Margaret Iverson (Manchester, 1992), pp. 159–79.

13. Carter, *The Sadeian Woman* (London, 1979), pp. 150–1.

14. Carter, *Nights at the Circus* (London, 1984), p. 286.

15. Carter, 'Notes from the Front Line', p. 73.

16. Clare Hanson, '"The Red Dawn Breaking Over Clapham": Carter and the Limits of Artifice', in *The Infernal Desires of Angela Carter*, ed. Bristow and Broughton, pp. 64–5. As Carter herself remarked, 'The whole point about the feast of fools is that things went on as they did before, after it stopped' (Lorna Sage, 'Angela Carter Interviewed by Lorna Sage', in *New Writing*, ed. Malcolm Bradbury and Judith Cooke [London, 1992], p. 188).

17. Carter, *The Sadeian Woman*, p. 106. Carter is talking here about the 'theory of maternal superiority', but earlier she had included 'all mythic versions of women' (p. 5).

18. See Carter's comments on how she herself read: 'I remember ... having a great argument with somebody about feeling the need to identify with characters in fiction. I'd never felt this at all, I didn't see that there was any need to do this' (Watts, 'An Interview with Angela Carter', 167).

19. Lorna Sage, *Angela Carter* (Plymouth, 1994), p. 50.

20. Haffenden, *Novelists in Interview*, p. 79.

21. See Anna Katsavos, 'An Interview with Angela Carter', *Journal of Contemporary Fiction*, 14:1 (1994), 12; speaking of the 'continuum' of her work and beliefs, she comments, 'I've been publishing fiction since 1966, and I've changed a lot in the way I approach the world and in the way that I organise the world'.

22. Haffenden, *Novelists in Interview*, p. 87.

23. Ibid., p. 82.

24. See Carter's comments on *Wise Children* in interview: 'It's very broadly about class, our two distinct cultures in Britain. ... The absolute fissure between bourgeois culture and non-bourgeois culture' (Scott Bradfield, 'Remembering Angela Carter', *Review of Contemporary Fiction*, 14:3 [1994], 91).

25. Sage, *Angela Carter*; Sarah Gamble, *Angela Carter: Writing from the Front Line* (Edinburgh, 1997); Linden Peach, *Angela Carter* (Basingstoke, 1998); Aidan Day, *Angela Carter: The Rational* Glass (Manchester 1998); Sage (ed.), *Flesh and the Mirror*; Bristow and Broughton (eds), *The Infernal Desires of Angela Carter*.

26. See this volume, p. 174

27. Sage, *New Writing*, p. 188.

28. Sage, *Angela Carter*, p. 35.

29. Elaine Jordan, 'Afterword', in *The Infernal Desires of Angela Carter*, ed. Bristow and Broughton, p. 219.

30. Ellen Cronan Rose, 'Through the Looking Glass: When Women Tell Fairy Stories', in *The Voyage In: Fictions of Female Development* (Hanover, NH, 1983), pp. 209–27. See also Sandra M. Gilbert and Susan Gubar, *The Madwoman in the Attic: The Woman Writer and the Nineteenth-Century Literary Imagination* (New Haven, CT, 1979).

31. Patricia Dunker, 'Re-Imagining the Fairy Tales: Angela Carter's Bloody Chambers', *Literature and History*, 10:1 (1984), 3–14; and Robert Clark, 'Angela Carter's Desire Machine', *Women's Studies*, 14 (1987), 146–61.

32. Suzanne Kappeler, *The Pornography of Representation* (Cambridge, 1986), pp. 133–47. For a different view, see Gamble, *Angela Carter*, pp. 97–104.

33. Carter, 'Notes From the Front Line', p. 76.

34. See also Robin Ann Sheets, 'Pornography, Fairy Tales, and Feminism: Angela Carter's "The Bloody Chamber" ', *Journal of the History of Sexuality*, 1:4 (1991), 633–57, for a detailed consideration of those feminist debates round pornography.

35. Carter, *The Sadeian Woman*, p. 9.

36. See this volume, p. 61.

37. Sally Robinson, *Gendering the Subject: Gender and Self-Representation in Contemporary Women's Fiction* (Albany, NY, 1991), p. 3; for the comment by Mary Russo, see this volume, p. 143.

38. See this volume, p. 99.

39. See this volume, p. 153.

40. See this volume, p. 162.

41. See also Carter's comments on how race and colonialism impact on white Europeans, including herself: Haffenden, *Novelists in Interview*, pp. 94–5; Carter, 'Notes from the Front Line', pp. 72–3; and Kerryn Goldsworthy, 'Interview', pp. 10 and 13.

42. Lorna Sage, 'The Savage Sideshow: A Profile of Angela Carter', *New Review*, 4: 39/40 (1977), 53.

43. Sage, *Women in the House of Fiction: Post-War Women Novelists* (London, 1992), p. 168. See also Gamble, *Angela Carter*.

44. Sage, *Women in the House of Fiction*, pp. 173 and 174.

45. Judith Butler, *Gender Trouble: Feminism and the Subversion of Identity* (London, 1990). See this volume, p. 185, note 5.

46. Goldsworthy, 'Interview', p. 12.

47. See this volume, p. 194.

48. Watts, 'An Interview with Angela Carter', 175.

Angela Carter's *The Bloody Chamber* and the Decolonisation of Feminine Sexuality

MERJA MAKINEN

The last thing you'd ever need to do with an Angela Carter text is to send it on an assertiveness training course. With her death (and no one has spoken more effectively on that than her last novel, *Wise Children*, 'a broken heart is never a tragedy. Only untimely death is a tragedy') the obituaries have started to evoke her as the gentle, wonderful white witch of the north. But far from being gentle, Carter's texts were known for the excessiveness of their violence and, latterly, the almost violent exuberance of their excess. Many a reader has found the savagery with which she can attack cultural stereotypes disturbing, even alienating. Personally I found (and find) it exhilarating – you never knew what was coming next from the avant-garde literary terrorist of feminism.

Margaret Atwood's memorial in the *Observer* opens with Carter's 'intelligence and kindness' and goes on to construct her as a mythical fairy-tale figure: 'The amazing thing about her, for me, was that someone who looked so much like the Fairy Godmother ... should actually *be* so much like the Fairy Godmother. She seemed always on the verge of bestowing something – some talisman, some magic token ...'Lorna Sage's obituary in the *Guardian* talked of her 'powers of enchantment and hilarity, her generous inventiveness' while the *Late Show*'s memorial on BBC2 had the presenter calling her the 'white witch of English literature', J. G. Ballard a 'friendly witch', and Salman Rushdie claimed 'English literature has lost its high sorceress, its benevolent witch queen ... deprived of the fairy queen we cannot find the magic that will heal us' and finished by describing her as 'a very good wizard, perhaps the first wizard de-luxe'.[1] But this concurrence of white witch/fairy godmother mythologising needs watching; it is always the dangerously problematic that are mythologised in order to make them less dangerous. As Carter herself argued strongly in *Sadeian Woman*, 'if women allow themselves to be consoled for their culturally determined lack of access to the modes of intellectual debate by the invocation of hypothetical great goddesses, they are simply flattering themselves into submission (a technique often used on them by men).'

The books are not by some benign magician. The strengths and the dangers of her texts lie in a much more aggressive subversiveness and a much more active eroticism than perhaps the decorum around death can allow. For me, the problematics of Carter's writing were captured with more frankness when *New Socialist* dubbed her – wrongly, I think, but wittily – the 'high-priestess of post-graduate porn' in 1987. For Carter's work has consistently dealt with representations of the physical abuse of women in phallocentric cultures, of women alienated from themselves within the male gaze, and conversely of women who grab their sexuality and fight back, of women troubled by and even powered by their own violence.

Clearly, Angela Carter was best known for her feminist re-writing of fairy-tales; the memorials blurring stories with story-teller stand testimony to that. *The Bloody Chamber and Other Stories*, published in 1979, is also midway between the disquietingly savage analyses of patriarchy of the 1960s and 1970s, such as *The Magic Toyshop, Heroes and Villains, Passion of New Eve*; and the exuberant novels of the 1980s and early 1990s, *Nights at the Circus* and *Wise Children*. This is not to argue that the latter novels are not also feminist, but their strategy is different. The violence in the events depicted in the earlier novels (the rapes, the physical and mental abuse of women) and the aggression implicit in the representations, are no longer foregrounded. While similar events may occur in these two last texts, the focus is on mocking and exploding the constrictive cultural stereotypes and in celebrating the sheer ability

of the female protagonists to survive, unscathed by the sexist ideologies. The tales in *The Bloody Chamber* still foreground the violence and the abuse, but the narrative itself provides an exuberant
re-writing of the fairy-tales that actively engages the reader in a
feminist deconstruction. I am therefore focusing my discussion on
Carter's fairy-tales to allow a specific analysis of Carter's textual
uses of violence as a feminist strategy, alongside a case study assess-
ing the relationship of such a strategy to an assessment of her
readership.

Fairy-tale elements had been present in Carter's work as early as
The Magic Toyshop in 1967, but she didn't come to consider them
as a specific genre of European literature until the late seventies. In
1977 she translated for Gollancz a series of Perrault's seventeenth-
century tales, and in 1979 published *The Bloody Chamber*, her re-
writing of the fairy-tales of Perrault and Madame Leprince de
Beaumont. In 1982 she translated another edition, which included
the two extra stories by Madame de Beaumont, 'Beauty and the
Beast' and 'Sweetheart'. Three of the stories from *Bloody Chamber*
were rewritten for Radio 3,[2] and she took part in adapting one of
them, 'Company of Wolves', into the film by Neil Jordan (1984).
Finally, she edited the *Virago Book of Fairy Tales* in 1990, and the
Second Virago Book of Fairy Tales for 1992.

Carter saw fairy-tales as the oral literature of the poor, a literature that spanned Europe and one that encoded the dark and mysterious elements of the psyche. She argued that even though the
seventeenth- and eighteenth-century aristocratic writers 'fixed' these
tales by writing them down and added moral tags to adapt them
into parables of instruction for children, they could not erase the
darkness and the magic of the content.[3] She argued that both literature and folklore were 'vast repositories of outmoded lies, where
you can check out what lies used to be a la mode and find the old
lies on which new lies are based'. But folk-tales, unlike the more
dangerous myths (which she tackled in *Passion of New Eve*), were
straightforward devices whose structures could easily be re-written
with an informing, feminist tag, where the curiosity of the women
protagonists is rewarded (rather than punished) and their sexuality
is active (rather than passive or suppressed altogether). Carter's Red
Riding Hood in 'Company of Wolves' is more than a match for her
werewolf:

> What big teeth you have ...
> All the better to eat you with.

The girl burst out laughing; she knew she was nobody's meat. She laughed at him full in the face, she ripped off his shirt for him and flung it into the fire, in the fiery wake of her own discarded clothing.[4]

Feminist critics who have written on *Bloody Chamber* argue that the old fairy-tales were a reactionary form that inscribed a misogynistic ideology, without questioning whether women readers would always and necessarily identify with the female figures (an assumption that Carter too shares in). They argue that Carter, in using the form, gets locked into the conservative sexism, despite her good intentions. Patricia Duncker uses Angela Dworkin's *Pornography: Men Possessing Women* to argue that Carter is 're-writing the tales within the strait-jacket of their original structures' and therefore reproducing the 'rigidly sexist psychology of the erotic'. Avis Lewallen agrees, Carter has been unable adequately to revision the conservative form for a feminist politics, and so her attempts at constructing an active female erotic are badly compromised – if not a reproduction of male pornography.[5]

I would argue that, conversely, it is the critics who cannot see beyond the sexist binary opposition. In order to do this, two issues need to be addressed: whether a 'reactionary' form can be rewritten; and the potential perversity of women's sexuality. The discussion of the first issue will lead to an argument for a feminist strategy of writing and also of reading, and hence throw some light on Carter's potential audiences.

Firstly, the question of the form of the fairy-tale: is it some universal, unchangeable given or does it change according to its specific historic rendition? Narrative genres clearly do inscribe ideologies (though that can never fix the readings), but later re-writings that take the genre and adapt it will not necessarily encode the same ideological assumptions. Otherwise, one would have to argue that the African novels that have sought to decolonise the European cultural stereotypes of themselves, must always fail. One would need to argue that Ngugi's or Achebe's novels, for example, reinforce the colonial legacy because they use the novel format. This is clearly not true. When the form is used to critique the inscribed ideology, I would argue, then the form is subtly adapted to inscribe a new set of assumptions. Carter argued that *Bloody Chamber* was 'a book of stories *about* fairy stories' (my emphasis) and this ironic strategy needs to be acknowledged. Lewallen complains that Duncker is insensitive to the irony in Carter's tales, but then agrees with her assessment of the patriarchal inscriptions, seeing the irony as merely

'blurring the boundaries' of binary thinking. Now I want to push
the claim for irony a lot further than Lewallen, and argue that
rather than a blurring, it enacts an oscillation that is itself
deconstructive.

Naomi Schor, in an essay on Flaubert's ironic use of
Romanticism, states that irony allows the author to reject and at
the same time re-appropriate the discourse that s/he is referring to,
(i.e., Romanticism is both present and simultaneously discredited in
Flaubert's texts).[6] Schor historicises the continuity between nineteenth-century and modernist irony as inherently misogynistic
(because linked to the fetishisation of women) and calls for a feminist irony that incorporates the destabilising effects, while rejecting
the misogyny. She cites Donna Haraway's opening paragraph from
'A manifesto for cyborgs': 'Irony ... is a rhetorical strategy and political method, one I would like to see more honoured within socialist
feminism.' Utilising this model of an ironic oscillation, I want to
argue that Carter's tales do not simply 'rewrite' the old tales by
fixing roles of active sexuality for their female protagonists – they
're-write' them by playing with and upon (if not preying upon) the
earlier misogynistic version. Look again at the quote from 'Company
of Wolves' given earlier. It is not read as a story read for the first
time, with a positively imaged heroine. It is read, with the original
story encoded within it, so that one reads of *both* texts, aware of
how the new one refers back to and implicitly critiques the old. We
read 'The girl burst out laughing; she knew she was nobody's meat'
as referring to the earlier Little Red Riding Hood's passive terror of
being eaten, before she is saved by the male woodman. We recognise
the author's feminist turning of the tables and, simultaneously, the
damage done by the old inscriptions of femininity as passive. 'I am
all for putting new wine in old bottles, especially if the pressure of
the new wine makes the old bottles explode.'[7]

What should also not be overlooked, alongside this ironic deconstructive technique, is the role of the reader; the question of *who* is
reading these tales. These are late twentieth-century adult fairy-tales
conscious of their own fictive status and so questioning the very
constructions of roles while asserting them. When a young girl res-
olutely chops off the paws of the wolf threatening her, and we read
'the wolf let out a gulp, almost a sob ... wolves are less brave than
they seem' – we are participating in the re-writing of a wolf's characteristics and participating not only in the humour but also the
arbitrariness. 'Nature' is not fixed but fluid within fiction.

Carter was insistent that her texts were open-ended, written with a space for the reader's activity in mind. She disliked novels that were closed worlds and described most realist novels as etiquette manuals. And she placed Marilyn French's *The Women's Room* in such a category, as well as the novels of Jane Austen. The fact that the former was feminist didn't let it off the protocol hook. Books written to show the reader how she should behave, were not only an insult to the reader but also a bore to write. Carter's own fiction seems always aware of its playful interactions with the reader's assumptions and recognitions.[8] *The Bloody Chamber* is clearly engaging with a reader historically situated in the early 1980s (and beyond), informed by feminism, and raising questions about the cultural constructions of femininity. Rather than carrying the heavy burden of instruction, Carter often explained that for her 'a narrative is an argument stated in fictional terms'. And the two things needed for any argument are, something to argue *against* (something to be overturned) and someone to make that argument *to* (a reader).

The question therefore arises of whether this deconstructive irony is activated if the reader is uninformed by feminism. The answer must be, on the whole, no. *Bloody Chamber* draws on a feminist discourse – or at least an awareness that feminism is challenging sexist constructions. Mary Kelly, the feminist artist, when challenged on the same question of the accessibility of her *Post Partum Document* to a wider audience, cogently argued, 'there is no such thing as a homogeneous mass-audience. You can't make art for everyone. And if you're enjoyed within a particular movement or organisation, then the work is going to participate in its debates.' Lucy Lippard goes on to suggest that Kelly's art 'extends the level of discourse within the art audience for all those who see the art experience as an *exchange*, a collaboration between artist and audience – the active audience an active art deserves'.[9] I would argue that Carter's tales evoke a similar active engagement with feminist discourse.

At first sight, such a conclusion may sound odd, because if anyone has taken feminist fiction into the mainstream, it is Carter. But if a feminist writer is to remain a feminist writer (rather than a writer about women) then the texts must engage, on some level, with feminist thinking. There is a wide constituency of potential readers who satisfy the minimum requirement of having an awareness that feminism challenges sexist constructions. One does not need to be a feminist to read the texts, far from it, but if the reader does not appreciate the attack on the stereotypes then the payback for that level of engagement, the sheer cerebral pleasure and the enjoyment of the iconoclasm, will be missing. And without the humour or the interest in deconstructing cultural gender stereotypes, the textual anger against the abuse of women in previous decades can prove very disquieting, even uncomfortable, to read. To enjoy the humour – the payback with many of Carter's texts – readers need to position themselves outside phallocentric culture (at least for the process of reading). The last two novels, with their lighter tone and more exuberant construction of interrelationships, probably have the widest readership of all. This mellowing of textual aggression is not the only explanation for the increasing popularity of Carter's later texts. Helen Carr notes that the mid-eighties saw the arrival of South American magic realism on the British scene.[10] From that moment, Carter's readers could assign her anarchic fusion of fantasy and realism to an intelligible genre, and so feel more secure.

However, a fuller explanation of Carter's popularity needs to take account of marketing and distribution: not just accessibility of ideology, but accessibility of purchase. Is the text on the general bookshop shelves? Is it marketed under a feminist imprint, thus signalling to the potential reader, for feminist eyes only? Nicci Gerrard in her examination of how feminist fiction has impacted on mainstream publishing, argues that Carter, along with Toni Morrison and Keri Hulme, have been more widely read because while still remaining explicitly feminist, they have brought feminism out of its 'narrow self-consciousness'.[11] Narrow is always a difficult adjective to quantify. In Britain, Angela Carter – like Morrison and Hulme – has been published by mainstream publishers from the beginning. The publishing history for her hardback fiction runs: Heinemann 1966–70, Hart Davis 1971–2, Gollancz 1977–84, Chatto & Windus 1984–92. As far as marketing and distribution are concerned, Carter has always been presented directly to mainstream audiences.

Both *Passion of New Eve* (1977) and *Bloody Chamber* (1979) initially came out under Gollancz's 'Fantasy' series, placing them within a specific genre, and the former was the first into paperback – being issued by Arrow in 1978. In 1981 Penguin issued *Bloody Chamber* along with *Heroes and Villains* and *The Infernal Desire Machine of Doctor Hoffman*. In the same year Virago published the paperback of *Magic Toyshop*, followed by *Passion of New Eve* the year after, and *Fireworks* in 1987. The covers of both publishing houses initially focused on the surreal, vaguely sci-fi elements, Penguin doing a nice line in suggestive plants, designed by James Marsh. (Thankfully, Virago has scrapped the original tawdry cover of the sci-fi couple embracing, on *Fireworks*, for the more tasteful modernist depiction of a Japanese urban environment.) Virago also published Carter's non-fiction and commissioned her to edit collections of stories.

Nights at the Circus reached a very large audience, in paperback. Picador published it in 1985 and it was taken up as a major lead title for Pan to promote and distribute. Gerrard cites Virago's average fiction print-run as 5000–7000 in the second half of the eighties. By the early nineties, *Nights at the Circus* had achieved sales which exceeded this figure ten times over. But even this success needs to be placed in context. It still only reaches about 20 per cent of the sales for a number one best seller, such as Martin Amis's *London Fields* or Julian Barnes's *History of the World in 10½ Chapters*.[12]

So Carter's involvement with feminist publishers came relatively late in the day and seems to have stemmed from Virago's publishing of her first piece of non-fiction, *Sadeian Woman: An Exercise in Cultural History* (1979). Her fiction's reputation was made from mainstream publishing houses and was reinforced by the awards of mainstream literary prizes: the John Llewellyn Rhys Prize for *Magic Toyshop*; Somerset Maugham Award for *Several Perceptions*; Cheltenham Festival of Literature Award for *Bloody Chamber*; and the James Tait Black Award for *Nights at the Circus*. The shortlisting of the 1984 Booker Prize caused a minor furore when *Nights at the Circus* was not included (it was won that year by Anita Brookner's *Hotel du Lac*). Even many of the individual tales from *The Blooody Chamber* first saw the light of day in small but fairly prestigious literature reviews such as *Bananas, Stand, Northern Arts Review*, and *Iowa Review* (the only academic journal), none of them notably feminist in their editorial policy. And 'The Courtship of Mr Lyon' was first published in the British edition of *Vogue*.

Clearly I am arguing that texts that employ a feminist irony, that engage activity with a feminist discourse, do not automatically confine themselves to a feminist ghetto. There is a wide and growing audience for at least some kinds of feminist fiction. But I am also arguing that exuberance sells better than discomfort. The

more textually savage books are published by Virago in paperback; the more magical by Penguin; and two celebratory ones by the big-money bidders, Picador and Vantage.

But what also sells in this commodified age of ours, as everyone knows, is sex, and Carter's texts have always engaged with eroticism. The quotes included by Penguin on the book covers invariably make reference to 'the stylish erotic prose', 'erotic, exotic and bizarre romance'. And this clearly also has a lot to do with her popularity. In order to counter Lewallen and Duncker's perception of her work as pornographic, I need to examine the feminist strategies of her representations of sexuality, particularly the debate surrounding the construction of sexuality within the *Bloody Chamber* stories. I believe Carter is going some way towards constructing a complex vision of female psychosexuality, through her invoking of violence as well as the erotic. But that women can be violent as well as active sexually, that women can choose to be perverse, is clearly not something allowed for in the calculations of such readers as Duncker, Palmer and Lewallen.[13] Carter's strength is precisely in exploding the stereotypes of women as passive, demure cyphers. That she therefore evokes the gamut of violence and perversity is certainly troubling, but to deny their existence is surely to incarcerate women back within a partial, sanitised image only slightly less constricted than the Victorian angel in the house.

Carter was certainly fascinated by the incidence of 'beast marriage' stories, in the original fairy-tales, and she claimed they were international. In discussing how the wolves subtly changed their meaning in the film of the story, she comments that nevertheless they still signified libido. Fairy-tales are often seen as dealing with the 'uncanny', the distorted fictions of the unconscious revisited through homely images – and beasts can easily stand for the projected desires, the drive for pleasure of women. Particularly when such desires are discountenanced by a patriarchal culture concerned to restrict its women to being property (without a libido of their own, let alone a mind or a room).[14]

In all of the tales, not only is femininity constructed as active, sensual, desiring and unruly – but successful sexual transactions are founded on an equality and the transforming powers of recognising the reciprocal claims of the other. The ten tales divide up into the first, 'The Bloody Chamber', a re-writing of the Bluebeard story; three tales around cats: lion/tiger/puss in boots; three tales of magical beings: erl-king/snow-child/vampire; and finally three tales of werewolves. Each tale takes up the theme of the earlier one and comments on a different aspect of it, to present a complex variation of female desire and sexuality.

In the Finale to *Sadeian Woman* Carter discusses the word flesh in its various meanings:

> the pleasures of the flesh are vulgar and unrefined, even with an element of beastliness about them, although flesh tints have the sumptuous succulence of peaches because flesh plus skin equals sensuality.
> But, if flesh plus skin equals sensuality, then flesh minus skin equals meat.[15]

This motif of skin and flesh as signifying pleasure, and of meat as signifying economic objectification, recurs throughout the ten tales, and stands as an internal evaluation of the relationship shown. The other recurring motif is that of the gaze, but it is not always simply the objectification of the woman by male desire, as we shall discover.

In each of the first three tales, Carter stresses the relationship between women's subjective sexuality and their objective role as property: young girls get bought by wealth, one way or another. But in the feminist re-write, Bluebeard's victimisation of women is overturned and he himself is vanquished by the mother and daughter.

> The puppet master, open-mouthed, wide eyed, impotent at the last, saw his dolls break free of their strings, abandon the rituals he had ordained for them since time began and start to live for themselves.
> (p. 39)

In the two versions of the beauty-and-the-beast theme, the lion and the tiger signify something other than man. 'For a lion is a lion and a man is a man' argues the first tale. In the first, Beauty is adored by her father, in the second, gambled away by a profligate drunkard. The felines signify otherness, a savage and magnificent power, outside of humanity. In one story, women are pampered, in the other treated as property, but in both cases the protagonists chose to explore the dangerous, exhilarating change that comes from choosing the beast. Both stories are careful to show a reciprocal awe and fear in the beasts, as well as in the beauty, and the reversal theme reinforces the equality of the transactions: lion kisses

Beauty's hand, Beauty kisses lion's; tiger strips naked and so Beauty chooses to show him 'the fleshly nature of women'. In both cases the beasts signify a sensuality that the women have been taught might devour them, but which, when embraced, gives them power, strength and a new awareness of both self and other. The tiger's bride has her 'skins of a life in the world' licked off to reveal her own magnificent fur beneath the surface.

Each of the three adolescent protagonists has been progressively stronger and more aggressive, and each has embraced a sensuality both sumptuous and unrefined. With the fourth story, 'Puss in Boots', the cynical puss viewing human love and desire in a light-hearted *commedia dell'arte* rendition, demythologises sex with humour and gusto.

If the wild felines have signified the sensual desires that women need to acknowledge within themselves, the three fictive figures signify the problematics of desire itself. 'Erl-king' is a complex rendering of a subjective collusion with objectivity and entrapment within the male gaze. The woman narrator both fears and desires entrapment within the birdcage. The erl-king, we are told, does not exist in nature, but in a void of her own making (hence his calling her 'mother' at the end). The disquieting shifts between the two voices of the narrator, first and third person, represent the two competing desires for freedom and engulfment, in a tale that delineates the very ambivalence of desire. 'Snowchild' presents the unattainability of desire, which will always melt away before possession. No real person can ever satisfy desire's constant deferral. 'Lady of the House of Love', with its lady vampire, inverts the gender roles of Bluebeard, with the woman constructed as an aggressor with a man as the virgin victim. But with this construction of aggressor, comes the question of whether sadists are trapped within their nature: 'can a bird sing only the song it knows or can it learn a new song?' And, through love and the reciprocal theme – he kisses her bloody finger, rather than her sucking his blood – this aggressor is able to vanquish ancestral desires, but at a cost. In this tale the overwhelming fear of the cat tales, that the protagonist might be consumed by the otherness of desire, is given a new twist.

The three wolf stories also deal with women's relationship to the unruly libido, but the werewolf signifies a stranger, more alienated otherness than the cats, despite the half-human manifestations. Old

Granny is the werewolf in the first tale, and the girl's vanquishing of her is seen as a triumph of the complaisant society (the symbolic) that hounds the uncanny. The tiger's bride had been a rebellious child and chooses desire over conventional wealth; now we have a 'good' child who sacrifices the uncanny for bourgeois prosperity. In the second tale, 'Company of Wolves', the list of manifestations of werewolves, the amalgam of human and wolf, symbolic and imaginary, concludes with the second Red Riding Hood story. This time the wolf does consume the granny, but is outfaced by Red Riding Hood's awareness that in freely meeting his sensuality, the libido will transform 'meat' into 'flesh'. After the fulfilment of their mutual desire, he is transformed into a 'tender' wolf, and she sleeps safe between his paws. The final tale is of a girl raised by wolves, outside of the social training of the symbolic. Alluding to Truffaut's *L'Enfant sauvage*, Lewis Carroll and Lacan, the young girl grows up outside the cultural inscriptions and learns a new sense of self from her encounters with the mirror and from the rhythms of her body. She learns a sense of time and routine. Finally her pity begins to transform the werewolf Duke into the world of the rational, where he too can be symbolised.

Reading Carter's fairy-tales as her female protagonists' confrontations with desire, in all its unruly 'animalness', yields rich rewards. However, Patricia Duncker simplistically reads the tales as 'all men are beasts to women' and so sees the female protagonists as inevitably enacting the roles of victims of male violence. Red Riding Hood of the twice mentioned quotation, according to her 'sees that rape is inevitable ... and decides to strip off, lie back and enjoy it. She wants it really, they all do.' Reading 'The Tiger's Bride' Duncker claims the stripping of the girl's skin 'beautifully packaged and unveiled, is the ritual disrobing of the willing victims of pornography'. Because she reads the beasts as men in furry clothing, Duncker argues Carter has been unable to paint an 'alternative anti-sexist language of the erotic' because there is no conception of women as having autonomous desire. But Carter is doing that. Read the beasts as the projections of a feminine libido, and they become exactly that autonomous desire which the female characters need to recognise and reappropriate as a part of themselves (denied by the phallocentric culture). Isn't that why at the end of 'Tiger's Bride' the tiger's licking reveals the tiger in the woman protagonist, beneath the cultural construction of the demure? Looked at again, this is not read as woman re-enacting pornography for the male gaze, but as woman reappropriating libido:

> And each stroke of his tongue ripped off skin after successive skin, all the skins of a life in the world, and left behind a nascent patina of shining hairs. My earrings turned back to water and trickled down my shoulders; I shrugged the drops off my beautiful fur.
>
> (p. 67)

Lewallen does read the beasts as female desire, but argues that the female protagonists are still locked within a binary prescription of either 'fuck or be fucked'. However, I would argue she too brings this binary division into the discussion with her, when she asserts 'Sade's dualism is simple: sadist or masochist, fuck or be fucked, victim or aggressor'. She uses a reading of Carter's reading of Sade, in *Sadeian Woman*, to inform the stories and argues, wrongly I think, that Carter is putting forward woman as sexual aggressor (Sade's Juliette), rather than victim (Sade's Justine). I would suggest that Carter is using de Sade to argue for a wider incorporation of female sexuality, to argue that it too contains a whole gamut of 'perversions' alongside 'normal' sex. My main problem with Lewallen's dualism is that it incorporates no sense of the dangerous pleasures of sexuality and that is not necessarily simply a choice between being aggressor or victim. Her 'fuck or be fucked' interpretation ignores the notion of consent within the sado-masochistic transaction, and the question of who is fucking whom. Pat Califia's novel of lesbian S&M illustrates how it is usually the masochist who has the real control, who has the power to call 'enough'.[16] While asking for a more mutual sexual transaction, Lewallen dismisses the masochism in 'The Bloody Chamber', as too disturbing, 'my unease at being manipulated by the narrative to sympathise with masochism'.

Now I don't deny that it is disturbing (except, perhaps, for the reader who is a masochist). And if it was the only representation of female sexuality, I would be up in arms against its reinforcement of Freudian views. But it is only one of ten tales, ten variant representations. Moreover, the protagonist retracts her consent halfway through the narrative, when she realises her husband, Bluebeard, is planning to involve her in real torture and a 'snuff' denouement. Up until then, the adolescent protagonist has not denied her own interest in the sado-masochist transaction:

I caught myself, suddenly, as he saw me, my pale face, the way the muscles in my neck stuck out like thin wire. I saw how much that cruel necklace became me. And, for the first time in my innocent and confined life, I sensed in myself a potentiality for corruption that took my breath away.

(p. 11)

Throughout the narrative, this 'queasy craving' for the sexual encounters ('like the cravings of pregnant women for the taste of coal or chalk or tainted food') is admitted by the narrator, until she discovers the torture chamber and the three dead previous wives. Then she removes her consent and, with the help of an ineffectual blind piano-tuner[17] and her avenging mother, Bluebeard is defeated. Of course I would not deny that the tale, through its oscillation with the original fable, also comments on male sexual objectification and denigration of women. Clearly much of its representation draws on this – but the male violator is also portrayed as captured within the construction of masculinity (just as the female vampire was trapped within hers). The protagonist can recognise his 'stench of absolute despair ... the atrocious loneliness of that monster'. Carter's representations of sexuality are more complex than many of her critics have allowed.

Maggie Anwell, in an excellent analysis of how the film *The Company of Wolves* was unable to get past the binary divide of victim/aggressor, does argue for a more complex psychic reading of female sexuality represented in the tale.[18] She suggests that the confrontation between 'repressed desire' (wolf) and the 'ego' (Red Riding Hood) ends with the ego's ability to accept the pleasurable aspects of desire, while controlling its less pleasurable aspects:

The story, with its subversion of the familiar and its structure of story-telling within a story, suggests an ambiguity and plurality of interpretations which reminds us of our own capacity to dream ... Not only does the material world shift its laws; we experience our own capacity for abnormal behaviour.

(p. 82)

Are we to call only for constructions of sexuality with which we feel at ease, at this point in time, still within a phallocentric society? Especially when all we have to inscribe our own sexual identities from are cultural constructions? I would argue that just as it is the debates around the marginalised and pathologised 'perversities' that

Lewallen does read the beasts as female desire, but argues that the female protagonists are still locked within a binary prescription of either 'fuck or be fucked'. However, I would argue she too brings this binary division into the discussion with her, when she asserts 'Sade's dualism is simple: sadist or masochist, fuck or be fucked, victim or aggressor'. She uses a reading of Carter's reading of Sade, in *Sadeian Woman*, to inform the stories and argues, wrongly I think, that Carter is putting forward woman as sexual aggressor (Sade's Juliette), rather than victim (Sade's Justine). I would suggest that Carter is using de Sade to argue for a wider incorporation of female sexuality, to argue that it too contains a whole gamut of 'perversions' alongside 'normal' sex. My main problem with Lewallen's dualism is that it incorporates no sense of the dangerous pleasures of sexuality and that is not necessarily simply a choice between being aggressor or victim. Her 'fuck or be fucked' interpretation ignores the notion of consent within the sado-masochistic transaction, and the question of who is fucking whom. Pat Califia's novel of lesbian S&M illustrates how it is usually the masochist who has the real control, who has the power to call 'enough'.[16] While asking for a more mutual sexual transaction, Lewallen dismisses the masochism in 'The Bloody Chamber', as too disturbing, 'my unease at being manipulated by the narrative to sympathise with masochism'.

Now I don't deny that it is disturbing (except, perhaps, for the reader who is a masochist). And if it was the only representation of female sexuality, I would be up in arms against its reinforcement of Freudian views. But it is only one of ten tales, ten variant representations. Moreover, the protagonist retracts her consent halfway through the narrative, when she realises her husband, Bluebeard, is planning to involve her in real torture and a 'snuff' denouement. Up until then, the adolescent protagonist has not denied her own interest in the sado-masochist transaction:

Carter's most discussed texts, engages directly with material issues which have been central to recent feminist politics, in particular its debates about sexuality, violence and pornography. Makinen also participates in an early but already heated debate about Carter's work in relation to the politics of women's rewriting of the patriarchal literary tradition. In Makinen's hands the focus of this debate is moved to the politics of reading and the textual positioning of the reader. Her insistence on a historically specific analysis of readers leads to a sense of a reading process which is productive of irony, destabilisation and the opening up of meaning. This brings about fresh thinking on the question of whether Carter's texts only reproduce what they intend to attack. Makinen argues that, in order to comprehend Carter's deliberately disturbing text, critics, specifically feminist critics, need both to move beyond an overly simple opposition of masculine and feminine (the binary of victim/aggressor), and to expand their criteria of what constitutes a feminist text. Makinen's essay is also illuminating on formal matters in that it reads *The Bloody Chamber* as a set of interacting rather than separate stories. Ed.]

1. Margaret Atwood, 'Magic Token Through the Dark Forest', *Observer*, 23 February 1992, p. 61; Lorna Sage, 'The Soaring Imagination', *Guardian*, 17 February 1992, p. 37; *The Late Show*, presented by Tracy McLeod, BBC2, 18 February 1992.

2. Later published with another of her radio plays, as *Come Unto These Yellow Sands: Four Radio Plays* (Newcastle, 1985).

3. For all that I will go on to question Patricia Duncker's reading of Carter's representation of female sexuality in 'Re-Imagining the Fairy Tales: Angela Carter's Bloody Chambers', *Literature and History*, 10:1 (1984), 3–14, she does give a good historical reading of fairy-tales, with much more analysis than Carter's version.

4. Angela Carter, *The Bloody Chamber and Other Stories* (London, 1979), p. 118. All subsequent quotations are from this edition.

5. Avis Lewallen, 'Wayward Girls But Wicked Women?', in *Perspectives on Pornography*, ed. Gary Day and Clive Bloom (Basingstoke, 1988).

6. Naomi Schor, 'Fetishism and its Ironies', *Nineteenth-Century French Studies*, 17:1–2 (1988–89), 89–97.

7. Carter, 'Notes from the Front Line', in *On Gender and Writing*, ed. Michelene Wandor (London, 1983), p. 69.

8. 'I try when I write fiction, to think on my feet – to present a number of propositions in a variety of different ways, and to leave the reader to construct her own fiction for herself from the elements of my fiction' (Carter, 'Notes from the Front Line').

9. Mary Kelly, *Post Partum Document* (London, 1984), p. xiii.

10. Helen Carr, ed. *From My Guy to Sci-Fi* (London, 1989).

11. Nicci Gerrard, *Into the Mainstream* (London, 1989).

12. I am indebted to Helena Blakemore's forthcoming doctoral thesis, 'Reading Strategies: Problems in the Study of Contemporary British Fiction' (Middlesex University).

13. Paulina Palmer, 'From Coded Mannequin to Bird Woman: Angela Carter's Magic Flight', in *Women Reading Women Writing*, ed. Sue Roe (Brighton, 1987), pp. 177–205.

14. Arguably Christina Rossetti's poetry, especially the notorious *Goblin Market*, employed a similar device in the nineteenth century and Ellen Moers in *Literary Women* (London, 1978) argued for a tradition of 'female gothic' tales that such strategies could belong to.

15. Carter, *The Sadeian Woman: An Exercise in Cultural History* (London, 1979).

16. Pat Califia, *Macho Sluts* (Boston, MA, 1989).

17. That Duncker argues the blind piano-tuner represents castrated male sexuality, referring to Rochester in *Jane Eyre*, situates her feminist strategy. She does not incorporate later psychoanalytic feminist readings, that could allow Carter's protagonist to elect for a man with whom she will not be the object of the male gaze, as she was with her husband.

18. Maggie Anwell, 'Lolita Meets the Werewolf', in *The Female Gaze: Women As Viewers of Popular Culture*, ed. Lorraine Gamman and Margaret Marshment (London, 1988), pp. 76–85.

19. Carter, 'Notes from the Front Line', p. 75.

2

Angela Carter's *The Sadeian Woman*: Feminism as Treason

SALLY KEENAN

Critical discussion of Angela Carter's *The Sadeian Woman* has tended to be oblique, focusing mainly on its relationship to her fiction, and the ways in which she worked through the theoretical issues it raises in fictional form. In particular, attention has been directed at her deconstruction of cultural myths of femininity and the repression of women's sexuality that those myths reinforce. Such studies give the impression that *The Sadeian Woman* has been read for the most part unproblematically, as a powerful feminist treatise, its attack on pornography constituting an attack on the pornographic representation of women in much cultural production past and present. Yet when it was first published in 1979, the book was widely reviewed in the press and received contradictory and in many cases ambivalent critical responses. The plenary discussion at the conference held in honour of Carter's work in 1994 at York University, 'Fireworks: Angela Carter and the Futures of Writing', suggested to me that many Carter enthusiasts still felt a considerable degree of ambivalence about *The Sadeian Woman* that was not evident in evaluations of her later work. What a retrospective reading of the text from the perspective of the mid-1990s reveals, however, is Carter's extraordinary capacity to tap into crucial critical debates relevant to feminism and cultural politics, long before those debates had been fully staged. If some of the book's reviewers in 1979 were either provoked or mystified by Carter's linking of Sade's work with the feminist project to promote women's sexual freedom, none of them could have anticipated how pornography was to become a key issue in feminist debates during the 1980s. It seems uncanny now that *The Sadeian Woman* was originally commissioned by Virago to launch the press in 1977 (although it did not finally appear until two years later). A controversial yet appropriate choice it proved to be, since it offered a prophetic intervention into the battle that was to ensue, writ most starkly between feminists campaigning against pornography and the counterarguments put forward by feminists opposed to censorship. Although the book has received no detailed critical treatment, two well-known feminist critiques of pornography, Susanne Kappeler's *The Pornography of Representation* (1986) and Linda Williams's *Hard Core* (1990), addressed *The Sadeian Woman*, albeit briefly, in strongly antithetical terms. As we shall see, Kappeler accused Carter of validating the pornographic – in the name of equal opportunity – by appealing to the literary. Williams, on the other hand, employed Carter's text in an argument which attempted to claim a positive value for women in pornography. Situated on opposite sides of the feminist controversy about pornography, Kappeler's and Williams's responses are symptomatic, and illustrate the significant role Carter's work has played in that debate. However, neither of their arguments, in my view, does justice to the complex way in which Carter negotiated this difficult terrain.

I will begin this chapter by giving some consideration to where I place *The Sadeian Woman* in Carter's work as a whole, in particular its relationship to *The Bloody Chamber and Other Stories*, which appeared in the same year (1979). I will also review some of the critical reactions to the book when it was first published and subsequently. In thinking about the source of Carter's interest in Sade, I will return to those antithetical responses by feminist critics, which will provide a context within which to examine the role of Carter's work in the controversies about pornography. Where are we to place Carter in that apparently intractable binary of antipornography/anti-censorship? And to what extent is Carter successful in her daring attempt to appropriate Sade, the arch misogynist, for her own project of 'demythologising' – that is, the demystification of those persistent, essentialising conceptions of women in our culture, especially regarding female sexuality and motherhood?

The Sadeian Woman may not have received the detailed and serious treatment it deserves because of the ways in which Carter reworked or worked out some of the issues it touches on in her fiction, notably in *The Bloody Chamber, The Passion of New Eve* (1977), and later in *Nights at the Circus* (1984). In *Nights at the Circus*, it might be argued, she finally laid the ghost of Sade to rest in her presentation of the circus as a parody of some Sadeian orgastic nightmare. The figure of the circus clown, Buffo, whose mask is described as 'a fingerprint of authentic dissimilarity, a genuine expression of [his] own autonomy', is perhaps an avatar of the libertine in his ultimate Sadeian form, Sovereign Man, splendid in his isolation, detached even from his own pleasure.[1] And Fevvers herself can be read as the image of Sade's Juliette transformed. Like Juliette, Fevvers is bold and transgressive, bearing not a trace of passivity, but humanised, invoking wonder rather than horror. She does not play the victimiser, only attempting to use her sexuality to dupe the master at his own game. More endangered than dangerous, she nearly loses.

Although I do not read Carter's *oeuvre* as a neat chronological progression towards a more utopian feminist perspective, it is possible to see *The Sadeian Woman* as a watershed moment in her thinking about feminism, a moment when her fictional narratives became increasingly bound up with theoretical considerations. Returning to examine *The Sadeian Woman* in the light of the later fiction and its reception, one is brought face to face with the radical nature of Carter's work: its complex paradoxes, its theoretical seriousness, and that characteristic refusal to settle in one fixed place. Perhaps, above all, what a retrospective examination of the text highlights is its almost heretical disagreement with certain aspects of feminist thinking current in the 1970s. First, her suggestion that women too readily identify with images of themselves as victims of patriarchal oppression, that in effect they are frequently complicit with that oppression, was a distinctly unfashionable notion in the mid-1970s. Her savage indictment of the figure of Sade's Justine as an extreme embodiment of this complicity made her argument the more treasonable since she was using the arch misogynist in support of it. Second, there was the attack she launched on the idealisation of motherhood in its various forms. The wide spectrum of that idealisation manifested in much 1970s feminist theorising is rejected in *The Sadeian Woman*, either explicitly or implicitly: the recreation of mother goddesses or the eco-feminists' reassertion of Nature as

Mother, for instance.[2] Third, there is her challenge, albeit an oblique one, to the revisionary psychoanalytic theories of the French feminists, especially Hélène Cixous and Julia Kristeva, in whose work during the 1970s, motherhood and the maternal body assume crucial significance in a whole variety of ways.[3]

If *The Sadeian Woman* was a response to certain assumptions current in feminist thinking in the 1970s, what was the critical reaction to the book? How was Carter's provocative intervention into debates about female sexuality received in 1979? What is most striking is the wide range of the media giving it review space – both tabloids and broadsheet papers in the mainstream press as well as the alternative press. That diversity of coverage is matched by a diversity of critical responses: the anticipation of sexual titillation (from a clearly disappointed reviewer in the *Birmingham Sun*); an interesting failure with little relevance to modern women (the *Financial Times*); a serious contribution to contemporary cultural politics (*Gay News*). The book was clearly controversial, and with some notable exceptions, many of the reviewers expressed puzzlement as to the main thrust of its argument. Several feminist reviewers, while conceding Carter's claim that Sade may be useful for women in that he separates women's sexuality from their reproductive function, nevertheless expressed qualms about 'the ethics of the connection' (Ann Oakley) between Sade and feminism, an imaginative leap they could not make. A repeated point was that Carter failed to sustain her argument in support of Sade and was forced to throw him over in an abrupt and unsatisfactory conclusion (Sara Maitland, Julia O'Faolain, *Women's Report*), and that she had led her readers on a 'wild goose chase', as Maitland called it.[4] The implicit desire for a clear conclusion that could be slotted into a feminist agenda fails to acknowledge certain characteristic features of Carter's writing: an intention to provoke questions rather than to provide answers, to engage with contradictions without seeking necessarily to resolve them. In the 'Polemical Preface' where Carter sets out her thesis, it is clear that the use of Sade is paradoxical. This is the point and challenge of the book: an attempt to jolt the reader out of customary associations and habits of thought. Carter was not looking to Sade for a model, but rather to provide a speculative starting point. The most positive reactions to the book in 1979 came from those who acknowledged Carter's understanding of Sade's work as a founding moment for our modern sensibility regarding sexual matters. Marsaili Cameron, writing in *Gay News*, made the valid point that

> This book is not primarily a study of de Sade himself either as a writer or as an historical figure ... Ranging from pornography and mythology to psychoanalysis to points west, it is mainly concerned with the elucidation of our own tortured ideas of sexuality inherited from the past.

In thinking of Carter's work as a complete body of work, as we now must, I am interested in the location of this text in that body of writing, and even more perhaps in the place I sense that it has occupied in many women's reading of Carter, and in the formation of their feminist politics. In thinking about this chapter, I asked Carter readers of my acquaintance about their responses on first encountering *The Sadeian Woman*, and also crucially at what point in time they had read it. I was interested to learn that for several it had not only been the book of Carter's that had first engendered their interest in her work, but that it had played a significant role in forming or reformulating their feminism. For some, it presented a puzzling mix of the fascinating and disturbing which prompted them to think through questions about their own sexuality and their attitudes to pornography in new ways. Yet for others, it provided a turning point that caused them to dispel previously unchallenged assumptions about being on the side of 'innocence'. One woman described her first reading as a shock of recognition, of how Carter had crystallised her own not fully formulated ideas about the issue of women's complicity with their sexual oppression.

It is more than coincidental that 1979 marked the publication of both *The Sadeian Woman* and *The Bloody Chamber*. Carter's revisionary fairy-tales brilliantly display how the discursive structures we inherit are not inevitably monolithic, or resistant to recasting. Through them, she wittily presents the relationship between cultural structuration and human agency as dynamic and malleable. Simultaneously exposing the structures of power manifest in our most conventional narratives of gender relations, she transforms those stories into images of erotic experience from the perspective of heterosexual women, reimagining the heroines as active agents in their own sexual development. However, the route she takes towards that revision constitutes what could be called a scandalous liaison with the book on Sade. Taken together, her revisionary fairy-tales (traditional literature for children) and her analysis of Sade's work (considered adult reading – that euphemism for pornographic literature) are deeply implicated in one another; they are, it could be said, contrasting sides of the same genre.

That year, 1979, also saw the publication of several works of feminist revision in which an analysis of fairy-tales played a part, most notably of course Sandra M. Gilbert and Susan Gubar's *The Madwoman in the Attic*. Thinking about the conjunction of *The Madwoman in the Attic* and *The Bloody Chamber* draws attention to Carter's capacity to tap into the *Zeitgeist*. At the same time, in measuring the distance between the two works one can gauge the extent to which Carter resisted being pulled into prevailing ways of thinking. In their introduction, Gilbert and Gubar map those feminine stereotypes of the nineteenth-century cultural imagination, the angel in the house and the whore in the street, on to the fairy-tale of Snow White and her counterpart the wicked queen, just as Carter does in her story, 'The Snow Child'. If the Victorian domestic angel, an avatar of the divine virgin of Christian mythology, represented an eternal feminine whose purity rendered her virtually lifeless (an angel of death), her antithetical mirror image was to be found in the monstrous whore, who constituted, in Gilbert and Gubar's reading, an embodiment of female autonomy, threatening to the social status quo. The only escape from the prison of the glass coffin, according to Gilbert and Gubar, is not through the prince's kiss, which will only enclose her in the mirror of his own desires, but through the wicked queen's '"badness", through plots and stories, duplicitous schemes, wild dreams, fierce fictions, mad impersonations'.[5]

Carter's revision of the same story focuses on the older of the two women just as Gilbert and Gubar do, but emphasises her recognition that neither position is desirable: each still represents the reverse side of the same coin. In 'The Snow Child', the wicked queen's vindictiveness is not regarded as subversive, nor an escape from her patriarchal inscription. Witnessing the fate of the compliant pure virgin enables her to acknowledge that her story is also mapped out by the king's authority. For Carter, rebellious rage at her victim status is not enough to release the female heroine from her powerlessness.[6]

The countess (queen) in Carter's story is clad in a manner befitting a brothel, echoing Sade's Juliette, just as the innocent but deathly snow child is an avatar of Sade's Justine. Justine, writes Carter in *The Sadeian Woman*, is 'a good woman according to the

rules for women laid down by men and her reward is rape, humiliation and incessant beatings ... a beautiful penniless orphan, the
living image of a fairy-tale princess in disguise but a Cinderella for
whom the ashes with which she is covered have become part of her
skin'. Juliette's story is 'Justine-through-the-looking-glass, an inversion of an inversion ... in a world governed by god, the king and
the law, the trifold masculine symbolism of authority, Juliette
knows better than her sister how useless it is to rebel against fate'
(p. 80). While Justine martyrs herself to the pursuit of virtue,
Juliette responds to the same assaults on her honour by turning
herself into the perfect whore.

If Carter's analysis of Sade's texts emphasises their fairy-tale-like
abstraction, then her revision of traditional fairy-tales serves to
highlight the pornographic nature of the stereotypes of women that
they have recirculated. Both texts stress the connections between
sexual and economic relations in a patriarchal society. The archetypes of both the pornographic and fairy-tale worlds confuse the
'historical fact of the economic dependence of women upon men'.
Although, as she points out, this is largely a fact of the past, its
effect lives on as a 'believed fiction and is assumed to imply an emo-
tional dependence that is taken for granted as a condition inherent
in the natural order of things' (p. 7).

Both pornography and fairy-tales are typically anonymous, a
feature which contributes to the sense that they are products of a
universal experience. Lorna Sage points out that Carter takes advantage of the 'anonymous' voice from our communal oral culture,
'multivoiced, dialogic, hybrid', capturing part of that old fluid
power that seems to blend together author and community.[8] But
there are dangers in that anonymity, too. It is after all the very
quality that enables an interpreter of fairy-stories like Bruno
Bettelheim to assign them a fixed meaning.[9] Far from asking who
authored them, he assumes they emerge out of some primordial cultural unconscious. The producer of pornographic literature is likewise usually 'invisible', his very anonymity lending power to the
suggestion that the pornographic scenario is invoking universal fantasies. But as Susanne Kappeler emphasises, this assumption of
anonymity disguises the actual structure of the pornographic scenario which is always tripartite: the master/producer, the object
(typically the woman/victim), and the onlooker (the producer's
guest). What makes Sade different and useful for Carter is that he is
the least invisible of pornographers, his name having become

synonymous with the sexual practices he describes (although he actively denied writing his most infamous texts). In his own life, long years of imprisonment could not bury the subversive potential of his writing, or the infamy of his name which 200 years later still has the power to discompose, provoking cries for its suppression.

The source of Carter's fascination with Sade is his potency as a satirist of his times, in particular his understanding and exposure of the central role of sexuality in the maintenance of the social status quo: 'since he is not a religious man but a political man, he treats the facts of female sexuality not as a moral dilemma but as a political reality' (p. 27). '[T]he prophet of the age of dissolution, of our own time, the time of the assassins', she calls him, the man whose danger lay in naming as his 'pleasure' what society sanctioned only as licensed legal crimes to be exercised as punishment by institutional authority (p. 32).

Furthermore, Carter argues, unlike all other pornographers, Sade claimed the 'rights of free sexuality for women', and created 'women as beings of power in his imaginary worlds' (p. 36). In her fairy-stories, she seeks to expose a truth that those old tales have only thinly disguised (just as Sade did in his black fairy-tales): that female virginity is the precious jewel of the ruling classes, token and guarantor of their property rights. This is something the Sadeian libertines understood, since it was the virgin daughters of the aristocracy who received the most vile treatment at their hands. The only real difference between pornographic and mythic archetypes, Carter suggests, is in the artful beauty with which sexual encounters are represented in the latter.

Carter claims that Sade is different from all other pornographers in that he discloses rather than hides the actuality of sexual relations:

> He creates, not an artificial paradise of gratified sexuality but a model of hell, in which the gratification of sexuality involves the infliction and the tolerance of extreme pain. He describes sexual relations in the context of an unfree society as the expression of pure tyranny.
>
> (p. 24)

The provocation in Carter's use of Sade is not her supposed validation of pornography, but her employment of his work to expose her female readers to their own complicity with the fictional representations of themselves as mythic archetypes. Such mystification of

femininity amounts, in her view, to a complicity with the pornographic scenario on which the unequal gender relations of our
society are founded. The figure of the innocent Justine – the
'repository of the type of sensibility we call "feminine"' (p. 47), 'the
broken heart, the stabbed dove, the violated sepulchre, the perse-
cuted maiden whose virginity is perpetually refreshed by rape'
(p. 49) – embodies the dangerous idealisation of the passive victim.
She is a figure of repression, 'repression of sex, of anger, and of her
own violence; the repression demanded of Christian virtue, in fact'
(pp. 48–9). Most provocatively of all, Carter says: 'In the looking-
glass of Sade's misanthropy, women may see themselves as they
have been and it is an uncomfortable sight' (p. 36).

It is important to remember that the vilification of Justine is part
of Carter's reaction to a mythicisation of female virtue that
infiltrated aspects of radical feminist discourse in the 1970s. Writers
such as Mary Daly and Susan Griffin popularised notions of
femininity as having innate qualities arising from women's reproductive functions: virtuous, nurturing and peace-enhancing. Such
ideas inevitably reinforced a conception of women as the passive
victims of male victimisers. Carter does not deny that women are
frequently victims of male violence and exploitation, but she is
arguing forcefully against the danger of turning that victimisation
into a virtue, of becoming enthralled by it. In doing so she runs the
risk of seeming to blame the victim for 'choosing' to 'collaborate',
as Kappeler puts it. But it needs pointing out that in *The Sadeian
Woman* she is careful to say: 'let us not make too much of this
apparent complicity. There is no defence at all against absolute
tyranny' (p. 139).[10]

On the whole, contemporaneous and subsequent critical responses to *The Sadeian Woman* reveal a profound unease, especially on the part of feminist critics, about Carter's precise
intentions. In *Heroes and Villains* (1969), *The Infernal Desire
Machines of Doctor Hoffman* (1972) and *The Passion of New Eve*,
she had already displayed her strong nerves in representing vivid
scenes of sexual violence. Several radical feminist critics in the
decade following the publication of *The Sadeian Woman* took
Carter to task, accusing her of reinforcing patriarchial representations of women that degraded them.[11] Even worse was Kappeler's
accusation that she implies women can liberate themselves through
exercising violence, that they should behave just as men do. This attention to Carter's work coincided with a moment when debates

among feminists were increasingly focused on the issue of pornography and violence against women. In the context of those debates, Carter was seen by these critics to be running with the enemy.

In examining the reasons why pornography became such a central issue for feminists, Lynne Segal points to the overriding emphasis given to sexuality in much feminist thinking, that it 'was *the* primary, overriding, source of man's oppression of women, rather than the existing sexual division of labour, organisation of the state or diverse ideological structures'. Secondly, she says, pornography came to be regarded by many as 'the cause of men's sexual practices, now identified *within* a continuum of male violence'. Such views, she adds, were commensurate with another shift in feminist thinking in the late 1970s and 1980s, from a celebration of sexual - pleasure and a belief in 'the *similarity* between men's and women's sexuality' that marked the earlier stages of the women's movement in the 1960s, to an emphasis on 'a fundamental *difference* between women's sexuality and men's, with women's sexuality once again the inverse of men's: gentle, diffuse and, above all, egalitarian'.[12] With her decidedly materialist conception of human sexuality and sexual practices, Carter staunchly opposed the implicit essentialism and ahistorical implications of such views. What was so controversial about Carter's response to these issues was not simply that she would reject the censorship of all pornography, but her argument that in examining the pornographic scenario we can learn as much about the cultural conditions that help to determine women's sexuality as we can about men's sexuality. The potency of Carter's writing is indicated by the fact that nearly a decade later *The Sadeian Woman* was used by feminist critiques of pornography when the debate was at its most intense. Her work was cited to reinforce the arguments of those situated on either side of the divide: those who viewed pornography as a central problem for women, and those who regarded the anti-pornography campaign as posing another danger, the policing and proscribing of women's sexual desires.

Kappeler's *The Pornography of Representation* offers a powerful indictment not simply of pornography itself, but of how the pornographic scenario, seen as the objectification and brutalisation of women, underpins much cultural production in Western societies. For Kappeler, the problem is not so much pornography as a distinct mode of representation or set of practices, but rather that it is ubiquitous, endemic to contemporary culture. Kappeler offers a complex thesis, and she certainly does not fall into the trap of naturalising women's difference from men. For Kappeler as for Carter, the pornographic scenario holds a mirror up to heterosexual relations, and yet Kappeler rejects Carter's conclusions and especially her use of Sade, accusing her of 'playing in the literary sanctuary' by vindicating Sade's work 'in the service of women' and of falling into the trap of claiming equal opportunities by proclaiming that women should '"cause suffering", just as men do'.[13] In fact, Carter's analysis of the antithesis Justine/Juliette, sacrificial victim and female libertine, is not fundamentally at variance with Kappeler's formulation of what she calls the 'cultural archeplot' of patriarchal power in which the female participants have two alternatives: willing victim or unwilling victim. Carter makes it clear that no matter how much control Juliette appears to assume over herself in the relentless pursuit of pleasure and the transgression of every social boundary, the king, master of the game, is still in place: 'her triumph is just as ambivalent as is Justine's disaster' (p. 79). But Carter cannot help betraying a preference for Juliette, the Nietzschean superwoman, because she is the female rebel, transgressor of the laws that conventionally control women's sexual behaviour. Juliette understands the master's game and plays it according to his rules. 'Since she specialises in *realpolitik*, it is not surprising that she is more like a real woman than Justine could ever be' (p. 101). Here Carter is on the verge of trying to have it both ways, subverting the binary of good/bad woman, and reinforcing it. The attraction to the bold, transgressive sister, the one who at least has her political analysis correct, over the submissive sister who clings to the fake myths of virginity as a woman's most valuable treasure, is understandable, but it almost betrays her purpose, and provides Kappeler with a space to make her accusation. Nevertheless, Kappeler fails to acknowledge Carter's conclusion, which finally throws over the whole Sadeian scene as 'this holy terror of love ... the source of all opposition to the emancipation of women' (p. 150), and insists on the necessity of reciprocity between the sexes.

Since the early 1990s, Kappeler's own work has been severely criticised for, among other things, a somewhat totalising view of men. 'With lovers like men,' she asks, 'who needs torturers?'[14] This provocative question suggests that the pornographic scenario is an inevitable element in heterosexual relationships. Lynne Segal makes explicit the connection between a suspicion of heterosexuality on the part of many feminists since the late 1970s and the reduction of feminist discussion about sexuality to the issue of pornography. Faced with Kappeler's belief that '"sexual liberation" is not the liberation of women, but the liberation of the female sex-object, which is now expected to orgasm (in response)',[15] Segal argues that many feminists 'who criticise pornography today mostly see themselves as rejecting the heritage of the sexual revolution'.[16] This point is crucial to understanding Kappeler's critique of Carter's thesis in *The Sadeian Woman*, with its assertion that women can gain pleasure in heterosexual relations, and its utopian conclusion that looks towards sexual reciprocity between men and women. Carter was as aware as anyone of the limitations of the sexual revolution. *The Infernal Desire Machines of Doctor Hoffman* can be read as a critique of 1960s notions of sexual liberation and their potential for exploiting women. But one of the most significant aspects of Carter's work, and which *The Sadeian Woman* exemplifies so profoundly, is its insistence on the empowerment of heterosexual women in a climate of opinion that suggested its impossibility. The questions that Segal places at the crux of the pornography debate within feminism – *'Is it, or is it not, possible for women to conceive of, and enjoy, an active pleasurable engagement in sex with men? Is it, or is it not, possible to see women as empowered agents of heterosexual desire?'* – are precisely the same questions that Carter addresses here and in her fiction.[17]

The figure of Juliette is the key to understanding Carter's use of Sade in rethinking female heterosexuality. She represents a heterosexual woman who uses her sexuality to explode the mythicisation of femininity that has kept women trapped and enthralled for centuries:

> She is a little blasphemous guerilla of demystification in the Chapel. ... She lobs her sex at men and women as if it were a hand grenade; it will always blow up in their faces.
>
> (p. 105)

As such, Juliette can be read as a figure of Bataillean excess, triumphing 'over the barriers of pain, shame, disgust and morality until her behaviour reverts to the polymorphous perversity of the child ...' (p. 148). Through Juliette, Sade claims this transgressive excess for women, but, Carter stresses, she is a figure of satire, not a role model. Nevertheless, it is a hazardous claim, as misreadings of the nuances of Carter's text testify. Opposing Kappeler in the feminist pornography debate is Linda Williams, who in her book *Hard Core* states that Carter 'argues for pornography on the grounds of Sade's politicisation of sexuality, and his insistence on the right of women to fuck as aggressively, tyrannically, and cruelly as men'.[18] Careful examination of the relevant passage from *The Sadeian Woman*, however, reveals that Carter's Sade does not actually say this at all. Carter says that he implies that it may be inevitable since '[a] free woman in an unfree society will be a monster'. But the point she is stressing here is that Sade 'urges women to fuck as actively as they are able ... to fuck their way into history and, in doing so, change it' (p. 27). That said, Williams is right to see in Carter an ally in her attempt to think beyond the binary of pornography or censorship that has polarised the debate. Williams's *Hard Core* played an important role in opening up the arguments through its exploration of the subversive and pleasurable possibilities of some pornography for women, and in moving away from the tendency in some feminist rhetoric to proscribe multiple, even 'perverse', expressions of female desire.

As an embodiment of a woman claiming responsibility for her own sexual behaviour, Juliette infiltrates many of the female protagonists of Carter's fiction: the rebellious heroines of the stories in *The Bloody Chamber*, and most explicitly Fevvers in *Nights at the Circus*. As Carter points out, if Apollinaire, at the turn of the century, could call Juliette the New Woman, to us she is only 'a New Woman in the mode of irony' (p. 79). But reflecting on current media images of sexually free, 'post-feminist' women – Madonna, Camille Paglia and the like – Nicole Ward Jouve asks if Juliette has nevertheless won, suggesting that Carter provided us in 1979 with an uncanny prophecy. But Ward Jouve's answer to her own question is a firm negative. These figures 'only seem to be the flesh-and-blood fulfilment of what *The Sadeian Woman* praised in Juliette', and like Lady Purple and other such figures in Carter's fiction, they serve to 'embody media fantasies'. Carter, she adds, 'unpicks the fabrication process: never promotes the illusion'.[19] In Fevvers, Carter creates a mediated version of this New Woman/sexual terrorist, who uses her sexuality as a device for survival, but who grows to understand that the price to be paid for playing the game according to the master's rules is ultimately annihilation.

The figure of Juliette carries one more resonance for Carter. She and the other female libertines in the Sadeian world 'like

Scheherazade ... know how to utilise the power of the word, of narrative, to save their lives' (p. 81). So for Carter she becomes a metaphor for the woman writer as rebel, the woman story-teller who tells the tales that do not quite fit into the social order of things. This analogy between the power of narration and survival – a significant theme in the whole feminist literary-critical enterprise of the last thirty years and more – recurs in her subsequent fiction. The successful heroines of the fairy-tales are the ones who become the authors of their own stories, inscribing their own desire into those old narrative frames. Fevvers constitutes a revision of Juliette, breaking out of that victim/victimiser frame by controlling the narration of her own story through a mixture of flagrant self-display and subterfuge.

The transformations of Juliette aside, and despite the rejection of Sade's binary of victim and victimiser, there remains the question of Carter's designation of Sade as a prototype of the 'moral pornographer', who

> might use pornography as a critique of current relations between the sexes. His business would be the total demystification of the flesh and the subsequent revelation, through the infinite modulations of the sexual act, of the real relations of man and his kind.
>
> (p. 19)

As Kappeler argues, if the pornographer as producer/director of the scene is an inherent element in the repressive and exploitative structures of representation in our culture, of which the pornographic scenario is simply an explicit case, how can pornography be invested with a different ideology, one aimed at exposing its own assumptions and exploitations? Both Carter's and Kappeler's texts provide critiques of prevailing modes of representation and of the political realities that produce them. Kappeler insists that '[t]he history of representation is the history of the male gender representing itself to itself – the power of naming is men's. ... Culture, as we know it, is patriarchy's self-image.'[20] This is an argument that Carter has elaborated in fictional terms in *The Passion of New Eve*. And in *The Sadeian Woman* she is as explicit as Kappeler about the relationship between pornography and other modes of representation, describing the literary as 'the imaginary brothel where ideas of women are sold' (p. 101).

Yet Kappeler's point that 'the root problem behind the reality of men's relations with women, is the way men see women, is Seeing'[21] draws attention to a structural feature of pornographic representation that Carter's discussion elides. Kappeler claims that women are objectified twice over, 'once as object of the action in the scenario, and once as object of the representation, the object of viewing':[22] that is to say, a collusion between producer and viewer is an essential element in the representation itself. Kappeler quotes Luce Irigaray, who, like Carter, has argued for the advantages of a 'Sadeian showing forth':

> Perhaps if the phallocracy that reigns everywhere is put unblushingly on display, a different sexual economy may become possible? Pornography as 'catharsis' of the phallic empire? As the unmasking of women's sexual subjection?[23]

Kappeler's rejoinder to this is to stress the statement's uncertainty as to its address: 'who will see with her, and who will, on the basis of what they see, want "another sexual economy"'. This is a question that Carter, like Irigaray, does not confront. It is not a more egalitarian economy of desire that the Sadeian libertines hope to achieve 'but profit from the one that institutionalises their advantage'. But Kappeler concedes that 'Irigaray's criticism tries at least to break through the boundaries and asks beyond the sanctuary's own terms';[24] and so, I would suggest, does Carter's. She points out, just as Georges Bataille does, that the Sadeian libertine, Sovereign Man, remains isolated and alone, because he does not wish to relinquish one bit of his profit by sharing his pleasures with anyone else, even with his fellow libertines.

Kappeler's accusation that Carter is 'playing in the literary sanctuary' suggests a refusal to accept that some pornographic writing may be subversive of the social status quo. Susan Rubin Suleiman's analysis of Carter's elaborate intertextual engagement with Surrealism provides a convincing rejoinder to Kappeler's assumption. In *Subversive Intent*, Suleiman examines the tradition of pornographic writing that begins with Sade and continues through to Lautreamont, Dada, the Surrealists and Bataille, and explores convincingly how contemporary feminist writers like Carter have used that tradition in an attempt to rethink and rewrite the female body and female sexuality. But Suleiman stresses the critical use they have made of that tradition, refusing to regard the female body as simply a figure in the text as the Surrealists and Bataille customarily do. She characterises Carter's work, along with some other postmodern feminist writing, as informed by 'a double allegiance': 'on the one hand to the formal experiments and some of the cultural aspirations of the historical male avant-gardes; on the other hand, to the feminist critique of dominant sexual ideologies, including those of the very same avant-gardes'. It is that double perspective, so much a feature of *The Sadeian Woman*, that has provoked such critical uncertainty. Suleiman describes this feature as possibly 'the most innovative as well as the most specifically "feminine" characteristic of contemporary experimental work by women artists'.[25] In *The Sadeian Woman*, Carter acknowledges the play of forces at work in Sade's writing, between its revolutionary subversion and conservative reaction, its power and its danger. It is her fearless confrontation of those contradictions that makes her contribution to contemporary feminist discourse so valuable. In Suleiman's words, she 'expands our notions of what it is possible to dream in the domain of sexuality, criticising all dreams that are too narrow'.[26]

In quoting Emma Goldman at the conclusion of *The Sadeian Woman*, Carter deconstructs her own claims for Sade:

> History tells us that every oppressed class gained true liberation from its masters through its own efforts. It is necessary that woman learn that lesson, that she realise that her freedom will reach as far as her power to achieve her freedom reaches.
>
> (p. 151)

Carter's analysis of Sade finally reveals that he is in allegiance with the very assumptions he is endeavouring to transgress. If she regards his demystification of the maternal function as a contribution to the emancipation of women, it is in this area that she also locates a central contradiction in his position. The theory of maternal superiority, she argues,

> is one of the most damaging of all consolatory fictions and women themselves cannot leave it alone, although it springs from the timeless, placeless, fantasy land of archetypes where all the embodiments of biological supremacy live.
>
> (p. 106)

She regards the flagrant abuse and denial of the mothering function by Sade's female libertines as the key to this demystification, the most extreme instance of which is the abuse of Mme de Mistival by her own daughter, Eugenie, in *Philosophy in the Boudoir*. The mother is raped by the daughter with the aid of a dildo, the daughter's revenge against the mother's inhibition of the free expression of her sexuality. Before she reaches climax, however, the mother faints, and so, like Justine, experiences sexuality only 'as a theft from herself'. In one of those moments of searing clarity, Carter concludes from this that Sade has scared himself so badly at this prospect of the sexualised mother that he performs an act of self-censorship to prevent it:

> Sade, the prisoner who created freedom in the model of his prison, would have put himself out of business; he is as much afraid of freedom as the next man. So he makes her faint.
>
> (p. 132)

The eroticised mother is dangerous, signalling as she does a transgression of the ultimate taboo because she implies change, a shift away from the moral absolutes of vice and virtue on which the Sadeian system depends. Carter speculates on the source of Sade's fear of the mother, locating it in two places: in the Freudian castration complex, the son's simultaneous horror at and denial of the mother's apparent castration, and his fear of being engulfed in the dark abyss between her legs, an insatiable hole that he can never close. But Carter also sees the attack on the mother in terms of Kleinian anger and envy at the good breast, the child's fury at the delusory promise of perpetual satisfaction that it offers, which in the libertine's frenzy turns into 'a helpless rage at the organs of generation that bore us into a world of pain where the enjoyment of the senses is all that can alleviate the daily horror of living' (p. 135). These ambiguous interpretations are perhaps indicative of Sade's own ambivalence, having brought himself to the boundaries where desire, fear and hate meet. But, more to the point, can we accept the claim that Sade demystifies the maternal function when his hatred of it is based on the very mystification she is talking about? The veneration of motherhood in Western culture is derived precisely from fear of that specifically female function, two sides of the same coin, and amounts to an attempt to keep the mother in her proper place. Carter is right to suggest that the sexualisation of the mother would inevitably unravel the straitjacket of myths surrounding her, but Sadeian anger, founded on that old fear and loathing, can hardly provide the means to that demystification.

It is this aspect of Carter's writing, especially in *The Sadeian Woman*, that most troubles Ward Jouve. She writes that having 'hunted the maternal archetype down to extinction' in *The Passion of New Eve*, Carter continues to reject the mother's body even in her more utopian fictions that follow. Ward Jouve asks if paradoxically this 'downgrading and refusal of motherhood was the ultimate phallocracy, the perpetuation of women's subjection? Does she, in her rejection of the mother, produce another form of suppression?'[27] Perhaps. Yet the argument Carter makes linking the demythicisation of motherhood and the emancipation of women remains as potent as when she first made it. Surely the surrogate mothers of *Nights at the Circus* and *Wise Children* (1991) are figures that speak very much to our times, when notions of mothering and fathering are so much a part of political agendas. In Carter's last two novels the threat of the perpetuation of an essentialised, naturalised concept of motherhood, employed for political purposes as it always has been, confronts us yet again. Once more Angela Carter catches the prevailing mood of her times and offers a challenge to it.

Bataille says that '[t]he truth of eroticism is treason'.[28] Carter's text can be read as an attempt to transform a Sadeian treason into a feminist one. Bataille also writes that 'admiration' of de Sade 'exalts his victims and transforms them from the world of physical horror to a realm of wild, unreal, sheerly glittering ideas'.[29] I would suggest that to seek to assimilate Carter's reworking of Sade into some feminist orthodoxy would be to diminish the force of her attempts to extend the limits of feminist thought. *The Sadeian Woman* aims to provoke and discompose as much as it seeks to convince. Ward Jouve, in plotting with such clarity the history of her own readings of Carter's work, her ambivalent responses to it and her wariness that in celebrating Carter we somehow diminish her power to provoke, touches on the very aspect of *The Sadeian Woman* that I believe takes it beyond its moment of publication and continues to speak to present readers.

From *The Infernal Desires of Angela Carter: Fiction, Femininity, Feminism*, ed. Joseph Bristow and Trev Lynn Broughton (London, 1997), pp. 132–48.

NOTES

[Sally Keenan's essay should be read in conjunction with Merja Makinen's above; *The Sadeian Woman: An Exercise in Cultural History* is a central text in Carter's *oeuvre* and was published the same year as *The Bloody Chamber*. *The Sadeian Woman* is an analysis of the writings of the Marquis de Sade, exploring what these tell us about the economic and sexual gender relations of Western modernity, in particular women's possibilities within this. Carter's study has generated unease, bafflement, hostility and controversy. Sally Keenan's historicist and politically engaged essay helps to clarify the arguments which this unsettling work proposes, by positioning *The Sadeian Woman* back in the context of 1970s and 1980s feminist debates and issues, and hence in relation to how this work has been read by certain feminist critics. Keenan then considers how one might read *The Sadeian Woman* now. She is sensitive to the work's textual strategies, and demonstrates that only a close and very careful textual reading combined with a willingness to be provoked by the book will yield Carter's idiosyncratic meanings. Ed.]

1. Angela Carter, *Nights at the Circus* (London, 1984), p. 122.

2. Mary Daly's *Gyn/ecology: The Metaethics of Radical Feminism* (London, 1979) and Susan Griffin's *Women and Nature: The Roaring Inside Her* (1978; repr. London, 1984), for instance, were two widely read texts which tended to reinforce notions of women's moral superiority as derived from their reproductive capacity and their supposed closeness to nature.

3. See Hélène Cixous's use of maternal metaphors to represent *écriture féminine* (the practice of a specifically feminine writing) in 'The Laugh of the Medusa' (1975), and Julia Kristeva's conception of maternity as a potential challenge to phallogocentricism in 'Héréthique de l'amour' (1977). I believe that Carter makes explicit reference to the maternal theories of Cixous and Kristeva in *The Passion of New Eve*, and an implicit criticism of them underpins her attack on the mythicisation of motherhood in *The Sadeian Woman*. 'The Laugh of the Medusa' appears in Elaine Marks and Isabelle de Courtivron (eds), *New French Feminisms: An Anthology*, trans. Keith Cohen and Paula Cohen (Amherst, MA, 1980), pp. 245–64. 'Héréthique de l'amour' appears as 'Stabat Mater' in Toril Moi (ed.), *The Kristeva Reader*, trans. Léon S. Roudiez (Oxford, 1986), pp. 161–86.

4. I would like to thank Lisa Day of Virago Press for access to the follow-
ing cuttings from the Virago library: Jan Tomczyk, review of *The
Sadeian Woman* in the *Birmingham Sun,* 29 May 1979; Rachel
Billington, 'Beware Women', in the *Financial Times,* 31 March 1979;
Marsaili Cameron, 'Whip Hand', in *Gay News,* March 1979; Ann
Oakley, review in *British Book News,* August 1979; Julia O'Faolain,
'Chamber Music', in *London Magazine,* August/September 1979; Sara
Maitland, review in *Time Out,* 4 May 1979; anonymous review in
Women's Report, June 1979. Page numbers are not available.

5. Sandra M. Gilbert and Susan Gubar, *The Madwoman in the Attic: The
Woman Writer and the Nineteenth-Century Literary Imagination*
(New Haven, CT, 1979), p. 42.

6. Lorna Sage makes the point that Carter's writing is 'in an oblique and
sometimes mocking relation to the kind of model of female fantasy deployed by Gilbert and Gubar in *The Madwoman in the Attic,* where
fantasy is a matter of writing against the patriarchal grain'. In Carter's
fictional worlds female madness, marginality and anger are not automatically equated with subversion. Neither, as Sage also points out,
are Carter's heroines ever simply the innocent victims of their entrapment. In her fiction 'the structures of power (literary and otherwise)
are a lot less obvious'. Lorna Sage, *Women in the House of Fiction*
(Basingstoke, 1992), p. 168.

7. Angela Carter, *The Sadeian Woman: An Exercise in Cultural History*
(London, 1979), pp. 38–9. Further page references to this edition are
given in the text.

8. Lorna Sage (ed.), *Flesh and the Mirror: Essays on the Art of Angela
Carter* (London, 1994), p. 3.

9. Bruno Bettelheim, *The Uses of Enchantment* (Harmondsworth, 1975).
In some of the stories in *The Bloody Chamber,* Carter was clearly
countering Bettelheim's classically Freudian readings of fairy-tales.

10. It might be argued that these days we have finally left Justine behind
us. And, what is more, that the old misogynist pornographer has been
dethroned by female-authored erotic writing. On the other hand,
perhaps things have not moved so far after all. Reviewing recent erotic
fiction by women, Rebecca Abrams writes: 'Women are writing about
sex, oh yes! But what they are describing is not the joyous burgeoning
of sexual possibility, but the burden of sexual misery, of deeply rooted
collective memories, of degradation, subjection, and victimisation'
(*Guardian,* 19 July 1994, p. 10).

11. In an article on *The Bloody Chamber,* Patricia Duncker attacked
Carter's representation of female sexuality, arguing that she reinforced
the pornographic scenario of the woman as willing victim. What also
disturbed Duncker was Carter's apparent emphasis on 'the animal

aspects of sexuality'. Duncker fails to take into account the references to surrealism and to Bataille's writing in Carter's language of eroticism. In *Eroticism,* Bataille wrote: 'Sexuality, thought of as filthy or beastly, is still the greatest barrier to the reduction of man to the level of the thing' (trans. Mary Dalwood [London, 1962], p. 158). Carter's story 'The Tiger's Bride', in particular, is imbued with this Bataillean sense of the erotic, but she reworks it, investing it with the mark of gender. Paulina Palmer also expressed reservations about Carter's use of animal motifs with reference to female sexuality in *Contemporary Women's Fiction: Narrative Practice and Feminist Theory* (Brighton, 1989), p. 26.

12. Lynne Segal, 'Introduction', in *Sex Exposed: Sexuality and the Pornography Debate*, ed. Lynne Segal and Mary McIntosh (London, 1992), pp. 3–4.

13. Susanne Kappeler, *The Pornography of Representation* (Cambridge, 1986), p. 134.

14. Ibid., p. 214.

15. Ibid., p. 160.

16. Segal, 'Sweet Sorrows, Painful Pleasures: Pornography and the Perils of Heterosexual Desire', in *Sex Exposed*, ed. Segal and McIntosh, p. 78.

17. Ibid., p. 79.

18. Linda Williams, *Hard Core: Power, Pleasure and 'The Frenzy of the Visible'* (London, 1990), p. 11.

19. Nicole Ward Jouve, 'Mother is a Figure of Speech', in *Flesh and the Mirror,* ed. Sage, pp. 147–8.

20. Kappeler, *The Pornography of Representation*, pp. 52–3.

21. Ibid., p. 61.

22. Ibid., p. 52.

23. Luce Irigaray, *This Sex Which Is Not One*, trans. Catherine Porter (Ithaca, NY, 1977), p. 203.

24. Kappeler, *The Pornography of Representation*, p. 210.

25. Susan Rubin Suleiman, *Subversive Intent: Gender, Politics and the Avant-Garde* (Cambridge, MA, 1990), pp. 162–3.

26. Ibid., pp. 139–40.

27. Ward Jouve, 'Mother is a Figure of Speech', p. 163.

28. Bataille, *Eroticism*, p. 171. Bataille's study was first published in French in 1957.

29. Ibid., p. 179.

3

The Violence of Gendering: Castration Images in Angela Carter's *The Magic Toyshop*, *The Passion of New Eve*, and 'Peter and the Wolf'

JEAN WYATT

In an essay on life in the 60s, Angela Carter describes how she became committed to 'demythologising' 'the social fictions that regulate our lives': 'I began to question ... the nature of my reality as a woman. How that social fiction of my "femininity" was created, by means outside my control, and palmed off on me as the real thing.'[1] Her novels and short stories take on some of the master narratives that continue to construct femininity in Western culture – giving us, for instance, in *The Bloody Chamber*, reconstructed fairy tales that transform the original tales' helpless virgins into active sexual subjects. The best defence against a social myth is, perhaps, another myth: by telling the old stories differently, Carter both points up the age-old patriarchal preference for certain kinds of heroines – passive, inert – and sets an alternative model of womanhood in place of the old. If fairy tales are among the 'mind-forged manacles' that circumscribe female identity ('Notes', p. 70), so, to judge from Carter's essays and interviews, are Freud's tales. I argue that Carter rewrites Freud's story of a little boy's discovery of sexual difference in 'Peter and the Wolf', explores the narrative possibilities of Freud's concept of woman as a castrated man in *The Passion of New Eve*, and rewrites Freud's account of a girl's oedipal transformation in *The Magic Toyshop*, exposing the power relations masked by Freud's emphasis on female anatomical lack.

The castrated female body, a pivotal image in Freud's narratives of sexual difference, strikes Carter as a powerful ideological tool for inscribing and so ensuring women's inferiority. On the other hand, the image of woman's castration serves Carter's own polemical purposes as a metaphor for the painful curtailment of a woman's erotic potential and active impulses when she accepts the limitations of the feminine role. Carter returns to the image of castrated woman again and again, addressing it as ideological issue, as narrative device, as image.

The Sadeian Woman, Carter's essay on pornography, describes the cultural reverberations of the castration image:

> The social fiction of the female wound, the bleeding scar left by her castration, ... is a psychic fiction as deeply at the heart of Western culture as the myth of Oedipus, to which it is related in the complex dialectic of imagination and reality that produces culture. Female castration is an imaginary fact that pervades the whole of men's attitude towards women and our attitude to ourselves.[2]

On the one hand, Carter emphasises the force of the physical image: because it is present to our imaginations not as metaphor but as anatomical fact – as 'bleeding wound' – the image of castrated woman provides a powerful physical correlative to the cultural assumption of women's inferiority. In an interview, Carter attributes the image to Freud: 'he could only think of women as castrated men'.[3] And it is Freud who is Carter's target when she is working the physical register of culture. 'Peter and the Wolf' challenges the story of Freud's generic little boy, who discovers with horror that a little girl's body has 'nothing there', where the penis should be: when Carter's little boy, Peter, catches a glimpse of his girl cousin's body he sees what *is* there – and the text describes in precise detail the complex configuration of female genitalia.

On the other hand, the passage from *The Sadeian Woman* reveals Carter's interest in the way that the image of woman as castrate interacts with other mythic images 'in the complex dialectic of imagination and reality' that sustains patriarchy. It is Lacan, rather than Freud, whose theories are most helpful in understanding Carter's reflections on the cultural uses of the castrated woman image. *The Magic Toyshop* not only describes what lures are offered, what pressures exerted, to seduce and coerce a girl into accepting the limitations of femininity. It also explores how woman as castrated, silenced object supports the ideal of masculinity as mastery, self-sufficiency, control. But it offers an alternative as well, a deviation that upsets the power balance of gender: a young man, refusing to aspire to the mastery his gender entitles him to, rejects the phallic legacy – most graphically by chopping off and throwing away a clear and obvious symbol of the phallus.

CARTER'S DIALOGUE WITH FREUD: 'PETER AND THE WOLF' AND *THE PASSION OF NEW EVE*

In 'Peter and the Wolf', as I read it, Carter challenges Freud's image of woman as castrate, attempting to displace it by entering into the cultural imaginary her own picture of an intact female body. In Freud's narrative of sexual discovery, a boy catches sight of a little girl's genitals, and seeing there no penis assumes she has been castrated; the idea that castration could be visited upon him, too, precipitates the boy's flight from his mother and his alignment with his father's authority, resolving the oedipal crisis and positioning him appropriately in the sex/gender system. Throughout Freud's many versions of this story, he endorses the small boy's 'recognition that women are castrated' ('Passing', p. 179), referring in his own voice to the 'discovery of her organic inferiority' ('Female Sexuality', p. 200), 'the reality of castration' ('Infantile', pp. 231; 275), 'the fact of her castration' ('Inhibitions', p. 123; 'Anatomical', p. 188; 'Female Sexuality', p. 202).[4] Backed by Freud's authority, the fiction of female castration probably influences not only men's images of women, but, as Carter says in the passage quoted above, 'our attitudes toward ourselves'. That is, the material terms in which woman's inferiority has been encoded undermine the bodily basis of woman's self-esteem, giving her a foundational sense of inferiority.

'Peter and the Wolf' attempts to revise this founding narrative of sexual difference by articulating the female genitalia as material presence. The plot need concern us only insofar as it brings about an encounter between Peter, a seven-year-old boy, and his cousin of the same age, who has been raised by wolves. When the family traps her and brings her into their house, she sits on the hearth howling for her brethren wolves:

> Peter's heart gave a hop, a skip, so that he had a sensation of falling; ... he could not take his eyes off the sight of the crevice of her girl-child's sex, that was perfectly visible to him as she sat there square on the base of her spine. ... Her lips opened up as she howled so that she offered him, without her own intention or volition, a view of a set of Chinese boxes of whorled flesh that seemed to open one upon another into herself, drawing him into an inner, secret place in which destination perpetually receded before him, his first, devastating, vertiginous intimation of infinity.[5]

Carter answers Freud's 'no thing' with a complex whorl of fleshly things, his 'nothing' with a material 'infinity'. (Carter may be deliberately troping Freud here, her intact wolf girl playing off the figure of castrated wolf central to the 'Wolf Man's' castration anxiety dream ['Infantile', pp. 213–34].)

Carter revises the male look crucial to the oedipal turn. Peter doesn't reduce female difference to a logic of the same (having/not having the penis): he sees his cousin's vagina in all its 'puzzling otherness', its 'unresolved materiality', its heterogeneity (Gallop, *The Daughter's Seduction*, p. 61). Freud's cognitive alliance with the little boy who sees only that the girl's body is penis-less leaves him open to the criticism (made most persuasively by Irigaray) that he himself refuses to see what *is* there: if the female genitalia were admitted 'as the signifier of the possibility of an other libidinal economy' (*Speculum*, p. 48), the social and linguistic categories constructed along the axis presence/absence – in fact the whole system of phallocentric meanings – would collapse. Indeed, when Peter, years later, gets a second glimpse of his cousin's radically other sexuality he ceases to believe in the masculinist systems – Catholic theology and Latin language – he has lived by: 'What would he do at the seminary, now? ... He experienced the vertigo of freedom' (p. 86). He enters a world unmapped by linguistic and doctrinal meanings, a world wide open to his discovery (p. 87). Carter's story suggests that the vision of real difference, taken in without denial or defensive categorisation, opens the mind to the previously unsignified, springing the subject free from established categories of thought.

'Peter and the Wolf' performs an important service for women by honouring the female body through representation. If representation governs what we believe in as real, the absence of representation has the effect of erasing reality. The occlusion of female sex organs from cultural representations, as well as their resurgence in pornography as a 'desexed hole' (*Sadeian Woman*, p. 20), has doubtless diminished female sexual capacity and undermined female self-esteem. Michele Montrelay's 'Inquiry into Femininity' implies that verbal articulation is a crucial dimension of sexuality itself. Claiming that women generally have a 'blank' where a representation of their sexuality should be, she cites several cases recorded by Maria Torok in which a female patient, following a session in which the analyst provides a description of her sexuality, has a dream which includes orgasm. Apparently a dialectic between body and word is necessary to a full experience of physical sensation. 'Pleasure is the effect of the word of the other':[6] hence the pleasure that women readers (at least this reader) derive from Carter's description. By entering the female body into a structuring discourse, Carter supplies a missing dimension of female sexual identity.

The Passion of New Eve deals with a literal castration: Evelyn, a man, is surgically deprived of his penis, and a female anatomy is constructed on the basis of that castrated body: he becomes Eve. Carter seems to be giving body to Freud's myth of woman as a castrated man and so reinforcing it – till it becomes evident that Eve, 'the perfect woman', is constructed according to the specifications of male desire. The relevant question then becomes, Why does man (including Freud) need to represent woman as castrated?

Feminist answers to this question begin with de Beauvoir's notion of woman as man's other: a man needs a defective other to reflect back to him his own full manly reality. If woman's lack is integral to a male sense of sufficiency, then it is imperative to make a plausible case for her deficiency: what more convincing way to argue the inferiority of woman than to ground that inferiority in her body? It then seems to be a part of factual reality – irrefutable. Freud's insistent iteration of 'the fact of her castration' then responds to a cultural imperative. (Thomas Laqueur's work shows that women's social subordination has always been encoded as genital inferiority. Before European science discovered her difference, it was her similarity to men that established her inferior status: pre-eighteenth century medical texts describe woman's uterus, ovaries, and vagina, as inverted and inferior imitations of, respectively, the male scrotum, testicles, and penis.[7])

Lacan carries the logic of the other one step further. In his lexicon everyone is 'castrated' – but masculinity is founded on the denial of that fundamental lack. 'Castration' is the founding term of subjectivity: when a child enters language and the social order it loses the direct and immediate relation to things (including the mother's body) that it had before signifiers intervened; and it is divided from itself, losing to the unconscious the part of the self split off from the socially determined narrow 'I' of the linguistic register. The subject feels the loss of an originary wholeness, imagined retrospectively, from a site within the symbolic order, as a lost unity with the maternal body. 'Through his relationship to the signifier, the subject is deprived of something of himself, of his very life.' 'Castration' in the Lacanian system represents the loss of that part one thought one had, the vital part that made one whole, 'that pound of flesh which is mortgaged in [the subject's] relationship to the signifier'.[8] The relevant point here is that no one retains the 'pound of flesh', no one has the missing link to completeness: 'no one has the phallus – it is a signifier, the initial signifier of "the lack-in-being that determines the subject's relation to the signifier"'.[9] But conventional masculinity is founded on a pretence of wholeness, and on a pretension to the phallus as the insignia of masculine power, authority, and invulnerability – founded, in other words, on a denial of the 'castration' that is the unavoidable price of entering the symbolic order. This affirmation of phallic intactness is both 'central to our present symbolic order' and 'precariously maintained', since it rests on 'a negation of the lack installed by language'.[10]

The fiction that a man can embody the phallic ideal can only be sustained through a series of props – and the first of these is woman. 'The subject is constituted in lack and the woman represents lack' (Heath, 'Joan Riviere', p. 52). In order to be 'the woman men want', then, a woman must put on the masquerade of femininity: as 'the Real is full and "lacks" nothing',[11] a woman has to disguise herself as 'castrated' in order to appear desirable. In Lacanian symbology the veil constitutes the exemplary disguise: 'Such is the woman behind her veil: it is the absence of the penis that makes her ... object of desire.' *The Passion of New Eve* and *The Magic Toyshop* deploy veils as Lacan does – to signify the castrated female body whose lack confirms the value of what man has.[12]

In *The Passion of New Eve* the masquerade is literal: Tristessa, a Hollywood star who is every movie-goer's ideal of femininity, hides a male body beneath her veils. At the moment of her/his unveiling the narrator, Eve, understands that Tristessa has been 'the most beautiful woman in the world' because 'she' has been constructed by a man: 'That was why he had been the perfect man's woman! He had made himself the shrine of his own desires … How could a real woman ever have been so much a woman as [he]?'[13] And what are the characteristics of this quintessential woman, this archetype of man's desire? Tristessa's attractiveness rests, the narrator says, on 'your beautiful lack of being, as if your essence were hung up in a closet … and you were reduced to going out only in your appearance' (p. 72). Here Carter spells out the meaning of Tristessa's veils: she is costumed as 'lack-of-being'. She is equal to 'the secret aspirations of man' (p. 128) because she can act out man's lack – so he need not assume it. This Lacanian perspective focuses the otherwise puzzling behaviours of Tristessa on screen: throughout her many screen roles she weeps, seeming to 'distill … the sorrows of the world'; her 'melancholy', her 'ache of eternal longing' take on significance as elaborate rituals of mourning over some loss too fundamental to name (pp. 121, 110, 72).

'The woman men want' is a castrated woman. As if to hammer in the point, Carter doubles Tristessa's representation of lack with a literally castrated body: the narrator Eve, originally Evelyn, is (involuntarily) castrated, then surgically reconstructed as the 'ideal woman' (p. 78). Modelled on a blueprint 'drawn up from a protracted study of the media', including the *Playboy* centrefold, she is made to incarnate male fantasies of Woman (pp. 78, 75). Eve and Tristessa thus literalise the notion of femininity as a male construct. At their first encounter, the narrator Eve mentally addresses Tristessa in language that approaches the theoretical level of a Lacanian polemic on femininity.

> The abyss on which [Tristessa's] eyes open, ah! it is the abyss of myself, of emptiness, of inward void … With her glance like a beam of black light, she ordered me to negate myself with her.
>
> (p. 125)

It is as 'emptiness', 'void', 'negation' that 'Woman' exists, as the negative sign – 'minus phallus, minus power' – that establishes the man as the standard of positive value.[14]

BECOMING AN OBJECT: *THE MAGIC TOYSHOP* (I)

Beneath its patina of Gothic thrills, *The Magic Toyshop* presents a careful, if parodic, inventory of the practices, cultural and familial, that rob a young girl of agency – indeed, of subjectivity – reducing her to the position of feminine object. The fifteen-year-old protagonist, Melanie, puts on the veils of femininity twice: once before her mirror, where she decks herself out in the gauzy costumes pictured by various male artists, recreating herself as the object of their gaze; and again when her uncle Philip forces her to play a chiffon-draped Leda in a family theatrical.

Shortly after the novel opens, Melanie's parents are killed in an aeroplane crash, and she is placed in her Uncle Philip's household. Philip's only passion is making life-sized puppets and putting on puppet shows. Philip sees in Melanie the potential for embodying his idea of a naïve young ingenue and casts her as Leda opposite his puppet swan in a production of 'Leda and the Swan'.

I read this episode as a parodic enactment of the violence implicit in father–daughter relations. For despite its touches of the fantastic and macabre, *The Magic Toyshop* is at bottom a family novel. In an extreme but recognisable schematic of the lines of power in a patriarchal nuclear family, Philip's family is structured by his paternal authority. He effectively controls the time and labour of his wife Margaret and his 'children' – Finn and Francie, Margaret's two brothers – from whom he exacts unquestioning filial obedience. His wife Margaret is correspondingly passive, without will and without voice (struck dumb on her wedding day, she has remained mute ever since). When Melanie goes to live with them, she slips into the position of daughter to Philip. Given the hyperbolic imbalance of voice and authority in Philip's family, it comes as no surprise that Carter dramatises the 'daughter's' oedipal crisis in a way that heightens the power dimensions of father–daughter relations.

The play, 'Leda and the Swan', fulfils the function of the oedipal stage: that is, it organises Melanie's sexuality to accord with her gender role. And, as in the theories of feminist theorists like de Beauvoir, Chodorow, and Benjamin, it is the 'father' who is the agent of Melanie's transformation from active girl to woman-as-object.[15] As Leda, she goes on stage swathed in the white chiffon costume Philip has designed; and she is utterly dependent upon his voice-on-high for direction. 'She halted, at a loss what to do next.

... She prayed for a cue. Uncle Philip read out: "Leda attempts to flee her heavenly visitant but his beauty and majesty bear her to the ground".'[16] Melanie sees approaching from the wings a grotesque puppet-swan: 'It was nothing like the wild, phallic bird of her imaginings. It was dumpy and homely and eccentric. She nearly laughed aloud to see its lumbering progress' (p. 165). Crude or not, Philip's fantasy (as well as, by implication, the male sexual fantasies dramatised in myths like Leda and the Swan) is effective, holding the woman to her role within the male imaginary:

> All her laughter was snuffed out. She was hallucinated; she felt herself not herself, wrenched from her own personality, watching this whole fantasy from another place. ... The swan towered over the black-haired girl who was Melanie and who was not. ... The swan made a lumpish jump forward and settled on her loins. She thrust with all her force to get rid of it but the wings came down all around her. ... The gilded beak dug deeply into the soft flesh. She screamed, ... She was covered completely. ... The obscene swan had mounted her. She screamed again. There were feathers in her mouth. ... After a gap of consciousness, she ... looked around for her swan.
>
> (pp. 66–7)

While the swan is, mercifully, not anatomically correct, the 'act' of rape retains the psychological effect that theorists and survivors of rape report: that is, women experience rape not only as a physical violation, but as a denial of their humanity, of their agency and self-determination: 'the real crime is the annihilation by the man of the woman as a human being'.[17] *The Sadeian Woman* makes clear that Carter shares this understanding of rape: 'In a rape ... all humanity departs from the sexed beings. ... Somewhere in the fear of rape is ... a fear of psychic disintegration, ... a fear of a loss or dismemberment of the self' (p. 6). In *The Magic Toyshop*, then, Carter uses rape as a metaphor for the psychic 'dismemberment' of a young girl. Like Gayle Rubin, Carter revises Freud's notion that it is the recognition of her anatomical lack, of her actual 'castration', that persuades a girl at the oedipal juncture to acknowledge her 'inferiority',[18] rather, oedipal socialisation itself is shown as a castrating process that strips a girl of her active impulses, her agency, and indeed her subjectivity, reducing her to the feminine object required by a patriarchal social order.

For the play teaches Melanie to define herself as object: 'The swan towered over the girl who was Melanie and who was not'

(p. 166). John Berger has given us the paradigm for this doubling: existing within a world defined by the male gaze and dependent upon male approval for her welfare, a woman learns to see herself as men see her, carrying 'the surveyor and the surveyed within her'.[19] But Carter's description suggests a still more radical self-division. 'The black-haired girl who was Melanie' is the girl seen from outside, not from the position of 'surveyor within her', not from a subjective (if colonised) centre, but 'wrenched from her own personality, watching this whole fantasy from another place' – from a place that approximates the site of the male gaze; and 'the black-haired girl ... who was not [Melanie]' is the void within. Rather than being split into an object which is seen and a subject who sees, Melanie is split into an object – viewed from a male perspective external to her – and, perceived from within, a nothing.

At tea after the play, Melanie retains the consciousness – paradoxically – of an object. Since she lacks a subjective centre from which to organise the world, reality haemorrhages from the things she perceives, flowing toward the subject who now organises *her* as an object in his world. 'The cake seemed extremely unlikely, a figment of the imagination. She ate her slice but tasted nothing. The company round the tea-table was distorted and alien ... Everything was flattened to paper cut-outs by the personified gravity of Uncle Philip as he ate his tea' (p. 169). There is only one subject now, and 'his silence reached from here to the sky. It filled the room' (p. 168). Since Philip is silent, giving Melanie no script (or rather, no voice-over) she is silent too.

The violence of gendering is usually masked by the dynamic of love that produces it: according to the feminist theorists cited by Nancy Chodorow, a father 'bribes' his daughter with 'love and tenderness' when she explains the passive feminine behaviours that please him and so gradually trains her to derive self-esteem from his praise rather than from her own actions – to become, in the familiar phrase, the apple of his eye, the submissive object of his affection.[20] The idealisation of the father as powerful subject in relation to a passive and dependent self 'becomes the basis for future relationships of ideal love, the submission to a powerful other who seems to embody the agency and desire one lacks in oneself' (Benjamin, 'Desire', p. 86). By stripping the oedipal conversion from subject to object of compensatory fatherly affection and condensing a process of adaptation that usually takes years into the space of a single scene, Carter dramatises the violence of the father–daughter relations which force the identity of passive object on a girl – a violence already implicit, if unexplored, in de Beauvoir's description of a daughter's normal oedipal resolution: 'It is a full abdication of the subject, consenting to become object in submission [to the father]' (p. 287).

The oedipal stage which transforms an active girl into a passive object is always governed by the needs of a male-dominant social order;[21] but the social dimension is usually hidden by the family's enclosure within a seemingly private space. Carter emphasises that the closed space of the family doubles as cultural space by superimposing the myth of Leda and the Swan on Melanie's oedipal initiation. At a founding movement of Western civilisation – for the rape of Leda engendered Helen, hence the Trojan War, hence the master epic of the Western tradition, Homer's *Iliad* – as in every girl's oedipal experience, Carter implies, woman's subjectivity is erased as she is inserted into the patriarchal order. As the exaggerated conventionality of his patriarchal traits suggests, Philip's puppet workshop represents more than a family business: it doubles as a cultural site where the myths that sustain patriarchy are fabricated. (Philip's other puppet plays also dramatise a particular idea of womanhood: in 'The Death of the Wood-Nymph', for instance, his chiffon-draped ballerina puppet is exquisitely graceful and then in death, exquisitely graceful, silent, and quiescent.[22])

If Philip's imagination is crude, incapable of reaching beyond the terms of brute power, so, Carter implies, is the patriarchal imaginary. Rape is a basic trope of our Western cultural heritage: by Amy Richlin's count, Leda's is one of fifty rapes in Ovid's *Metamorphoses* alone. And Yeats's modernist update of 'Leda and the Swan' manages to celebrate rape as an act of power and beauty by eliding, again, the woman as subject. Leda is reduced to a body part, her sensations of pain and feelings of violation dead-ended in a synecdoche: 'How can those terrified vague fingers push / The feathered glory from her loosening thighs?' Carter's clumsy swan is a joke on patriarchal mythmakers who dress up the principle of male domination in grandiose poetry – but it is a serious joke. Yeats mystifies rape as a moment of divine transcendence ('Did she put on his knowledge with his power?'); Carter shows it to be an act of brute force.[23]

That Philip represents a cultural site for the production of social myths as well as a domestic tyrant, that the 'rape' of Melanie's subjectivity is meant to represent not just the plight of one abused daughter but the structural alienation of woman in patriarchy – these larger meanings are reinforced by the parallel between Philip's ideal of a womanhood effaced behind white veils and the diaphanous white costumes that Melanie designs for herself at the beginning of the novel, before her parents' death and her move to Philip's house. Melanie is just coming into womanhood as the novel opens:

> The summer she was fifteen, Melanie discovered she was made of flesh and blood. O, my America, my new found land. She embarked on a tranced voyage, exploring the whole of herself, clambering her own mountain ranges, penetrating the moist richness of her secret valleys, a physiological Cortez, da Gama or Mungo Park.

The metaphors of exploration indicate that Melanie is discovering herself for herself – her body an uncharted territory for her delectation alone. But the text immediately suggests the impossibility of discovering anything new:

> For hours she stared at herself, naked, in the mirror of her wardrobe; ... she posed in attitudes ... Pre-Raphaelite, she combed out her long, black hair to stream straight down from a centre parting and thoughtfully regarded herself as she held a tiger-lily from the garden under her chin ... She was too thin for a Titian or a Renoir but she contrived a pale, smug Cranach Venus with a bit of net curtain wound round her head ... After she read *Lady Chatterley's Lover*, she secretly picked forget-me-nots and stuck them in her pubic hair. Further, she used the net curtain as raw material for a series of nightgowns suitable for her wedding-night which she designed upon herself.
>
> (pp. 1–2)

The sequence of artists' names draws the reader's attention to the male hand, the male gaze, that direct and define Melanie even in the apparently unmediated act of self-exploration. Melanie continues to think of herself as exuberant subject when she is already part of a system of representations that defines her as object. 'A la Toulouse Lautrec, she dragged her hair sluttishly across her face and sat down in a chair with her legs apart and a bowl of water and a towel at her feet. She always felt particularly wicked when she posed for Lautrec' (p. 1). Between taking on the man's image of woman and presenting that same image to his gaze ('posing for Lautrec'), there is no room for an autonomous female subject; such a closed circuit makes a mockery of self-discovery. Rather than ask, as Melanie does, 'What am I?' (p. 141), a woman might well ask, 'What do I represent?' Limiting her analysis to the visual register of culture, Carter condenses the process of interpellation, dramatising 'the passage from cultural representations to self-representations' (de Lauretis, p. 12). Melanie accepts the culture's representation of woman as her own because she believes it will give her power – the sexual power to attract a romantic bridegroom who will carry her off to 'honeymoon Cannes. Or Venice'. But when she fancies her veiled self 'gift-wrapped for a phantom lover' (p. 2) she unwittingly acknowledges her subjection. As passive visual object offered to the man's gaze, she is utterly dependent on his desire to 'invest her veils' with 'charm', to quote Emily Dickinson. In fact (as Dickinson's poem goes on to suggest) the 'charm' attaches not to the woman, but to the veil: the woman herself is meant to recede behind the identity of the veil, a screen onto which the male viewer can project his ideal of womanhood.[24]

Lacan's theory of the gaze, because it is also limited to the visual register, can help explain how Melanie 'becomes' a representation – how she is interpellated into the symbolic order. According to Lacan's schema of the visual field (diagrammed in *The Four Fundamental Concepts*), when I look at an object an 'image' comes between my gaze and the object: when I in turn become the object of the gaze, the gaze surveys me through an intervening 'screen'.[25] What is this image through which I view an object? What is the screen through which the gaze fixes me? Lacan doesn't say; but Kaja Silverman treats both image and screen as cultural artifacts ('Male Subjectivity' pp. 145–52). The first proposition obviously fits Melanie's case: she cannot see her reflection directly, but only in a form dictated by the culture. The second part of Lacan's algorithm seems at first not to apply: the other looks at me through a cultural screen – or, more precisely (since, Lacan says, the screen is opaque), the gaze fits me into the configuration of the cultural screen it projects upon me. But Melanie is alone in her room: that is what gives her the illusion of creating her own image in an autonomous space. Lacan goes to great lengths, however, to distinguish the gaze from any specific eye. He repeatedly insists on our status as objects of the gaze, even if no one else is present: 'That which makes us consciousness institutes us by the same token as *speculum mundi* ... that gaze that circumscribes us ... makes us beings who are looked at, but without showing this' (Lacan, *Four*, p. 75). The gaze is all around us, a function of our existence in a visual field; being the object of the gaze is an inalienable dimension of human being. Although she is alone Melanie is nevertheless subject to the world's gaze, and that gaze fits her into a screen of cultural images. To credit oneself as possessor of the gaze, as Melanie does in this scene of presumed visual power, is to be deluded: 'In the scopic field, the gaze is outside, I am looked at, that is to say, I am a picture' (Lacan, *Four*, p. 106). Further, Lacan implies that being turned into a 'picture', being mapped onto a background of pre-existing images, pressures us to adopt their forms. 'If I am anything in the picture, it is always in the form of the screen' (Lacan, *Four*, p. 97). Carter literalises 'the process whereby the subject assumes the form of representation – becomes a picture' (Silverman, 'Male Subjectivity', p. 148) by having Melanie mould herself to the shapes of the cultural screen, step into the canvases of Lautrec, Cranach, the Pre-Raphaelites.

Compared to his analysis of the gaze, Lacan's notion of the mirror stage is relatively straightforward: the child takes on, assumes as his own identity, the unified body image in the mirror. Carter gives the mirror stage a cultural edge as Melanie accepts the icon in the mirror as her own self-image. In a final veiling, decked out in her mother's wedding dress, Melanie jubilantly declares, 'she *was* ... the beautiful girl ... in her mirror. Moonlight, white satin, roses. A bride' (italics mine; p. 16), and so embraces her function as a cultural sign in a symbolic system not of her own making.[26] Visually articulated into the cultural screen, Melanie leaves the prolonged mirror stage of the novel's opening pages not as agent, but as object of the gaze: to borrow Lacan's phrase, she defines herself as *speculum mundi*, offering her bridal-veiled self as spectacle to the world's gaze. '"Look at me!" she cried to the apple tree ... "Look at me!" she cried passionately to the pumpkin moon' (p. 16).

Melanie has already absorbed her cultural identity as object, then, well before she acts out Philip's script. Carter's idea of how 'the social fiction of [her] femininity' is 'palmed off' on a woman ('Notes', p. 70) is by no means simple. She complicates the psychoanalytic model of a femininity produced largely through father–daughter relations by connecting Philip's ideal of femininity as veiled impotence to the representations of women in Western art and myth.

Philip's brutal theatre of gender does add some important information to the messages about womanhood that Melanie gets from the better known artisans of femininity whose images crowd her solitude. Throughout the mirror scene, Melanie is seduced by a hypocritical culture's promise that dressing provocatively gives a young woman sexual power. Philip's dramatisation offers a more realistic assessment of the veils' power. The rape of Leda by a figure of omnipotent masculinity illustrates the power relations that patriarchal culture misrepresents as love relations. As in feminist accounts of rape as a political instrument of oppression that intimidates *all* women, Philip deploys rape to 'teach the objective, innate, and unchanging subordination of women'.[27] Negated as subject, Melanie is forcibly instructed in what the veils mean in a masculine symbolic system: they represent the erasure of the female subject, her transformation into a place-marker signifying lack. As Lacan suggests, the veils' allure stems from their capacity to suggest an absence beneath – to suggest the nothing that supports the something of man. 'Adornment *is* the woman, she exists veiled: only thus can she represent lack, be what is wanted' (Heath, 'Joan Riviere', p. 52).

'DISMEMBERING' THE PHALLIC BODY: *THE MAGIC TOYSHOP* (II)

The Magic Toyshop offers an alternative as well as a critique of patriarchal sexual relations. Melanie forms a romantic alliance with Finn, her counterpart in age, status, and subordination to the father – her 'brother', in a word, in this family structure. Choosing the more egalitarian structure of the brother–sister bond defeats the aim of the father–daughter relation, which is meant to shape female desire to the passive responsiveness that sustains male dominance.[28] It is not that Melanie suddenly changes from the impressionable girl that I have been describing into an autonomous and self-defining heroine; rather, it is Finn who makes the revolutionary gesture of forfeiting the privileges of masculinity, opening up the possibility of a different relationship between man and woman.

During the night following the play, Finn comes to Melanie's bedside asking for comfort. He has destroyed the puppet swan, he says, and he is trembling with shock at his own audacity and with fear at the terrible vengeance that awaits him – for Philip loves all his puppets inordinately, especially the newly-created swan. Finn describes chopping up the swan and carrying the pieces to a park nearby to bury:

> 'First of all, I dismembered [the swan] ... with Maggie's little axe ... the swan's neck refused to be chopped up; the axe bounced off it. It kept sticking itself out of my raincoat when I buttoned it up to hide it and it kept peering around while I was carrying it, along with all the bits of the swan ... It must have looked, to a passer-by, as if I was indecently exposing myself, when the swan's neck stuck out. I was embarrassed with myself and kept feeling to see if my fly was done up ... it seemed best ... to bury it in the pleasure garden.'
>
> (pp. 171–3)

It is from his own body that the false 'phallus' pokes out, so in chopping it off Finn refuses the masquerade of masculinity: he acknowledges his own castration. In the family structure, Finn is in the position of son to Philip, 'apprenticed' to him ostensibly to learn the art of toymaking, but implicitly to learn the art of male dominance. 'He is a master', says Finn, referring to Philip's skills as dollmaker; but in the field of gender relations as in woodcraft Finn is meant to identify with the father figure, become 'master' in relation to woman. (Before the play, for instance, Philip sent Finn to 'rehearse' Melanie in the role of Leda – in other words, to play the part of the rapist swan; Finn initially complied, but bolted in the middle of the act.) Severing and throwing away the paternal symbol is equivalent to refusing the phallic function. In Lacan's terms, Finn acknowledges the lack that is everyone's inevitable lot. He presents himself at Melanie's bedside as castrated – that is, as incomplete, insecure, in need of comfort: 'Sick and sorry, he came creeping to her bed ... "Melanie ... can I come in with you for a little while? I feel terrible"' (p. 170). Finn not only derails the family agenda; by rejecting 'the affirmation central to our present symbolic order that the exemplary male is adequate to the paternal function' (Silverman, p. 135) Finn subverts the power relations of patriarchy.

A remark dropped during an interview suggests what Carter was up to when she staged this male castration:

> 'But you see, one of the things I love about Charlotte Brontë, about *Jane Eyre*, is that she won't look at Rochester until she's castrated him ... [Then] she's very nice to him, she can afford to be, this is where she can start behaving like a human being. Actually, in Freudian terms (not Freudian, Freud would be terribly upset) what she's done is to get him on an egalitarian and reciprocal basis,

because in fact she hasn't castrated him at all, she's got rid of his troublesome *machismo*.'

(Sage p. 56)

Carter's nod to Freud's discomfiture suggests that she is aware of the revolutionary potential of shifting castration from woman to man. Freud would be 'terribly upset' because he inscribed his notion of gendered power relations across the genitals, with the active penis representing the triumphant male subject and the corresponding blank representing a necessarily passive female space. Fixing the sign of castration on the male body, dispensing with a 'troublesome *machismo*', with the aspiration to invulnerable masculinity – with the phallus, not the penis – would shift the balance of power to which Freud subscribed, opening the way for an 'egalitarian and reciprocal' relation between man and woman.

Indeed, Melanie responds to Finn's display of neediness with a new set of responses:

> He must have been through a great ordeal. ... 'I have been in that place, too,' she thought. She could have cried for them both. ... 'You must have had a time of it, poor Finn.' She felt that somehow their experience ran parallel. She understood his frenzy. 'Poor Finn.'
>
> (pp. 172–3)

Finn's refusal to disavow castration has started a general collapse of the fortifications that defend the system of sexual difference. Melanie's recognition that she and Finn are alike undermines gender hierarchy. A founding principle of the sex/gender system, Gayle Rubin shows, is 'the idea that men and women are mutually exclusive categories'; that social fiction contradicts 'nature', where 'men and women are closer to each other than either is to anything else – for instance, mountains, kangaroos, or coconut palms. ... Far from being an expression of natural differences, exclusive gender identity is the suppression of natural similarities' (pp. 79–80). Jessica Benjamin, analysing the principles governing erotic dominance in 'The Story of O', finds that each act of the master 'signifies the male pronouncement of difference over sameness'.[29] Absolute mastery depends on absolute differentiation from the subjugated woman, especially on a denial of mutual dependency. In less extreme cases of male dominance as well, a man's fear of being demoted to the feminine position safeguards the system of sexual difference from an admission of similarity. 'Psychological domination is ultimately the failure to recognise the other person as like, although separate from oneself' (Benjamin, 'Master', p. 283).

Finn is released from the fear that he will be reduced to similarity, he is already there. And Finn's renunciation of all claim to phallic sufficiency necessarily releases Melanie from the task of patriarchy's good woman – seeing and desiring a man 'only through the mediation of images of an unimpaired masculinity' (Silverman, 'Male Subjectivity', p. 42). The dangers to gender hierarchy of admitting resemblance are immediately clear, as Melanie moves from empathy to a geometry of equality: 'their experience ran parallel' (p. 173). The image of lives lived along parallel lines implies the replacement of hierarchy by a lateral relationship, 'egalitarian and reciprocal'.

Angela Carter does not idealise the sibling model of erotic relations, either. A relationship with a vulnerable other who is needy like oneself entails giving up dreams of romantic love – and Melanie is reluctant to give up the fantasy bridegroom who would transport her to 'honeymoon Cannes. Or Venice' (p. 2). If the man doesn't have enormous power in relation to one's small self, then he doesn't have the power to sweep one off one's feet and carry one away to a new life. Melanie has to sacrifice transcendence in the passive mode.

> They were peaceful in bed as two married people who had lain in bed easily together all their lives. ... She knew they would get married one day and live together all their lives and there would be ... washing to be done and toast burning all the rest of her life. And never any glamour or romance or charm. Nothing fancy.
>
> (p. 174)

If the other is not markedly different from oneself, there is no hope of a radical break between the humdrum present and a glamorous future – only an infinitely protracted dailiness.

In the light of Finn's 'simple and honest' (p. 170) declaration of vulnerability and request for comfort, Philip's conventional masculinity takes on the appearance of masquerade (or parade, Lacan's term for masculinity). The assumption of phallic identity – of a masterful, coherent and self-contained sufficiency – entails an impossible consistency: Philip is invariably overbearing, always brutal and insensitive, single-minded in his determination to control everyone – with no lapses, no gaps, no needs. His one-dimensional consistency makes the model of dominant masculinity look implausible.

Likewise, Finn's relationship with Melanie, based on a recognition of mutual need, throws a parodic light on the standard patriarchal couple represented by Philip and Margaret. Since Philip pretends to the phallic ideal, his wife must support the fiction by revering him as the phallic ideal: in Silverman's phrase, the 'dominant fiction' requires that both the man and his attendant woman 'deny all knowledge of male castration by believing in the commensurability of penis and phallus, actual and symbolic father' (p. 42). Margaret attests to Philip's absolute power by applauding his omnipotence as puppet-master (p. 128) and by maintaining a consistent show of shrinking, cowed obedience.

In other words, the parade of phallic sufficiency requires the masquerade of castrated woman. If the man is to deny castration, the woman must serve as the site where he can deposit his lack. Margaret's lack is indeed conspicuous: she has no voice. And every Sunday she puts on a rather literal masquerade of femininity, donning the necklace Philip has made for her. This silver necklace, reaching from shoulder to chin, is alternately described as a 'choker' – it prevents any movement of the head – and a 'collar', worn like other collars in the spirit of subjection (pp. 112–13). Finn says that Margaret and Philip make love every Sunday: to attract the man the woman ornaments herself; but the ornament itself signifies her subjection to the man; and it is adornment as a sign of submission that makes her desirable.

Silent, passive, and compliant, Margaret appears to be the perfect 'castrated woman'. But if such true womanliness is 'a presentation for the man, ... as he would have her' (Heath, 'Joan Riviere', p. 50), a question lingers: what hides behind the presentation? In particular, if the masquerade ... is what women do ... in order to participate in man's desire, but at the cost of giving up their own' (Irigaray, *This Sex*, p. 133), what becomes of that displaced desire? Is there perhaps a hint of anxiety in Freud's question, 'What does a woman want?'

In the concluding pages of the novel, the reader, Melanie, and Philip all find out what is behind the mask. Margaret and Francie (Margaret's other brother) are lovers: 'They have always been lovers' (p. 194). When Philip finds his wife in her brother's arms, he burns down the house. Given Carter's affection for *Jane Eyre*, the parallel with Bertha and her fire seems inescapable: female desire, forced into a patriarchal lock-up by a system of repressive gender roles, gains in intensity from its very suppression until it explodes from within, destroying the patriarchal family structure that confined and silenced it.

Finn and Melanie, escaping to the garden next door[30] while 'everything' burns, 'faced each other in a wild surmise' (p. 200). This closing allusion to Cortez's discovery of the Pacific (in Keats's 'On First Reading Chapman's Homer') encourages readers to hope that the destruction of Philip's factory of patriarchal fantasies opens up before Melanie and Finn an uncharted space free of the old gender demarcations. Or does it? The opening page's metaphors of global exploration have taught us to be sceptical about the possibility of brave new worlds.

Critics have objected that Carter's early novels (*The Magic Toyshop*, 1967, *Heroes and Villains*, 1969, and *The Passion of New Eve*, 1977) critique patriarchy without offering any positive alternatives: thus Paulina Palmer comments that 'while presenting a brilliantly accurate analysis of the oppressive effects of patriarchal structures, [the novels run] the risk of making these structures appear even more closed and impenetrable than, in actual fact, they are' by discounting all possibilities for change.[31] I would argue that although Carter rewrites social myths in ways that bring out their hidden damages – the pain of Melanie's gendering, for instance, is not softened by parental tenderness – her revisions are liberatory not just because of their 'demythologising' effect: they also suggest alternative forms of masculinity – and therewith, since gender is a relational term, the possibility of revising notions of femininity as well. Both 'Peter and the Wolf' and *The Magic Toyshop* picture what would happen if a male subject refused the privileges of masculinity. 'Peter and the Wolf' revises the look central to male identity formation, substituting an active receptivity to female difference for Freud's defensive wrestling of difference into a familiar binary that separates those who have from those who don't. Finn's 'castration' undoes the rigid structural opposition between man and woman, suggesting the possibility of distributing strength and weakness, need and comfort, more equably between the sexes. What Carter is unwilling to compromise or soften in these early novels is her depiction of woman's structural position within patriarchy: becoming a woman requires, in *The Passion of New Eve*, a literal castration and, in *The Magic Toyshop*, a 'rape', an alienation of a woman's subjective agency that amounts to a mutilation.[32]

From *Women's Studies*, 25:6 (1996), 549–70.

NOTES

[Lacan's theories of subject formation have been important to much contemporary cultural analysis, including feminist studies. Jean Wyatt's essay, strongly based on a number of psychoanalytic texts, finds Lacan's ideas more useful than Freud's in understanding Carter's explorations of patriarchal formations and the whole system of social meanings based on this 'libidinal economy', including representations that make the masculine sign of the phallus central. In Wyatt's discussion of *The Passion of New Eve* and *The Magic Toyshop*, she makes use of Lacanian ideas of cultural 'castration' where men as well as women are subordinated within the socio-symbolic order (though the masculine must pretend to being still whole in order to have some power and authority). Also important to her analysis is the process of 'interpellation' – the way in which society seeks to call its subjects to predetermined roles (though we must also remember that this does not necessarily produce compliant subjects). Furthermore, Wyatt makes the issue of Carter's relation to these psychoanalytic theories central to her essay. She gives an account of Carter's rebellious rewriting of Freud in her story, 'Peter and the Wolf', and identifies other hints of parody and humour in Carter's handling of masculine subjectivity, thus demonstrating that ideological formulations are never identical with actual experience. This reprinting of Wyatt's essay has, with the author's permission, omitted two extended footnotes elaborating on certain complexities of Freud's ideas in relation to her argument. Ed.]

1. Angela Carter, 'Notes from the Front Line', in *On Gender and Writing*, ed. Michelene Wandor (London, 1983), pp. 71, 70.

2. Carter, *The Sadeian Woman: An Exercise in Cultural History* (London, 1979), p. 23.

3. Lorna Sage, 'The Savage Sideshow: A Profile of Angela Carter', *New Review*, 4.39–40 (1977), p. 56.

4. Sigmund Freud, 'The Passing of the Oedipus-Complex' (1924), reprinted in *Sexuality and the Psychology of Love*, ed. Philip Rieff (New York, 1963), pp. 176–82; Freud, 'Female Sexuality' (1931), reprinted in *Women and Analysis*, ed. Jean Strouse (Boston, 1985), pp. 73–94; Freud, 'From the History of an Infantile Neurosis' (1918) ('Wolf Man' case history), reprinted in *Three Case Histories*, ed. Philip Rieff (New York, 1965), pp. 187–316; Freud, *Inhibitions, Symptoms, and Anxiety* (1926), Standard Edition, ed. James Strachey, vol. 20, pp. 75–174; Freud, 'Some Psychological Consequences of the Anatomical Distinction Between the Sexes' (1925), reprinted in *Sexuality and the Psychology of Love*, ed. Rieff, pp. 183–93. Shortly after the publication of Freud's first essay on femininity in 1925, Karen Horney shrewdly observed that Freud's description of female development 'differs in no case by a hair's breadth from the typical ideas that

the boy has of the girl' ('The Flight from Womanhood' [1926], reprinted in *Woman and Analysis*, ed. Strouse, p. 174). See also Luce Irigaray's analysis of Freud's 'nothing there' (*Speculum of the Other Woman*, trans. Gillian Gill [Ithaca, NY, 1985], p. 48) and Jane Gallop's commentary on Irigaray (*The Daughter's Seduction: Feminism and Psychoanalysis* [Ithaca, NY, 1982], pp. 58–9; 65–6). Juliet Mitchell is more forgiving: she argues that Freud was consciously analysing women's condition under patriarchal oppression; recognising her 'castration' meant recognising her lack of phallic power ('On Freud and the Distinction Between the Sexes', in *Women and Analysis*, ed. Strouse, p. 34).

5. Carter, 'Peter and the Wolf', in *Black Venus* (London, 1986), p. 83.

6. Michele Montrelay, 'Inquiry into Femininity', trans. Parveen Adams. *m/f*, 1 (1978), 95.

7. Simone de Beauvoir, *The Second Sex*, trans. H. M. Parshley (New York, 1989), p. xxiii; Thomas Laqueur, *Making Sex: Body and Gender from the Greeks to Freud* (Cambridge, MA, 1990), pp. 4, 25–62, 236.

8. Jacques Lacan, 'Desire and the Interpretation of Desire in *Hamlet*', trans. James Hulbert, in *Literature and Psychoanalysis: The Question of Reading Otherwise*, ed. Shoshana Felman (Baltimore, MD, 1982), p. 28.

9. Lacan, *Ecrits* (Paris, 1966), p. 710, quoted in Stephen Heath, 'Joan Riviere and the Masquerade', in *Formations of Fantasy*, ed. Victor Burgin, James Donald and Cora Kaplan (London, 1986), p. 52.

10. Kaja Silverman, *Male Subjectivity at the Margins* (New York, 1992), pp. 135–6.

11. Lacan, 'La Relation d'objet et les structures freudiennes', *Bulletin de Psychologie*, 10.14 (1957), 851–2.

12. Lacan, *Ecrits: A Selection*, trans. Alan Sheridan (London, 1977), p. 322. This present essay deals with the veil as signifier in Western cultural discourse only. For the complex relation of the veil to gender and politics in Muslim countries, see Cynthia Enloe, *Bananas, Beaches and Bases* (Berkeley, CA, 1990), and Unni Wikan, *Behind the Veil in Arabia: Women in Oman* (Chicago, 1982).

13. Carter, *The Passion of New Eve* (London, 1992), pp. 128–9. All subsequent quotations are from this edition.

14. Josette Féral, 'Powers of Difference', in *The Future of Difference*, ed. Hester Eisenstein and Alice Jardine (New Brunswick, 1989), p. 89. Roberta Rubenstein, 'Intersexions: Gender Metamorphosis in Angela Carter's *The Passion of New Eve* and Lois Gould's *A Sea-Change*',

Tulsa Studies in Women's Literature, 12.1 (1993), makes the crucial point that Tristessa and Eve both suffer from the 'recognition that each is an Other, an object constructed by others – as in a mirror or in another's gaze – and not a subject or self (p. 111). Rubenstein thinks that Carter's story remains too bound by prevailing definitions of gender to provide a 're-gendered' vision of human possibility (p. 116). Likewise, Carol Siegel, 'Postmodern Women Novelists Review Victorian Male Masochism', *Genders*, 11(1991), comments that while the novel insists upon 'the constructed, anti-natural quality of gender', it does not 'release passion from determination by the concept of femininity as the binary opposite of masculinity or from the association of masochism with femininity'(p. 12). Susan Rubin Suleiman, *Subversive Intent: Gender, Politics, and the Avant-Garde* (Cambridge, MA, 1990), on the other hand, credits the novel with 'expand[ing] our notions of what it is possible to dream in the domain of sexuality. ... It is to the ... dream of going beyond the old dichotomies, of imagining "unguessable modes of humanity" that *The Passion of New Eve* succeeds in giving textual embodiment' (pp. 139–40).

15. Nancy Chodorow, *The Reproduction of Mothering: Psychoanalysis and the Sociology of Gender* (Berkeley, CA, 1978); Jessica Benjamin, 'A Desire of One's Own: Psychoanalytic Feminism and Intersubjective Space', *Feminist Studies/Critical Studies*, ed. Teresa de Lauretis (Bloomington, IN, 1986), pp. 78–101.

16. Carter, *The Magic Toyshop* (London, 1981), p. 166.

17. Susan Griffin, *Rape: The Power of Consciousness* (San Francisco, 1979), p. 39.

18. Freud, 'Female Sexuality', p. 200; Gayle Rubin, 'The Traffic in Women: Notes on the "Political Economy" of Sex', in *Toward an Anthropology of Women*, ed. Rayna Reiter (New York, 1975), pp. 157–210.

19. John Berger, *Ways of Seeing* (New York, 1973), p. 46.

20. Helene Deutsch, *Psychology of Women*, vol. 1 (New York, 1944), pp. 251–2; Eleanor Maccoby and Carol Jacklin, *The Psychology of Sex Differences* (Stanford, CA, 1974), p. 329; quoted in Chodorow, *Mothering*, p. 139.

21. As Irigaray says, 'In the last analysis, the female Oedipus complex is woman's entry into a system of values that is not hers, and in which she can "appear" and circulate only when enveloped in the needs/desires/fantasies of others, namely men' (*This Sex Which Is Not One*, trans. Catherine Porter [Ithaca, NY, 1985], p. 134).

22. Bram Dijkstra, *Idols of Perversity: Fantasies of Feminine Evil in Fin-de-Siècle Culture* (Oxford, 1986), documents the popularity of the dead beauty in nineteenth-century paintings; the dead woman repre-

sents 'the apotheosis of an ideal of feminine passivity and helplessness' (p. 36). See also Elizabeth Bronfen, *Over Her Dead Body: Death, Femininity, and the Aesthetic* (New York, 1992), pp. 59–64.

23. Amy Richlin, 'Reading Ovid's Rapes', *Pornography and Representation in Greece and Rome*, ed. Amy Richlin (New York, 1992), p. 158. This volume shows that the simultaneous inscription and erasure of sexual violence against women that characterises Yeats's poem occurs again and again in classical as well as modern texts. See especially Lynn Higgins and Brenda Silver, 'Introduction: Rereading Rape', *Rape and Reproduction*, ed. Higgins and Silver (New York, 1991), pp. 1–11, and the essays in the same volume by Patricia Kleindienst Joplin, 'The Voice of the Shuttle is Ours', pp. 35–64, and Brenda Silver, 'Periphrasis, Power, and Rape in *A Passage to India*', pp. 115–37.

24. Dickinson, Emily, *The Complete Poems of Emily Dickinson*, ed. Thomas Johnson (Boston, 1958), vol. 1, p. 421. The relevant stanza reads:

> A Charm invests a face
> Imperfectly beheld -
> The Lady dare not lift her Veil
> For fear it be dispelled.

I am indebted to Cay Strode's analysis of the poem's visual power dynamic ('The Dynamics of Feminine Representation: A Feminist Reading of Emily Dickinson's "A Charm Invests a Face"', unpublished thesis submitted for English departmental honours, Occidental College (Eagle Rock, CA, 1987).

25. Lacan, *The Four Fundamental Concepts of Psycho-Analysis*, trans. Alan Sheridan (New York, 1981).

26. It is the underlying male structure, the exchange of women between men, that gives the wedding dress its meaning: while a woman may think her wedding dress celebrates her power – the beauty and virtue that have secured her a husband – the white of the wedding dress refers to male interests only, signifying that the woman is unexchanged, unused, and so keeps her full value as commodity, as the gift that ratifies the bond between the father who gives her and the husband who takes her. Perhaps because it thus suggests the alienation of woman into a symbol, the wedding dress is often an accoutrement of femininity in Carter's novels. In *Heroes and Villains* Marianne is forced to put on an ancient wedding dress for her arranged marriage, becoming a signifier in Donally's symbolic system, which incorporates Lévi-Strauss's model of the exchange of women. In *Love* and 'The Bloody Chamber' a wedding dress is likewise imposed upon the woman rather than self-chosen.

27. Susan Brownmiller, *Against Our Will: Men, Women and Rape* (New York, 1975); and Barbara Mehrhof and Pamela Kearon, *Notes from the Third Year: Women's Liberation* (New York, 1971).

28. I have discussed the structural similarities (including power asymmetries) between father–daughter relations and romantic love relations in *Reconstructing Desire:The Role of the Unconscious in Women's Reading and Writing* (Chapel Hill, NC, 1990), pp. 26–31. Elizabeth Abel, 'Resisting Exchange: Brother–Sister Incest in Fiction by Doris Lessing', in *Doris Lessing: The Alchemy of Survival*, ed. Carey Kaplan and Elizabeth Cronan Rose (Athens, OH, 1988), pp. 115–26, analyses the subversive potential of the brother–sister bond in Sophocles' *Antigone* and in Doris Lessing's work: by making the familiar, the familial, man the object of desire in place of a stranger, brother–sister incest challenges 'the fundamental structure of partriarchy' by preventing the exchange of women.

29. Jessica Benjamin, 'Master and Slave: The Fantasy of Erotic Domination', in *Powers of Desire: The Politics of Sexuality*, ed. Ann Snitow, Christine Stansell, and Sharon Thompson (New York, 1983), p. 288.

30. Flora Alexander, *Contemporary Women Novelists* (London, 1989), finds a parallel between Finn and Melanie's new beginning in the garden and Adam and Eve's: 'They have quarrelled with a patriarchal figure like God the Father and it has been their good fortune to escape' (p. 65).

31. Paulina Palmer, 'From "Coded Mannequin" to Bird Woman: Angela Carter's Magic Flight', in *Women Reading Women's Writing*, ed. Sue Roe (NewYork, 1987), pp. 180, 181. Robert Clark, 'Angela Carter's Desire Machine', *Women's Studies*, 14.2 (1987), 147–61, faults Carter for not always providing enough cues to produce a parodic reading of the patriarchal tropes she incorporates into her fiction: 'The ideologic power of the form being infinitely greater than the power of the individual to overcome it', Carter risks reinscribing the ideology of erotic domination by presenting rape and other forms of sexual violence as thrilling, without the necessary 'moral and historical context' (pp. 152–3) to provide a critical perspective. Elaine Jordan, 'Enthralment: Angela Carter's Speculative Fictions', in *Plotting Change: Contemporary Women's Fiction*, ed. Linda Anderson (London, 1990), pp. 19–40, makes a spirited rejoinder to Clark's argument. She claims that 'Angela Carter is offering experiments in overcoming ideas, images, representations, that have determined our options for thinking and feeling' (p. 34).

32. In the later *Nights at the Circus* (1984) Carter offers a picture of female sexuality exuberant in its excesses rather than curbed of its potential. In that novel she rewrites 'Leda and the Swan' to a woman's

advantage, creating in the protagonist Fevvers her own mythic version of Leda's offspring. Because she is sprung from the egg laid by Leda, Fevvers has too many appendages rather than too few – and her wings are just one of the excesses that contribute, like her laughter and her verbal fluency, to stumping definitions of femininity (as spectacle, as sexual victim, and so on) that various male characters try to impose on her. See Sally Robinson, *Engendering the Subject: Gender and Self-Representation in Contemporary Women's Fiction* (Albany, NY, 1991), pp. 117–31.

4

History and Women's Time: *Heroes and Villains*

GERARDINE MEANEY

Doris Lessing's *Landlocked* and Hélène Cixous' 'The Laugh of the Medusa' [the subject of Meaney's previous chapter – Ed.] foreground the relationship between maternity and language and their treatment of that relationship poses one question very clearly.[1] What is the relationship between maternity, language and the feminine subject's access to history? Does participation in language and history necessarily involve a repudiation of maternity? Or is it the case that the celebration of a positive relationship to the maternal is necessary if women are to transform language and change history?

These questions are addressed in *Heroes and Villains* by Angela Carter and in the lyrical and philosophical essay 'Stabat Mater' by Julia Kristeva.[2] Both of these texts reimagine myths; Kristeva interrogates the myth of the Virgin Mother, Carter rewrites the myth of the hero. In interrogating myth, both analyse and attempt to revise the parameters and definition of history. It is, paradoxically, through their interrogation of the significance of maternity for feminine subjectivity that both texts engage with history (and historicity).[3]

Two strands of thought have emerged in feminism with regard to maternity. One concentrates on maternity as exile from history, the other on the maternal as a powerful disruption of the linear history from which women have been excluded. These appear to be incompatible positions, yet neither can ever be fully extricated from the other, as we will see. In general, Carter is more concerned with the

84

perils and snares in which maternity confines femininity and Kristeva with maternity's challenging and subversive aspects. Yet each of these positions is presented with reservations and qualifications. Maternity is not amenable to any one reading and the recurrent disruptive factor in any formulation of its significance is the recognition that the mother is always also a daughter. In other words, the discussion of the relation of the maternal and history returns us to the mother–daughter relationship.

Kristeva, like Cixous, explicitly addresses the question of language's function as mother and the mother's function in language. Unlike Cixous, however, she assumes neither that language holds no hidden enemies for the 'feminine' speaking subject nor that those aspects of language and literary practice closest to the 'maternal body' are unambiguously affirmative. On the contrary she posits a close relationship between the maternal, the poetic and death (or more specifically, the 'death drives'). Kristeva's recognition of the dangers implicit in the breakdown of the symbolic order is possibly closer to Lessing than Cixous. In *About Chinese Women* the dilemma crucial to the development of Lessing's fiction is succinctly stated:

> A woman has nothing to laugh about when the symbolic order collapses. She can take pleasure in it, if by identifying with the mother, the vaginal body, she imagines she is the sublime, repressed forces which return through the fissures of the order. But she can just as easily die from this upheaval ... if she has been deprived of a successful maternal identification and has found in the symbolic paternal order her one superficial, belated and easily severed link with life.
>
> (p. 150)

Kristeva appreciates how fragile the border is between 'the id ambiguously uttered'[4] and the bewildered and fragmented utterances of the psychotic, unable to 'get messages out'.[5] Lessing draws back from that border. At the end of *Landlocked* Martha throws Thomas Stern's testament to the insights and tortured possibilities of that dangerous psychic territory into a suitcase. The *Children of Violence* series[6] progresses to a refusal of such insights as well as a banishment of the spectre of madness. Kristeva's project in texts as diverse as *The Revolution in Poetic Language, About Chinese Women* and 'Stabat Mater' has consistently been to explore and to map out precisely this region of borders and boundaries, testing its limitations and its liberating excesses and exploring its significance for women as subject to and subjects of discourse.

Angela Carter's use of the genres of science fiction and fantasy, her willingness to experiment with form and her reinvention of myth give her also a certain amount of common ground with Lessing. Unlike Lessing, however, she does not appear to have written anything which could be mistaken for realism. Her first novel, *The Magic Toyshop* (1967), is the nearest she has come to writing traditional realism, but its use of fairy-tale motifs, fantasy and dreams ensures its exclusion from the ranks of the conventional or the realistic. Carter's use of traditional myths and images is closer to Cixous's iconoclasm than Lessing's revisions. Her appropriation of Freudian imagery and mythology operates on a quite different level from Lessing's use of Laing and is very much in harmony with the work of Cixous and Irigaray. ...

FANTASY, SPECULATIVE FICTION AND SUBVERSION

Angela Carter's fiction and theory stress the danger of enclosure more often than they celebrate marginality. None the less, they exploit marginal positions and subversive strategies quite as much as Kristeva's writings and, like them, they test limits. Novels such as *The Magic Toyshop* (1967) and *Love* (1971) blur the edges of realism, dissolving the rigours of plot and characterisation in phantasmagorical productions attributed to the disturbed and disturbing psyches of their protagonists. In some respects these novels have much in common with Lessing's *The Four-Gated City*. Like Lessing's novel they operate on the basis of a radical disruption of expectations, though they burst out of the conventions of the novel of plausibility into fantasy, not science fiction: 'Fantasy tells of limits, and it is particularly revealing in pointing out the edges of the real.'[7] It is as interrogations of the 'real' and as play in the field of limits that Carter's fantasy and Kristeva's theory will be seen to have most in common.

Such play is automatically an exploration of the (im)possibilities of language. Fantasy, by its very ability to make non-sense its sense and impossibility its reality, radically undermines the referential claims of language. It is the genre of 'thingless names'.[8] As self-reflexive linguistic artifice, fantasy has much in common with the science fiction mode employed by Lessing. Use of the term 'speculative' as opposed to 'science' fiction illuminates the difference between the two modes, however.[9] The interaction of cognition and alienation which characterises science fiction constitutes a speculative mode: it elaborates an hypothesis from given premisses. In other words speculative fiction asks, 'What if ...?' Its relation to perceived 'reality' is one of interrogation. Fantasy's relation to reality, however, is one of negation. 'Fantasy embodies a "negative subjunctivity" – that is, fantasy is fantasy because it contravenes the real and violates it.'[10] 'Negative subjunctivity' can contradict the real, but it cannot escape it. 'The actual world is constantly present in fantasy, by negation.' The negativity of fantasy has certain traits in common with the Kristevan concept of negativity as rejection, described as 'the fourth "term" of the dialectic',[11] the dynamic of change and of the (e)mergence and collapse of the subject, the symbolic and language. In this context 'negative subjunctivity' can be seen as allied to the death drives[12] and so as participating in the semiotic and concentrating its recurrent upheaval against the symbolic.

Such access and allies would appear to privilege fantasy as a genre of subversion. There is a danger, nonetheless, that fantasy's 'subversion' may be illusory if reality is contravened only in order to be reinstituted. If a simple opposition between fantasy and reality is established then the fantasy is not even escapist,[13] but reactionary. It becomes no more than a fit of freakishness which reinstitutes the norms on which it depends to define it by opposition.

Speculative fiction guards against such a relation by the device of alienation, by providing a futuristic or quasi-scientific context in which the unexpected rules. The presence of familiar elements gives plausibility to the 'What if ...?' and gives the reader a framework of references to work with. The cognitive elements are also there to be made strange, however, and the interaction of familiar and alien is, in truly speculative fiction, a mutual putting-into-question. The 'authorisation' of future possibility as an equal rival and sustained interruption of present 'reality' is a strategy best described as anachronic.

Three of Carter's novels can be described as speculative fiction: *Heroes and Villains* (1969), *The Infernal Desire Machines of Doctor Hoffman* (1972) and *The Passion of New Eve* (1977). These novels are situated in another border area, that between science fiction and fantasy. *Heroes and Villains* is set in a post-nuclear future, but the protagonists are mythic and the action is identified with the dreams of the 'heroine', Marianne (p. 137). In *The Infernal Desire Machines of Doctor Hoffman* advanced technology harnesses erotic energy to make the fantasies of individuals manifest as effective reality. *The Passion of New Eve* is set in a near-future, disintegrating America. This context is used to debunk the myth of maternal omniscience as well as masculinist arrogance and to explore bisexuality. A conjunction of interrogation and negation is achieved: in effect, these novels ask, what if reality was *not* so, was not what our most deeply held myths, beliefs and schemes say it is? The rigorous alienation of speculative fiction joins forces with fantasy and functions, like Doctor Hoffman's machines, to release the repressed. The particular disturbing force of Carter's work derives from this combination.

In *Heroes and Villains* the myths of the hero, the (tribal) mother and the phantasms of Freud's family romance form both the fantasy elements and the cognitive components of a science fiction romance. They may be unreal, but they are familiar. The main protagonist, Marianne, is a 'Professor's' daughter. The society of the Professors has evolved from the elite groups who were allocated refuge in the bunkers during a long-past nuclear war. Those who have survived outside the bunkers and the villages which replace them are divided into two groups: the Mutants, whose origin is obvious, and the Barbarians, who have escaped the worst effects of radiation and live a nomadic existence raiding the Professors' villages. As a child Marianne witnesses a raid on her village by the Barbarians and sees one of them kill her brother. After the death of her father she helps a Barbarian raider, Jewel, to escape and leaves with him herself to become eventually a Barbarian leader. The relationship of Jewel and Marianne is antagonistic as well as sexual. In the tradition of romance, Jewel turns out to be the Barbarian who killed her brother. In the tradition of the myth of the hero, Marianne is recognised by Jewel as a kind of doom upon him. Jewel's mentor and the tribe's witchdoctor is a renegade Professor, Donally, who manipulates the superstition of Jewel and the tribe. Donally attempts to integrate Marianne into the tribe by marrying her to Jewel. The uneasy alliance of Marianne and Jewel overthrows Donally's power in the tribe when Marianne becomes pregnant. Donally revenges himself by engineering Jewel's death, but Marianne survives and seems poised to combine both their roles at the novel's end.

MONUMENTAL TIME

The plot has much in common with that of Lessing's *The Marriages Between Zones Three, Four and Five*, though the opposing cultures in Carter's novel are not seen as ordered stages in the path of spiritual progress, but are engaged in a desperate dialectic, each anathema and necessary to the other. The repressive, settled and industrious society of the 'Professors' very gradually succumbs to the scavenging 'Barbarians', whose living will disappear with the enemies whose produce they raid. They kill and need each other. It is interesting that Lessing's allegory transforms historical stages into topographical areas and so endows them with spiritual significance. Carter, in contrast, projects the 'two nations' of the present into a post-apocalyptic death struggle and moves from an exploration of the economic to the symbolic basis of social relations. The *Marriages Between Zones Three, Four and Five* moves towards a restoration of dialectical struggle as the principle of life, but also endorses a dubious spiritual and political hierarchy. 'Primitive', tribal Zone Five is portrayed as furthest from the light. It is also closest to contemporary 'under-developed' societies. Zone Three, the highest stage of social organisation portrayed in the novel, may be said to embody the aspirations of an enlightened, social democratic, probably Scandinavian, republic.

The endorsement of such a hierarchy is weakened by the substitution of topography for temporality. The marriage of a Marxist concept of history to the traditional 'path' of spiritual progress in this novel paradoxically precipitates the collapse of history into geography and the disintegration of progress into flux. The 'dialectic of enlightenment'[14] erodes the boundaries that are the only points of reference in the attempt to approach 'truth'.

Travel occurs between the Zones, not only forwards, from Zones Five to Four and Four to Three, but backwards also. The first and most important journey in the novel is Al-Ith's journey back to Zone Four from the more advanced Zone Three. Only after such regression (for she does develop some of the characteristics of Zone Four's inhabitants) can she progress to the borders of Zone Two. Further, as Virginia Tiger has pointed out, the oppressed women of Zone Four are a major cataclysmic force in the novel.[15] They break down all the categories, moving backwards and forwards between Zones and violating the proper pace and mode of progress. Their

visit to Zone Three is premature though Dabeeb, who is their representative voice in the novel, insists: 'That it was their place and
their right to go, since it was they who had kept the old knowledge
alive for so long.'[16] This journey is inappropriate, however, and dis-
concerts the people of both Zones Three and Four: 'Their coming at
all was sensed to be ill-judged. Much worse damage had been done
by them than by the officious and doltish soldiers who had come to
fetch Al-Ith at the beginning. ... All of us questioned the marriage
again, and felt undermined: some were even wondering about the
Providers – if they had made a mistake or were careless in allowing
themselves to be wrongly interpreted. Such thoughts were new with
us, and an uneasy troubling current was set at work throughout the
Zone' (p. 231). Lessing repudiates the women's insistence on trans-
lating their new-found spiritual freedom into action. Dabeeb, earlier
so rebellious, must acknowledge: 'I don't know how it happened
that I was so sure we should all come – but I do see now ... what
got into me? And I have done harm, yes, we can all see that'
(p. 231). These unruly women are none the less the ones who have
'kept the old knowledge alive for so long', through their songs,
which, as they force the inhabitants of Zone Three to realise, 'are
not only known in the watery realms "down there" – just as theirs
are to us – but are also told and sung in the sandy camps and
around the desert fires of Zone Five' (p. 245). Once again the feminine and the poetic appear in Lessing's fiction as a dangerous alliance and once again these elements persist and insist on their
power. We can see the semiotic in dynamic action in such a novel.
The very inclusion of the tale of the women's disruptive journey is
testament to the impossibility of any final victory for symbolic
power. The feminine, poetic and unruly, cannot be banished. It is
perhaps inevitable that the other great threat in the novel to the
'Providers'' schemes to restore spiritual striving and a new order to
the Zones is Murti, who replaces Al-Ith as ruler of Zone Three and
who resembles nothing more than the fairy-tale jealous stepsister.

Under pressure from these feminine elements and the songs with
which they are associated, the programmatic structure of the Zones'
relation to each other breaks down. That structure had itself translated an historical continuum into spatial 'Zones'; when the boundaries between these are themselves transgressed and each Zone
becomes less distinct from the others, there are no reliable co-
ordinates, spatial, temporal, or even spiritual, remaining. The
chants and songs which the women bring from Zone to Zone blur

the distinction between progression and regression. Zone Six, described in *Shikasta*, stretches into infinity behind this narrative and Zones One and Two are beyond imagining. The limitless space/time which is the novel's landscape will not allow beginnings and ends to be identified.

It must be remembered that the novel 'sequence', *Canopus in Argos*, is nothing of the sort. No chronology can be established which relates all the texts in a temporal sequence (some obviously deal with simultaneous situations, but this relation is not constant).[17] *Canopus in Argos* possesses no form or structure which makes it inevitable or necessary to read any one before or after another.

What Kristeva calls 'monumental' time, 'all encompassing and infinite like imaginary space' (p. 191), confounds linear time in *The Marriages Between Zones Three, Four and Five* and precipitates the disintegration of both *telos* and origin.

CYCLICAL TIME

Conventional temporality fares no better in *Heroes and Villains*. Marianne tells Jewel he is an anachronism: '"What's an anachronism," he said darkly. "Teach me what an anachronism is." "A pun in time," she replied cunningly, so that he would not understand her' (p. 56). The sorcerer-priest Donally comments, 'Time is going backwards and coiling up; who let the spring go, I wonder, so that history would back on itself?' (p. 93).

Cyclical time takes over here. That is precisely what renders the novel so problematic. Cyclical time can be associated with stultifying 'immanence' or with the danger of petrification, as it is in *Children of Violence*. It could be described as the space to which women are banished when they are exiled from history. Kristeva describes it spectacularly differently, reclaiming it as a space dizzying in its vastness rather than as 'confinement or restriction to a narrow round of uncreative or repetitious duties'.[19] In 'Women's Time':

> There are cycles, gestation, the eternal recurrence of a biological rhythm which conforms to that of nature and imposes a temporality whose stereotyping may shock, but whose regularity and unison with what is experienced as extra-subjective time, cosmic time, occasion vertiginous visions and unnameable *jouissance*.[20]
>
> (p. 191)

Vertigo often precipitates a fall and the logic of this 'time' in *Heroes and Villains* is the eternal recurrence of a vicious circle, a shocking, stereotyping victory of maternity over the woman as protagonist, as thinker, as producer of her own story. Carter's text directly addresses the issue which disrupts any comfortable conclusions in the work of Cixous and Lessing and which sometimes threatens to overwhelm that of Kristeva: 'I think therefore I am, but if I take time off from thinking, what then?' (p. 98). This question is posed by Donally, the sinister architect of the symbolic in *Heroes and Villains*. He repeatedly scrawls epigrams, ciphers and questions on the crumbling walls of the shelters where Marianne takes refuge with the Barbarians. The question of the self's fate without consciousness or when consciousness is no longer in control is his greatest challenge to this girl who 'keeps on utilizing her perceptions until the very end' (p. 81). It is also, of course, the greatest challenge which the concept of a decentred self poses for feminism. Women have sought independence, autonomy, historical and political agency, all of those things which have traditionally defined 'human' subjectivity. That definition has collapsed under the onslaught of contemporary critical theory, perhaps primarily under the onslaught of feminism's claims that women will no longer guarantee the subject's autonomy and agency, but will instead exercise it. If the self is no more than a fragile illusion, sustained by a dualism inimical to women, prey to unconscious drives and produced by language, what is left to resist hegemony and seek change? Towards the end of *Heroes and Villains*, Marianne, pregnant, trapped, finds 'she was not able to think' (p. 149) and 'then' the age-old pattern recurs. Jewel dies, becomes a hero and so fulfils the destiny which Donally insisted would be his, that of the new Arthur, 'the Messiah of the Yahoos'. Marianne survives, becomes a mother and the 'Tiger Lady' (p. 150), 'Eve at the end of the world' (p. 124). Through Marianne and her child will be completed the process begun by Donally and, reluctantly, Jewel. The novel ends poised for the transformation of the tribe from a loose family grouping to a structured society. If a woman takes time off from thinking, it seems, she is in danger of becoming a mother goddess.

FEMALE FANTASIES CONCERNED WITH POWER

In *This Sex Which is Not One*, Luce Irigaray warns that inherent in 'the race for power', inextricably linked to the attempt of 'the female imaginary' to 'represent itself', is the danger 'yet again', of 'a privileging of the maternal over the feminine'.[21] In *Heroes and Villains* there are recurrent textual signals that the feminine protagonists claim on subjectivity is fragile. Her sexuality is projected on to a masculine figure, a demon lover. Marianne, significantly when both Jewel and her own situation are most beyond her control and comprehension, calls him 'the furious invention of my virgin nights' (p. 137). In this novel, as in *Landlocked*, it is the male protagonist who is closest to the libido – Jewel is more than reminiscent of Thomas Stern. This recurrent association of the masculine and the libidinal raises severe problems for the subversive alliance between the feminine and the unconscious postulated by Cixous, Kristeva and Irigaray (obviously, the nature and meaning of that alliance is treated very differently by each of these three). Marianne, who considers herself 'the only rational woman left in the whole world' (p. 55), is oriented towards ego – and, in view of her reverence for the memory of her Professor father, super-ego. Jewel, as a projection of egoistic fantasy and return of the repressed, is more complex. In reading *Landlocked* in terms of Gilbert and Gubar's analysis of the 'demon lover' figure in women's fiction and in my own reading of *Landlocked* it was assumed that the female protagonist would be identified with ego. The male 'character' that fulfils the function of non-identical double then becomes by turn alter-ego and projection of the dissociated id. This pattern in women's fiction would initially appear to confirm Freud's description of the libido in masculine terms:

> There is only one libido, which serves both the masculine and feminine sexual function. To it itself we cannot assign any sex: if following the conventional equation of activity and masculinity, we are inclined to describe it as masculine we must not forget that it also covers trends with a passive aim. Nevertheless the juxtaposition 'feminine libido' is without justification. Furthermore it is our impression that more constraint has been applied to the libido when it is pressed into the service of the feminine function, and that – to speak teleologically – Nature takes less careful account of its [the function's] demands than in the case of masculinity. And the reason for this may be – thinking once again teleologically – in the fact that the accomplishment of the aim of biology has been entrusted to the aggressiveness of men and has been made to some extent independent of women's consent.[22]

As Laura Mulvey points out, Freud shifts here from 'the use of active/masculine as *metaphor* for the function of libido to an invocation of Nature and biology that appears to leave the meta-phoric usage behind'.[23] This doom at the hand of biology and the denial of woman's autonomy is the substance of Martha Quest's nightmare. Freud's denial of 'feminine libido' is, however, at odds with the *telos* of that denial: 'Woman would be the basis, the in-scriptional space for the representatives of the masculine uncon-scious.'[24] The problem for Freud is that in the light of his assertion that 'sexual life is dominated by the polarity of masculine and fem-inine ... the notion suggests itself of considering the relation of the libido to its antithesis' (p. 131), but such a relation is unthinkable: 'the feminine cannot be conceptualised as different, but rather only as *opposition* (passivity) in an antinomic sense or as *similarity* (the phallic phase)'.[25] So following the 'conventional equation of mas-culinity and activity' Freud is 'inclined' to describe the libido as masculine. The unconscious, however, is inclined to be projected on to the feminine. The refusal to juxtapose the 'feminine' and the 'libido'[26] opens up a disjunction between libido and unconscious where the feminine disrupts the 'conventional equation of activity and masculinity'. The projection of the libido on to male figures in *Wuthering Heights, Landlocked* and *Heroes and Villains* would in-dicate on one level that the unconscious is always projected on to the 'opposite' sex and, as the extract from Freud above epitomises, woman is always the opposite sex. In the confrontation between the maternal and the feminine speaking, acting subject she is even the opposite of herself as protagonist, Perseus *and* Medusa. Jewel, Thomas Stern and Heathcliff are projections of libido, which need not be assigned a sex since only one is thinkable. They are also, however, the inscriptional space for the unconscious, thus fulfilling a function which Irigaray identifies as feminine. These demon lover figures thus confound the differentiation between masculine and feminine. This is the key to the ambivalence which Gilbert and Gubar detect in Brontë's Heathcliff and to the figure of Jewel in *Heroes and Villains*.

The fact that both of these ambiguously male figures are out-siders and foreigners and both wanderers is crucial:

> In the fascinated rejection that the foreigner arouses in us, there is a share of uncanny strangeness in the sense of the depersonalisation that Freud discovered in it, and which takes up again our infantile desires and fear of the other – the other of death, the other of woman, the other of uncontrollable desire. The foreigner is within

us, and when we flee from our struggle against the foreigner, we are fighting the unconscious, that 'improper' facet of our impossible 'own and proper'.[27]

Thomas Stern, the wandering Jew, Jewel, the itinerant Barbarian, are already *'unheimlich'* and homeless. As foreigners, others, they are already feminised.

THE ORIGIN OF CASTRATION

Carter rewrites the Heathcliff 'demon lover' motif in *Heroes and Villians*.[28] It is possible to compare the rape scene in *Heroes and Villains* with the scene in *Wuthering Heights* where Catherine is savaged by the Lintons' guard-dog. Gilbert and Gubar interpret the latter as simultaneously marking Catherine's entry into 'adult female sexuality' *and* castration. In *Wuthering Heights* this incident brings about Catherine's separation from Heathcliff. In *Heroes and Villians* Marianne and Jewel play out what might be a parody or grotesque inversion of the violent love scene of Brontë's protagonists, later in *Wuthering Heights*, which precipitates Catherine's death. Commenting on the wound inflicted by Skulker on Catherine, Gilbert and Gubar observe:

> Obviously such bleeding has sexual connotations, especially when it occurs in a pubescent girl. Crippling injuries to the feet are equally resonant, moreover, almost always signifying symbolic castration, as in the stories of Oedipus, Achilles and the Fisher King. Additionally, it need hardly be noted that Skulker's equipment for aggression – his huge purple tongue and pendant lips, for instance – sounds extraordinarily phallic. In a Freudian sense then, the imagery of this brief but violent episode hints that Catherine has been simultaneously catapulted into adult female sexuality and castrated.[29]

The otherwise gratuitously bloody defloration of Marianne is equally suggestive. In *Heroes and Villians* the 'totemic animal'[30] which rapes/castrates her and the other self of the heroine are one. Marianne makes this explicit. There is an ironic resonance of the Fall in her comparison of Jewel's attack on her with an earlier incident where she was bitten by a snake: 'It hurt far worse than the snake-bite because it was intentional' (p. 55). Like Brontë, Carter is engaged in rewriting the myth of the Fall. The 'snake', Jewel, has had Adam and Eve tattooed on his back by Donally:

> He took a fortnight and I was delirious most of the time but the needles didn't poison my blood because Mrs Greene looked after them. Though green in fact is the worst, green hurts most of all. You'll notice what a lot of green there is in the picture.
>
> (p. 86)

The relation of the feminine to the maternal once again forms a backdrop to the 'Fall' into castration. The outrageous conceit at the heart of Freud's denial of 'feminine libido' (p. 131) is its proposal that women are irrelevant to 'the aim of biology'. Childbirth is dissociated from the maternal body as well as the mother's will and is made an attribute of an abstract 'Nature'. The description of conception and childbirth in terms of *telos* again displaces reproduction from the realm of the physical into a quasi-metaphysical project of the 'idea', Nature. The possibility of a feminine libidinal economy[31] is eliminated under the same sign that banishes the maternal body, the sign of castration:

> This 'castration' that Freud accounts for in terms of 'nature', 'anatomy', could equally well be interpreted as that prohibition that enjoins woman – at least in this history – from ever imagining, fancying, re-presenting, symbolising, etc. (and none of these words is adequate as all are borrowed from a discourse which aids and abets that prohibition) her own relation to *beginning*. The 'fact of castration' has to be understood as a definitive prohibition against establishing one's own economy of the desire for origin. Hence the hole, the lack, the fault, the 'castration' that greets the little girl as she enters as a subject into representative systems.[32]

If a Lacanian perspective is superimposed on this Freudian framework another related pattern emerges. Marianne, in effect, is a subject striving to cohere, she 'thinks', she 'is'. Jewel sees in her 'the map of a country in which I only exist by virtue of the extravagance of my metaphors' (p. 120). *Heroes and Villains* 'brings into play'[33] the female imaginary, that is, it explores from a feminine perspective, 'the imaginary relation, that between the ego and its images'.[34] That process generates an intoxicating subversion by negation (fantasy) and interrogation (science or speculative fiction) of myth, history, sexuality, language and the novel. Yet its guerrilla tactics demonstrate the aptness of Carter's comment on de Sade's sexual guerrilla, Juliette: 'Juliette, secularised as she is, is in the service of the goddess too, even if of the goddess in her demonic aspect, the goddess as antithesis.'[35] The logic of the narrative is that if the feminine subject 'takes time off from thinking' (*Heroes and Villians*, p. 98), 'then', there occurs precisely that return to the privilege of the maternal over the feminine which Irigaray fears. It culminates in the collapse of sexuality into reproduction, an equation which Carter posits as the most insidious enemy of women. The female imaginary would appear to self-destruct.

MATERNITY AND HISTORY

> There is no way out of time.
> (*The Sadeian Woman*, p. 110)

In *The Sadeian Woman* (1979) Carter presents the notion of 'women's time' rather differently from Kristeva's exhilarating rewrite of woman's relation to history. Carter's formulation of the mother–daughter relationship appears close to that implicit in the early novels of the *Children of Violence* series: 'the daughter may achieve autonomy only through destroying the mother, who represents her own reproductive function, also, who is both her own mother and the potential mother within herself' (p. 124). Carter is commenting on de Sade's *Philosophy in the Bedroom*.[36] Irigaray, in 'And the One Does Not Stir Without the Other', comments that 'mother and daughter live as each one the other's image'.[37] The indistinct identities and interplay of voices between mother and daughter are also recognised in *The Sadeian Woman*:

> If the daughter is a mocking memory to the mother – 'As I am so you once were' – then the mother is a horrid warning to her daughter. 'As I am, so you will be.' Mother seeks to ensure the continuance of her own repression, and her hypocritical solicitude for the younger woman's moral, that is, sexual welfare masks a desire to reduce her daughter to the same state of contingent passivity she herself inhabits.
>
> (p. 124)

Carter's 'Exercise in Cultural History' goes further than Irigaray's 'Forgive me, Mother, I prefer a woman to you'.[38] It simultaneously postulates the radical separation of 'mother' and 'woman' and the explosive possibility of their combination.

Carter celebrates a radical and final disruption of 'the nightmare of repetition'. The medium of this revolution is quite simple. Carter is one of the few writers under discussion to ask specifically *why* maternity is now available for discussion as myth, for interrogation, acceptance, or rejection:

> Techniques of contraception and surgically safe abortion have given women the choice to be sexually active yet intentionally infertile for more of their lives than was possible at any time in history until now.
>
> (*The Sadeian Woman*, p. 107)

It could be said that both the theory and practice of women's writing in the late twentieth century are in the process of inscribing and must be inscribed in that transformation. The cultural lag between the advent of the dislocation of sexuality and reproduction and 'the several millennia in which this fact was not self-evident at all, since it was continually obscured by enforced pregnancies' and 'endless or at best lengthy series of childbirths and miscarriages'[39] appears to be closing in *The Sadeian Woman*:

> The goddess is dead.
>
> And, with the imaginary construct of the goddess, dies the notion of eternity, whose place on earth was her womb. If the goddess is dead, there is nowhere for eternity to hide. The last resort of home-coming is denied us. We are confronted with mortality, as if for the first time.
>
> There is no way out of time. We must learn to live in this world ... because it is the only world that we will ever know.
>
> I think that is why so many people find the idea of the emancipation of women frightening. It represents the final secularisation of mankind.
>
> (p. 110)

But is this not rejection of the mother and with her much that constitutes the specifically feminine, rejection (as with Lessing) of self as woman?

The Sadeian Woman acknowledges that this may be the price of the sexual and intellectual terrorism necessary 'to pare a good deal of the fraudulent magic from the idea of women' (p. 109). The discussion of *Philosophy in the Bedroom* identifies the point at which de Sade retreats from the erotic relation of mother and daughter as the point at which his aim of 'perpetual immoral subversion of the established order' (p. 132) is betrayed: 'He is on the point of becoming a revolutionary pornographer; but he, finally, lacks the courage. He reverts, now, to being a simple pornographer' (p. 132). That the maternal function is compatible with pleasure is too dangerous an admission, even for the most inveterate iconoclast. 'Mother' 'cannot be corrupted into the experience of sexual pleasure and so set free. She is locked forever in the fortress of her flesh, a sleeping beauty whose lapse of being is absolute and eternal' (p. 128). An explanation for the inevitability of such lapses is given in *The Sadeian Woman*. Eugenie, in her attack on her mother, 'attacks only that part of herself, her reproductive function, she can afford to lose' (p. 131). That loss is the price of autonomy, independence. However:

> The violation of the mother is no more than a performance, a show; it demonstrates and creates Eugenie's autonomy, but also the limits of her autonomy, for her freedom is well policed by the faceless authority beyond the nursery, outside the mirror,[40] the father who knows all, sees all and permits almost everything, except absolute freedom.
>
> (p. 131)

If mother is the threat of confinement(s), repression, repetition, exile, father is the guarantor of autonomy, action and independence to act – within 'history', which he defines.

BREAKING UP (HIS)STORY

A recurrent conflict emerges in the writings of Carter and Kristeva between resistance to history as the agent of determinism and desire for access to history as the arena of change. Each asks if to enter history is to become the slave of history:

> Women are caught ... in a very real contradiction. ... As long as women remain silent, they will be outside the historical process. But if they begin to speak and write *as men do*, they will enter history subdued and alienated; it is a history that, logically speaking, their speech should disrupt.[41]

'Woman's time', the cycles of gestation and the mo(nu)ments of eternity, is, for Kristeva, the place of just such a disruption. Carter calls it 'the great, good place' (*The Sadeian Woman*, p. 108) – that is, nowhere:

> The theory of maternal superiority is one of the most damaging of all consolatory fictions and women themselves cannot leave it alone, although it springs from the timeless, placeless, fantasy land of archetypes where all the embodiments of biological supremacy live.
>
> (p. 106)

The Sadeian Woman is very much at odds here with Cixous's description of the all-affirming mother, who 'will never be lacking' ('The Laugh of the Medusa', p. 893) The myth of 'Mother'

> puts those women who wholeheartedly subscribe to it in voluntary exile from the historic world, this world, in its historic time that is counted out minute by minute, in which no event exists for itself but is determined by an interlocking web of circumstances, where actions achieve effects and my fertility is governed by my diet, the age at which I reached puberty, my bodily juices, my decisions.
>
> (*The Sadeian Woman*, p. 106)

Kristeva, in 'Women's Time' and *The Revolution in Poetic Language*, puts the notion of exile from history in a new light. It is not simply absence from the temporal continuum of causation and so activity, but also access to another 'sphere', another space, which can disrupt, traverse and transgress history. Carter speaks of sexual terrorism as a mode of purging the old mystifications which have exiled women to eternity; that is, to maternity:

> The womb ... is a fleshly link between past and future, the physical location of an everlasting present tense that can usefully serve as a symbol of eternity, a concept which has always presented some difficulties in visualisation.
>
> (p. 108)

Kristeva posits the maternal as a border from which textual terrorism can be launched. The question remains whether access to history, because it requires the assumption of subjectivity, also requires subjection. If this is so, the option for women in relation to writing and to history is simply between two forms of exile, from articulation and action or from themselves.

So there is the 'Tiger Lady', the Goddess, or Juliette the guerrilla, and while Carter scorns the former, she distrusts the latter, 'but' wonders how she can be done without:

> With apologies to Apollinaire, I do not think I want Juliette to renew my world; but, her work of destruction complete, she will, with her own death, have removed a repressive and authoritarian super-structure that has prevented a good deal of the work of renewal.
>
> (p. 111)

Kristeva commented in *About Chinese Women* that 'A woman has nothing to laugh about when the symbolic order collapses' (*The Kristeva Reader*, p. 150). *Heroes and Villians*, like 'The Laugh of the Medusa' and some of Lessing's experiments with speculative fiction, explores the danger that such collapse merely initiates renewal. Goddess and guerrilla, the two forms of exile, present another form of the Medusan impasse which was explored in the texts of Lessing and Cixous: 'For Juliette, secularised as she is, is in the service of the goddess too, even if of the goddess in her demonic aspect, the goddess as antithesis' (p. 111). Eternal goddess, dying and (possibly) reviving god/hero: these are the elements to which the narrative structure of *Heroes and Villians* consistently alludes. Marianne finds the tribe's 'sign' against the evil eye is the sign of the cross, Jewel is to be the 'Messiah of the Yahoos', or the new Arthur (p. 124). These 'archetypes' and their myth are subjected to the alienating interrogation of a post-nuclear setting, however. In such a setting any renewal is inevitably warped, the concept of eternal continuity has become ironic. Carter engages in that mythologising of myth which Barthes advocates as the most effective method of revealing the signifying structure which myth must conceal if it is to operate as purveyor of universal unchangeability.[42] Indeed, one of Donally's aphorisms neatly summarises much of Barthes's argument, 'MISTRUST APPEARANCES; THEY NEVER CONCEAL ANYTHING' (p. 60). Donally's imperative is typical of this novel's 'negations'. The mythologist is also the literary and sexual terrorist: 'Juliette, as Theodor Adorno and Max Horkheimer say, embodies "intellectual pleasure in regression" [history wound back on itself]. She attacks civilisation with its own weapons. She exercises rigorously rational thought; she creates systems; she exhibits an iron self-control' (p. 148). There is much of the Marianne of *Heroes and Villains* in this, particularly Marianne as artist/dreamer, whose 'furious invention' this is. She never completes her work of destruction, however, and the renewal promised in the conclusion may be the establishment, not the removal, of 'a repressive and authoritarian superstructure' (p. 111). ...

The novel's conclusion points to the danger that the removal of the maternal guarantee and the subversion of the socio-symbolic order reduces sociality to blood-ties and the panic-stricken repudiation of the other which makes tribal warfare not only inevitable but constitutive of the tribe. *Heroes and Villains* asks if, in overthrowing a totalising ideology based on sameness, one may not unleash a totalitarian violence which cannot accept the otherness it can no longer evade. Marianne will be the greatest loser if this occurs: her assimilation to the 'eternal feminine' would form the linchpin of the frightening new order.

If there are dangers, there are also possibilities implicit in the novel's ending. Marianne has understood she is a stranger to herself. She knows who she is and is not when she stops thinking. As 'Eve at the end of the world' (p. 124) she has tasted knowledge.

Among the ever shifting names in *Heroes and Villains*, however, Marianne is also called 'a little Lilith' (p. 124), Lilith who absolutely refused to be party to the contract and whom the Law of the Father turned into a most Medusa-like monster instead.

Lilith with a little knowledge would be a dangerous woman indeed.

From Gerardine Meaney, *(Un)Like Subjects: Women, Theory, Fiction* (London and New York, 1993), pp. 78–80, 84–100, 120.

NOTES

[Gerardine Meaney's book *(Un)Like Subjects* traces connections between three important French feminist theorists (Cixous, Irigaray and Kristeva) and three British novelists (Doris Lessing, Carter and Muriel Spark). Meaney's decision to make the fiction illuminate and indeed question the theoretical ideas, rather than privilege theory as some kind of ready-constructed 'authority', chimes well with Carter's own sceptical engagement with political and cultural theory in her imaginative writings, and her prioritising of the political. For reasons of space only certain sections from Meaney's extended chapter on *Heroes and Villains* are printed here, and readers are directed to the original version both for her fuller theorising, via Kristeva, of women's space/time in ways which relate to ideas of speculative fiction, and for her analysis of Carter's fictional interrogation of how the origins and future of the socio-symbolic contract (which is not a contract for women) have been envisaged by the political utopians, Rousseau and Engels, and the anthropologist, Lévi-Strauss. Kristeva has suggested that women may be removed by maternity from linear historical time into cycles of gestation and birth. Meaney's chapter addresses this perceived relationship of the maternal to history (and consequently, to questions of political agency) as a key issue of female subjectivity, and asks in what ways one might rethink this through both Carter's speculative fiction and Kristeva's concern for border spaces where historical time is interrupted by something else. This leads Meaney to a rethinking of both Carter's and Kristeva's critiques of Freudian thinking on sexuality, particularly in relation to the idea of 'castration' (women's disempowerment – see also Essays 3 and 5 in this volume) and feminist notions of the Imaginary (the relation of the ego to its images). We should also note that, as Meaney explains earlier in her book, French feminists use the term, *féminine*, to refer to their notions of subversive aspects of female biology, creating, writing and the possibility of a different subjectivity, rather than to the social construction of women (as the term is normally used in Anglo-American feminist studies). Ed.]

1. Doris Lessing, *Landlocked* (London, 1965); Hélène Cixous, 'The Laugh of the Medusa', trans. Keith and Paula Cohen, *Signs* 1:1 (1976), 875–99.

2. Angela Carter, *Heroes and Villains* (1969; reprinted Harmondsworth, 1981), all quotations are from this edition; and Julia Kristeva, 'Stabat Mater', in *The Kristeva Reader*, ed. Toril Moi (Oxford, 1986), pp. 161–86. To simplify references, where possible and unless indicated otherwise, quotations and references to the work of Kristeva will be from the translated versions in *The Kristeva Reader*.

3. For analysis of history and its relation to the feminine and to feminism from a variety of very different perspectives, see Margaret J. M. Ezell, 'The Myth of Judith Shakespeare: Creating the Canon of Women's Literature', *New Literary History*, 21:3 (1990), 579–92; Jane Marcus, 'The Asylums of Antaeus: Women, War and Madness', in *The New Historicism*, ed. H. Aram Veeser (London, 1989), pp. 132–51; Judith Lowder Newton, 'History as Usual? Feminism and the New Historicism', in Veeser, *The New Historicism*, pp. 152–67; Alicia Ostriker, 'Dancing at the Devil's Party', *Critical Inquiry*, 13 (1987), 579–96; Lillian S. Robinson, 'Sometimes, Always, Never: Their Women's History and Ours', *New Literary History*, 21 (1990), 377–94; Janet Todd, *Feminist Literary History* (Oxford, 1988); and Jane Tompkins, 'Indians: Textualism, Morality and the Problems of History', *Critical Inquiry*, 13 (1986), 101–19.

4. Cixous, 'The Laugh of the Medusa', p. 889.

5. Lessing, *Landlocked*, p. 280.

6. Lessing, *Children of Violence* (London, 1952–69), her five novel series including *Landlocked* (1965), and *The Four-Gated City* (1969).

7. L. Bessière, *Le Récit fantastique: la poétique de l'incertain* (Paris, 1974), p. 62.

8. Samuel Beckett, *Molloy* (London, 1959); Rosemary Jackson, *Fantasy: The Literature of Subversion* (London, 1981), p. 38.

9. See Darko Suvin, *Metamorphoses of Science Fiction: On the Poetics and History of a Literary Genre* (New Haven, CT, 1979), and Robert Scholes, *Structural Fabulation* (London, 1975), for the definition of speculative fiction in terms of the interaction of alienating or unfamiliar elements with cognitive or familiar ones.

10. Joanna Russ, 'The Subjunctivity of Science Fiction,' *Extrapolation*, 15:1 (1973), 52.

11. Kristeva, *The Revolution in Poetic Language*, trans. Margaret Waller (New York, 1984), pp. 109–13.

12. See Kristeva, *Powers of Horror: An Essay in Abjection*, trans. Leon S. Roudiez (New York, 1982), p. 245, for a discussion of the relation between 'style' and the death drives in Céline.

13. I am distinguishing here between escape, an attempt to become free of reality's constraints, and escapism, an attempt to evade reality.

14. Max Horkheimer and Theodor W. Adorno, *The Dialectic of Enlightenment*, trans. John Cumming (London, 1973).

15. Virginia Tiger, 'Doris Lessing's Revision of Feminist Utopias', paper given at the Third International Congress on Women, 'Visions and Revisions', Dublin, July 1987.

16. Lessing, *The Marriages Between Zones Three, Four and Five* (London, 1980), p. 219. All subsequent quotations are from this edition.

17. Lessing, *Canopus in Argos: Archives* (London, 1979–83), including *Re: Colonized Planet 5 Shikasta* (1979) and *The Marriages Between Zones Three, Four and Five* (1980). Lessing may be adapting Jung's acausal principle of synchronicity as an alternative to deterministic, causal principles of plot.

18. Simone de Beauvoir, *The Second Sex*, trans. H. M. Parshley (Harmondsworth, 1972), p. 94.

19. Ibid., p. 63.

20. In a particularly condensed version of her encoding of modernist within feminist discourse, Alice Jardine, *Gynesis: Configurations of Women and Modernity* (London, 1986), p. 89, quotes Kristeva quoting Joyce:

'Father's time, mother's species', as Joyce put it; and indeed, when evoking the name and destiny of woman, one thinks more of the *space* generating and forming the human species than of *time*, becoming or history. The modern sciences of subjectivity, of its genealogy and accidents, confirm in their own way this intuition, which is perhaps itself the result of socio-historic conjecture.

(*The Kristeva Reader*, p. 190)

21. Luce Irigaray, *This Sex Which is Not One* (1977), trans. Catherine Porter with Carolyn Burke (Ithaca, NY, 1985), p. 30.

22. Sigmund Freud, *Standard Edition of the Complete Psychological Works*, ed. James Strachey, vol. 22, *New Introductory Lectures on Psycho-Analysis and Other Works* (London, 1981), p. 131.

23. Laura Mulvey, 'Afterthoughts on Visual Pleasure and Narrative Cinema', in *Psychoanalysis and Cinema*, ed. E. Ann Kaplan (London, 1990), p. 26.

24. Irigaray, *Speculum of the Other Woman* (1974), trans. Gillian C. Gill (Ithaca, NY, 1985), p. 111.

25. Mulvey, 'Afterthoughts', p. 26.

26. Freud, *Standard Edition*, vol. 22, p. 131.

27. Kristeva, *Strangers to Ourselves* (1988), trans. Leon S. Roudiez (London, 1991), p. 19.

28. Angela Carter indicated her use of Brontë and referred me to the ballad 'The Demon Lover', in response to queries made by me in June 1987. For variant texts of 'The Demon Lover' see Francis James Child (ed.), *English and Scottish Popular Ballads*, vol. 4 (New York, 1965), pp. 360–9.

29. Sandra M. Gilbert and Susan Gubar, *The Madwoman in the Attic: The Woman Writer and the Nineteenth-Century Literary Imagination* (New Haven, CT, 1979), p. 272.

30. Ibid., p. 272.

31. Susan Sellers (ed.), *Writing Differences: Readings from the Seminar of Hélène Cixous* (Milton Keynes, 1988).

32. Irigaray, *Speculum of the Other Woman*, p. 83.

33. Irigaray, *This Sex Which is Not One*, p. 30.

34. Jacques Lacan, *Ecrits*, ed. and trans. Alan Sheridan (New York, 1977), p. ix.

35. Carter, *The Sadeian Woman: An Exercise in Cultural History* (London, 1979), p. 111.

36. Donatien Alphonse François, Marquis de Sade, *Philosophy in the Bedroom*, trans. Richard Seaver and Austryn Wainhouse (New York, 1965).

37. Irigaray, 'And the One Does Not Stir Without the Other' (1979), trans. Hélène Vivienne Wenzel, *Signs*, 7:1 (1981), 63.

38. Ibid., 67.

39. Annis Pratt, 'Women and Nature in Modern Fiction', *Contemporary Literature*, 13 (1972), 488.

40. The play of images, the imaginary, Marianne's dream.

41. Xavière Gauthier, 'Is There Such a Thing as Women's Writing?', trans. Marilyn A. August, in *New French Feminisms*, ed. Marks and Courtivron, p. 163.

42. Roland Barthes, *Mythologies*, trans. Annette Lavers (London, 1972).

5

The Anti-hero as Oedipus: Gender and the Postmodern Narrative in *The Infernal Desire Machines of Doctor Hoffman*

SALLY ROBINSON

Angela Carter's novels, *The Infernal Desire Machines of Doctor Hoffman* and *Nights at the Circus*, present a postmodernist take on de Beauvoir's claim that 'one is not born, but becomes a woman'. These novels are much more obviously 'deconstructive' than Doris Lessing's, in that they operate a displacement of sexual difference as a 'natural' distinction between women and men based in biology. For Carter, to become Woman means to become naturalised into a subordinate position, regardless of one's 'official gender'. That is, she disrupts an essentialist equation between biological sex and social gender. At the same time, however, she *foregrounds* gender as constitutive of subjectivity by tracing the processes by which 'official' women – that is, individuals sexed female – are socially and discursively constructed as Woman according to the needs of the dominant, 'official' sex, men. For Carter, gender is a relation of power, whereby the weak become 'feminine' and the strong become 'masculine'. And, because relations of power can change, this construction is always open to deconstruction. These two novels inscribe a tension between the normative construction of gender and its subversive deconstruction. And, although the line between construction and deconstruction is unstable and uncertain, the overall effect of Carter's novels is to drive a wedge between Woman and women, between male-centred metaphysical representations of Woman and the feminine, and women's multiplicitous and heterogeneous self-representations. Both of these texts strategically engage with the theoretical concerns of postmodernism and, in my reading of them [reading of *Nights* omitted here – Ed.], I will focus on their engagement with one relatively new, and predominantly male, theoretical preoccupation which has emerged from the 'postmodern condition': a preoccupation with the place of 'woman' in the deconstruction of culture's master narratives.[1]

The Infernal Desire Machines of Doctor Hoffman presents an epistemological revolution, not unlike that heralded by theorists of the 'postmodern condition', in which culture's master narratives are losing the power and authority to order experience and, conversely, in which 'experience' is no longer considered the ground of epistemological certainty. One master narrative, however, remains intact in this world: an Oedipal narrative that places man in the position of questing, speaking subject, and woman in the non-position of object who is *subject to* male regulation, exploitation, and violence. This is the same mythical narrative that caused so much disturbance in Lessing's fictions of female subjectivity. But, in *The Infernal Desire Machines*, the hero's gender fits with the gender of the 'mythical hero'. Desiderio is a subject gendered male, but not in the falsely universal sense. Carter's revision of the Oedipal quest narrative *foregrounds*, rather than *transcends* gender, de-universalising the male subject by engendering him. In *Nights at the Circus*, Carter continues to explore male fictions of woman but, here, creates a counter-narrative that explodes these fictions from the outside, and implodes them from the inside. In this text, Carter engages with the postmodern desire to privilege what Linda Hutcheon calls the 'ex-centric': the Other(s) of Western culture, who have, historically, had limited access to the place(s) of enunciation.[2] With the postmodernist critique of the self-present, knowing subject, has come a desire to explore the 'difference' whose exclusion has guaranteed the identity of the liberal humanist self. These explorations, however, too often become appropriations that do not disrupt the politics of enunciation. The politics of the postmodern, thus, can approach a postfeminism in which the gender of the speaking and reading subject is all but beside the point. Such a politics makes irrelevant the historically constituted experience of gender difference, including the differences among and within women. I use the term 'experience' in Teresa de Lauretis's sense of a 'personal, subjective, engagement in the practices, discourses, and institutions that lend significance (value, meaning, and affect) to the events of the world'.[3] And, although experience, like gender, is a construct rather than an essence, it does not necessarily follow that it is, thus, without authority in constituting subjectivity. It is precisely the neglect of 'experience' in postmodern/poststructuralist theory that Carter critiques in her novels. ...

Angela Carter's novels employ a doubled feminist perspective by performing a movement between the 'inside' and the 'outside' of normative gender constructions, including the construction of Woman as Other to Man's self – whether that Other be denigrated or celebrated. For Carter, denigration and celebration of Woman as Other are both masculinist strategies within patriarchal cultures, whereby Man secures his hegemony over the places of enunciation. Woman, whether revered or reviled, is spoken through dominant representational practices, whereas women are prohibited from speaking. To speak, or write, as a woman means to enact the double relation of women to dominant representational practices. For Carter, this entails practising the double strategies of mimicry, parody, and masquerade. Each of these performative strategies negotiates between the terms of a series of oppositions: construction/deconstruction of 'natural' sexual difference; compliance/resistance to the ideologies of gender difference as offered through hegemonic discursive systems; and, inscription/subversion of the fit between Woman and women, between metaphorical figures constructed according to the logics of a desire encoded as masculine and social subjects who position themselves through processes of self-representation. Like Irigaray's strategy of mimicry, Carter's parodies and masquerades point to an 'elsewhere' of discourse, what de Lauretis refers to as the 'chinks and cracks' in dominant representational practices. That elsewhere is the space of radical critique that exceeds the performance of mimicry or parody, and gets the text, and its readers, off the fence of what Linda Hutcheon calls the 'political ambidexterity' of postmodernist parody.[4]

The Infernal Desire Machines of Doctor Hoffman chronicles a revolution in the relationship between reason and unreason in which Dr Hoffman – a renegade philosopher, whose theoretical framework echoes Nietzsche, Derrida, and others – has declared a war on reality, in order to liberate desire; he is intent on exploring and materialising the 'obscure and controversial borderline between the thinkable and the unthinkable'.[5] Eschewing binary and linear logic, Hoffman attempts to find the 'loopholes in metaphysics' (p. 212), rewriting the *cogito* to read: 'I DESIRE, THEREFORE I EXIST' (p. 211). Against the law of the city fathers – represented by the Minister of Determination who 'is not a man but a theorem, clear, hard, unified and harmonious' (p. 13) – Hoffman is 'disseminating' 'lawless images' (p. 12). The Doctor is attractive in his ability to think beyond binary oppositions, to read the world in ways not wholly dependent on a logic which would repress the unconscious in a hegemony of logocentrism. But, early in the novel, something sinister enters into the textual mapping of the Doctor's effects. In an absurd confrontation between Hoffman's Ambassador and the Minister, the former speaks for seduction and the latter for coercion; however, the two figures come closer together as the Ambassador describes the Doctor's terms for capitulation: he wants 'absolute authority to establish a regime of total liberation' (p. 38). The language here foregrounds the idea that the Doctor's liberatory schema is complicit in the same will to power that the Minister clings to.[6] The Minister, a representative of 'logical positivism' (p. 194) speaks for a humanist epistemology that cannot countenance contradiction in its systems. The Doctor speaks for a posthumanist epistemology where contradiction rules and where rationality has been put radically into question. Yet, the two systems are quickly seen to be complicit in the same ideological agenda: they both position Man as an imperialist subject whose desire gives free reign to exploitation and domination.

Desiderio, a postmodern Oedipus, is sent to destroy the doctor; but his quest is complicated by the fact that everything he sees and experiences turns out to be an emanation of his desires. The world across which Desiderio moves is literally a construction: the Doctor's desire machines have disrupted 'reality' to the extent that any epistemological certainty has become impossible. Objects, people, landscapes, and even time are subject to the whims of the desire machines which are generating 'eroto-energy' as a force in opposition to rational knowledge. This eroto-energy causes each subject to perceive and experience the world according to the logic – or, illogic – of his/her desires. Since we see everything through Desiderio's eyes, we are immersed in his desires and forced to experience them along with him. All of Desiderio's 'experiences', thus, are constructions of his desire. In reading this text, we are constantly aware that desire is, indeed, the 'motor force' of narrative, as Peter Brooks would have it; and, further, that the 'engine' behind the narrative, like the male 'eroto-energy' Dr Hoffman's revolution unleashes, is hostile to women.[7] Desiderio's desire participates in the fantasy of colonisation that, simultaneously, marks the Doctor's and the Minister's projects for 'liberation' – this despite his ambiguously claimed membership in a colonised group, due to his being 'of Indian extraction' (p. 16). Desiderio's discursive self-positioning throughout the narrative is dependent on his negation of the various exotic and erotic 'others' his desire invokes. Against these others, he claims the 'unique allure of the norm' (p. 101).

Despite the fact that Desiderio's narrative is anything but a traditional quest story, its structure follows pretty closely the form of that story: sent to seek and destroy the diabolical Doctor, Desiderio gets sidetracked and, in fact, seduced to the Doctor's side through the mediation of his daughter, Albertina. While his pursuit of the elusive woman disrupts his primary quest – a quest that originates through the imperative of a stern father figure – he nevertheless finally finds the Doctor, and it appears that he will get a bonus for his trouble: possession of Albertina. Finding himself duped, however, by Albertina – who turns out to be even more diabolical than her father – and his 'physicality thwarted by metaphysics' (p. 204), he kills them both, and returns to his city of origin, a hero. Like Oedipus, he has rid the city of its pollution and, also like Oedipus, must pay the price of his new knowledge: 'I knew I was condemned to disillusionment in perpetuity', he reminisces. 'My punishment had been my crime' (p. 220). While culture's master narratives are losing their authority in this deconstructing textual world, the power relations embedded within white capitalist patriarchy remain intact. Desiderio begins his quest from the 'thickly, obtusely masculine' city that 'settled serge-clad buttocks at vulgar ease as if in a leather armchair' (p. 15) – a city whose 'smug, impenetrable, bourgeois affluence' is achieved at the expense of 'indigenous' peoples whose names have now become 'unmentionable' (p. 16). At the end of his journey, instead of finding the disruption he expects through the Doctor's liberatory projects, Desiderio finds a 'chaste, masculine room ... with a narrow bed and a black leather armchair ... and a magazine rack containing current numbers of *Playboy*, *The New Yorker*, *Time* and *Newsweek*' (p. 199). Woman, in Desiderio's narrative, as in the classical quest story, occupies a range of traditional object positions: she is a fetish, a foil, the exotic/erotic object awaiting the hero at the end of his quest, but never a subject. She is, like Derrida's 'affirmative woman', an object put into circulation according to the logic of male desire.[8] As object of the male gaze, she is subject to regulation, exploitation and violence.

Desiderio's narrative is, then, an exaggerated form of the mythical quest plot that de Lauretis identifies with the prevalence of Oedipus as paradigm in patriarchal culture. It is exaggerated in that Carter brings to the surface what often remains underground in male-centred fictions: the trajectories of desire whereby Woman becomes merely a foil or a 'prize' in the stories of male subjectivity. For her part, Carter sees the primacy of the Oedipus story in culture's master narratives and would seem to agree with Laura Mulvey's observation that 'sadism demands a story', and perhaps vice versa.[9] Speaking to the prevalence of erotic violence in representation and other social practices, Carter invokes Oedipus. Acts of violence, she writes,

> reawaken the memory of the social fiction of the female wound, the bleeding scar left by her castration, which is a psychic fiction as deeply at the heart of Western culture as the myth of Oedipus, to which it is related in the complex dialectic of imagination and reality that produces culture. Female castration is an imaginary fact that pervades the whole of men's attitude towards women and our attitude to ourselves, that transforms women from human beings into wounded creatures who were born to bleed.[10]

The Infernal Desire Machines of Doctor Hoffman reinscribes this transformation, complete with erotic violence unleashed. Oedipal narrative not only keeps woman 'in her place', but does so in order to safeguard male subjectivity from the 'bleeding wound' of difference she represents. This text brings to the surface the violent excesses of the transformation of women into Woman by exaggerating the complicities between desire and domination in Western culture's master narratives.

The Infernal Desire Machines of Doctor Hoffman mimics male-centred fictions in a particularly ingenious and telling way. In this text, Carter assumes the mask of maleness, using Desiderio as the only locus of narrative voice and desire – a gendering of the 'I' that the reader cannot forget for one moment. Desiderio is the architect, or author, of a narrative of sexual exploitation and violence – a quasi-pornographic writer who enlists an array of misogynist sentiment and fantasy. In this novel, Carter is playing with a tradition of pornographic fiction she describes in *The Sadeian Woman*, a tradition marked by the appropriation of a woman's voice to speak for male sexuality:

> Many pornographic novels are written in the first person as if by a woman, or use a woman as the focus of the narrative; but this device only reinforces the male orientation of the fiction. John Cleland's *Fanny Hill* and the anonymous *The Story of O*, both classics of the genre, appear to describe a woman's mind through the fiction of her sexuality. This technique ensures that the gap left in the text is of just the right size for the reader to insert his prick into, the exact dimensions, in fact, of Fanny's vagina or O's anus. Pornography engages the reader in a most intimate fashion before it leaves him to his own resources.
>
> (pp. 15–16)[11]

In *The Infernal Desire Machines of Doctor Hoffman*, Carter appropriates a man's subjectivity to describe the fictions of his sexuality, but does so self-consciously; that is, the text foregrounds the problematics of gendered address by deliberately framing the female figures within the text, as well as the woman reader, as figments of a masculine imaginary. In containing women within a figure of Woman, Carter demonstrates how Woman is trapped *inside* gender. But, her strategic engagement with fictions of male subjectivity simultaneously demonstrates what it means to be *outside* hegemonic representations of gender, dismantling them from the margins. This text does, in fact, inscribe a 'hole' or gap; but it signifies an absence, rather than a presence. While Woman is everywhere present in this novel, women are conspicuously absent.

How, then, does a text that seems so violently to foreclose on female subjectivity be read as a feminist critique of narrative structures? Or, to put it in slightly different terms, if Carter's text details the dangerous economies of male desire lurking behind narrative and representation, does it simply reinforce the power of these economies, thus closing off the possibility of changing them? How can one tell the difference between construction and deconstruction?[12] Linda Hutcheon, for one, wonders if it is possible to tell the difference at all. She claims that postmodernist artistic practices both use and abuse history, tradition, representation, humanist ideology, and so on. Through parody, the texts of postmodernism *inscribe* in order to *subvert* the master narratives of Western culture, a practice that results in what she calls the 'political ambidexterity' of postmodernism. She writes: 'Postmodernism knows it cannot escape implication in the economic (late capitalist) and ideological (liberal humanist) dominants of its time. There is no outside. All it can do is question from within' (*Poetics*, p. xiii). However, Hutcheon notes that perhaps women have more to win, than to lose, from critique of the politics of representation; and, further, that feminist postmodern practice would have little to gain through a 'legitimation' of that which it critiques.[13] In other words, feminist postmodernist parody has a political stake in disrupting representations of woman, and such disruptions are marked by the desire to change these representations. The feminist postmodernist text

> parodically inscribes the conventions of feminine representation, provokes our conditioned response and then subverts that response, making us aware of how it was induced in us. To work it must be complicitous with the values in challenges; we have to feel the seduction in order to question it and then to theorise the site of that contradiction. Such feminist uses of postmodern tactics *politicise desire* in their play with the revealed and the hidden, the offered and the deferred.
>
> (*Politics*, p. 154, my emphasis)

Carter's text does, indeed, politicise desire, and does so by playing with the conventions of pornographic address, a strategy that Hutcheon notes in other feminist texts. Carter foregrounds the text's enunciative apparatus by making explicit the complicities between desire and domination. Throughout all of Desiderio's adventures, his subjectivity is guaranteed by his objectification of women – of all races, classes, and sexual orientations – who are never, in this text, 'fully human' (p. 73). They are 'erotic toys', mutilated bodies, phallic mothers, castrating Amazons who are all punished for the crime of being female. Except, that is, for Albertina, the Doctor's daughter, who is punished, to be sure – in a gang rape by a group of Centaurs; but she is also the supreme object of desire, the 'inexpressible woman' (p. 13) who takes different shapes according to the logic of Desiderio's desire. Because of the mechanisms of identification built into a first-person quest narrative, this text seems to address its readers as male: as subjects who can enjoy, along with Desiderio, the triumphs of his desire. As feminist theorists of narrative film have suggested, when a woman reader approaches such a text, she may well find herself engaged in a split identification: the narrative positions her to identify with the (male) protagonist by various mechanisms, such as first-person narration as the locus of desire; while, by virtue of her gender, she may also feel identification with the female or feminine forces in the narrative.[14] The overt masculinisation of the narrative in Carter's text, however, serves to subvert the mechanisms of identification that support the successful narrativisation of violence against women. Carter's mimicry of pornographic narrative – an exaggerated form of all narratives mobilised by male desire – confronts the issue of gendered address head-on by placing the woman reader in an impossible position. There is, quite simply, *no place* for a woman reader in this text; and that no place foregrounds the hom(m)osexual economy Carter is mimicking in it.

The text, then, paradoxically addresses its reader as *feminist* by de-naturalising the processes by which narrative constructs differences – sexual, racial, class, national – according to the twin logics of desire and domination; that is, it invites the reader to occupy a position not sanctioned by Desiderio's narrative itself but, rather, a position on the outside of that narrative. Carter's text offers this outsider position through a disruption of identification in a number of ways. First, and most obvious, is the fact that, because Desiderio is so clearly complicit in his adventures – which include a number of rapes and female mutilations – a reader who identifies with him will uncomfortably share in his complicity. Second, because the text makes explicit the economies of male desire behind representations of women, the reader does not so easily get seduced into identification – either with Desiderio, or with the female figures he encounters (constructs) on his journey. In other words, there is no illusion of 'reality' in this text which might mask the fact that Desiderio's desire is the motor force of the narrative, and we are, thus, constantly aware that none of his constructions of women are 'natural'. The text demonstrates how Woman is *produced*, rather than simply represented, in narratives of male desire and subjectivity. Finally, Carter makes explicit the 'underside' of narrative and history through the use and abuse of pornographic narrative conventions. This 'underside' – the mechanics of desire and pleasure as they function beneath the violent and de-humanising fictions of masculinist pornographic narrative – is brought to the surface and, thus, problematises the identification that is necessary in order for pornography to do its 'work'.[15]

The text contains a number of explicit references to pornographic representation, including a couple of scenes straight out of the pages of the Marquis de Sade, and a 'Peep Show', where very familiar representations are de-familiarised by being framed with ironic titles. If the text is pornographic, it is what Carter calls 'pornography in the service of women'. She speculates, in *The Sadeian Woman*, that a political 'pornographer would not be the enemy of women, perhaps because he might begin to penetrate to the heart of the contempt for women that distorts our culture even as he entered the realms of true obscenity as he describes it' (p. 20). The use of the masculine pronoun here, always gendered in Carter's work, foregrounds, I think, the reasons behind her appropriation of male subjectivity in her novel. Because, according to Carter, pornography is representation by and for men, her intervention into the politics of representation must be, as Linda Hutcheon puts it, from the inside. Yet something of the 'outside' of this representation remains in the novel, a critical perspective akin to the one Luce Irigaray claims as that which remains through women's mimicry.[16] The text refuses to guarantee a voyeuristic or narcissistic position for its readers – male and female – because its metafictional strategies continuously disrupt the 'pleasure' such positions traditionally afford. Take, for example, this description of the female figures who people the Sadeian 'House of Anonymity' that Desiderio visits:

> Each was as circumscribed as a figure in rhetoric and you could not imagine they had names, for they had been reduced by the rigorous discipline of their vocation to the undifferentiated essence of the idea of the female. This ideational femaleness took amazingly different shapes though its nature was not that of Woman; when I examined them closely, I saw that none of them were any longer, or might never have been, woman. All, without exception, passed beyond or did not enter the realm of simple humanity. They were sinister, abominable, inverted mutations, part clockwork, part vegetable and part brute.
>
> (p. 132)

Desiderio's confusion here marks the contradictions Carter sees in the construction of Woman through pornographic narrative. Are these figures women or Woman? Both and neither, it would seem, as Desiderio is forced to confront his complicity in the dehumanisation of the objects of his desire. This passage is more like literary criticism than it is like pornography: here, Carter deconstructs representations of women as the machines of male pleasure, bringing to its logical conclusion the ideology of pornography that reduces agents to mere functions. Such a reduction removes sexuality and erotic domination from the social world and makes the 'pursuit of pleasure' into 'a metaphysical quest' (*The Sadeian Woman*, p. 16). Carter aims in *The Infernal Desire Machines* to show how 'sexual relations between men and women always render explicit the nature of social relations in the society in which they take place' and how, 'if described explicitly, will form a critique of those relations' (*The Sadeian Woman*, p. 20).

Carter's critique of desire as domination works through a literalisation – or de-metaphorisation – of the structures of male fantasy underlying traditional, and not so traditional, quest narratives, including the kind of quest narrative that I read against the grain of Derrida's *Spurs* in the first part of this chapter [omitted here – Ed.]. The notion of woman as 'ideational femaleness' that 'can take amazingly different shapes' in Carter's text resonates thematically with the philosophical trend chronicled by Jardine in *Gynesis*. Hoffman is a figure intent on liberating the repressed of culture, on exploring the margins of philosophy and reason – precisely, the 'feminine' disorder that complements masculine order. At the end of the novel, we learn that the Doctor believes in the 'inherent symmetry of divergent asymmetry' modelled on the 'intercommunication of seed between male and female all things produced' (p. 213), and represented, predictably, by his daughter Albertina. This woman-figure, like Irigaray's Athena,[17] speaks the word of the father and makes that word flesh. The 'divergent asymmetry' to which the Doctor refers is gender difference and Albertina's gender fluidity throughout the novel serves, not to blur the boundaries of sexual difference in order to liberate us from the tyranny of absolute division by gender, but to perpetuate the whole metaphysical apparatus as it works around the question of sexual difference. The fact that Hoffman's metaphysics are *openly* based on sexual difference does not significantly differentiate them from the old system against which he is working; as in Derrida's appropriation of the feminine in a new narrative of sexual difference, here we see a female object put into circulation according to a male desire to control representation. The 'inherent symmetry' turns out not to be a symmetry at all; the male figures in the text retain power over the female, and put this power into play as Hoffman's 'liberation of desire' results in increased objectification of, and sexual violence against, women. As Alice Jardine suggests, there tends to be a congruence between valorisations of the 'feminine' as the repressed or 'unnameable', and increased narrativisation of violence against women in male-authored fictions.[18] ...

In Carter's text, Oedipus/Desiderio creates a fetish object, in the person of Albertina, a figure marked by undecidability. Like Derrida's woman-figure, Albertina is nearly impossible to pin down; she assumes numerous different identities, experiences gender fluidity, and takes any form that Desiderio's desire imposes on her. He seeks her as his 'Platonic other, [his] necessary extinction, [his] dream made flesh' (p. 215) and, as such, she can take any form; she is an idea, not a woman – for, more precisely, she is Woman, rather than *a* woman. As our protagonist himself comes to realise, she 'was inextricably mingled with [his] idea of her and her substance was so flexible she could have worn a left glove on her right hand' (p. 142). This woman-object serves as a decoy to mask the real object of desire – the father cum-phallus-cum 'Master'. What actually circulates in hom(m)osexual economies, then, is not the woman, but the phallus represented by the woman. As Gayle Rubin observes in her analysis of Freud and Lévi-Strauss, the interfamily exchange of women coincides with another, intrafamily, exchange: 'in the cycle of exchange manifested by the Oedipal complex, the phallus passes through the medium of women from one man to another. ... In this family *Kula* ring, women go one way, the phallus goes another. ... It is an expression of the transmission of male dominance. It passes through women and settles upon men.'[19] Desiderio himself eventually realises that 'perhaps the whole history of my adventure could be titled "Desiderio in Search of a Master". But I only wanted to find a master ... so that I could lean on him at first and then, after a while, jeer' (p. 190). Albertina's role here is to mediate between Desiderio and Hoffman, just as the affirmative woman's role in *Spurs* is to mediate between Derrida and Nietzsche.

Desiderio is literally fatherless: his mother, a prostitute, conceived him through her work in the Indian slums of the city. Thus, not only has his mother deprived him of a present father, but also, forced him to carry the 'genetic imprint' of this lost father 'on his face' (p. 16). And, while he disclaims his Indian heritage in his life before Hoffman's revolution, this repressed material gets released once the desire machines start their work. Thus it is that Desiderio finds himself 'adopted' by a family of 'River People' in an adventure that plays out his ambivalence toward his mother's actions and his father's race. During his time with the River People, Desiderio's colonialist imagination is given full scope, as he constructs this isolated society as 'ex-centric': primitive, naïve, living with 'a complex, hesitant but absolute immediacy' (p. 71).[20] Not surprisingly, this way of life is encoded as 'feminine': the River People don't 'think in straight lines', but in 'subtle and intricate interlocking circles'; concepts are relational, rather than absolute, opposites existing in 'a locked tension'; the written form of their language is 'beautiful', but 'utterly lacking in signification' (p. 75); and so on. Their society is 'theoretically matrilinear though in practice all decisions devolved upon the father' (p. 80). Because everything that happens to Desiderio is an emanation of his desires, we can read in this episode a nostalgic return to the 'feminine', to his (absent) mother and the threat that this return evokes.

That threat, of course, is castration, and Desiderio's adventure with the river family replays the Freudian family romance in a new, although still recognisable, way. It is assumed that he will become the husband of one of the clan's daughter, Aoi, whom Desiderio consistently refers to as an 'erotic toy' (p. 86). In preparation for her marriage, Aoi's grandmother has manipulated her clitoris over the years, until it approximates a penis. Desiderio cannot help approving this practice: '[I]t was the custom for mothers of young girls to manipulate their daughters' private parts for a regulation hour a day from babyhood upwards, coaxing the sensitive little projection until it attained lengths the river people considered both aesthetically and sexually desirable' (p. 84). What is important here is not so much this practice itself, but Desiderio's interpretation of it; from his male-centred frame of reference, the women are aspiring to masculinity.[21] His desire to masculinise the women amounts to a fetishistic desire to endow his 'erotic toy' with a penis. He leaves the River People, reluctantly, after it becomes clear that the father is about to make good on the threat of castration – but not, however, until he succeeds in sleeping with the mother. It is this experience which prompts Desiderio to remark, 'Indeed, I was growing almost reconciled to mothers' (p. 85).

Desiderio's desire constructs women as phallic in order to alleviate his anxieties over his own masculinity, evoked by the absence of his father. We have Mamie Buckskin, a 'freak' in a circus who is trapped within a conventional narrative from classical Hollywood Westerns. Mamie, Desiderio tells us, 'was a paradox – a fully phallic female with the bosom of a nursing mother and a gun, death-dealing erectile tissue, perpetually at her thigh' (p. 108). We have the tribe of Amazons on the coast of Africa who are much more threatening, the destructive mother of male fantasy, with a vengeance. The massive black chieftain who presides over this tribe, a figure of racist fantasy, tells Desiderio and his companions about why he has chosen women to be his warriors – that is, after all 'capacity for feeling' has been excised from them through clitorodectomy:

> Why, you may ask, have I built my army out of women since they are often held to be the gentler sex? Gentlemen, if you rid your hearts of prejudice and examine the bases of the traditional notions of the figure of the female, you will find you have founded them all on the remote figure you thought you glimpsed, once, in your earliest child-hood, bending over you with an offering of warm, sugared milk. ... Tear this notion of the mother from your hearts. Vengeful as nature herself, she loves her children only in order to devour them better and if she herself rips her own veils of self-deceit, Mother perceives in herself untold abysses of cruelty as subtle as it is refined.
>
> (p. 160)

Like the female figures in the House of Anonymity, these women 'have passed far beyond all human feeling' (p. 160), which is, of course, where both the chieftain and Desiderio want them. They are not 'human' because they have been de-humanised and it is the logic of Desiderio's desire that evokes these destructive, cannibalising women. While the chieftain, and Desiderio, thus, debunk one myth of femininity, they replace it with another: the all-good mother gives way to her opposite, both of whom are constructions of cultures where motherhood, whether revered or reviled, is the a priori condition of femaleness.

This adventure, like the episode with the River People, clearly shows how desire and domination are complicit and points to what I am reading as the text's inscription and subversion of a colonialist mentality. From here, Desiderio and Albertina move on to visit a tribe of centaurs who are evoked through a Western fantasy of 'primitive' cultures. The complex religious mythology that governs the centaurs' lives is merely a translation of Christian mythology, complete with a genesis story, a Christ figure, resurrection, and sal-vation. As Brian McHale points out, Carter 'has constructed an

Africa wholly derived from European fantasy. She populates its coast with cannibal tribesmen straight out of party jokes, comic-strips, and slapstick comedy; while in the interior she places centaurs, in effect suppressing indigenous mythology in favour of an imported European myth. This is imperialism of the imagination, and Carter knows it; indeed, her purpose is to foreground it and expose it for what it is' (p. 55). McHale further notes that these African figures are all 'reifications of European desire' – especially since they are the figments of Desiderio's imaginary. But what McHale does not note is the continuity of violent misogyny we can discern throughout all of these adventures, a misogyny that is as much a part of an imperialist imagination. The centaurs, for example, 'believed that women were only born to suffer' (p. 172), and, thus, 'the females were ritually degraded and reviled' (p. 176). Desiderio, while not exactly applauding this orientation to sexual difference, respects this culture for elevating the 'virile principle' to such a degree. He watches, 'indifferently', while Albertina suffers a gang rape by the centaurs, later observing that 'even the rape had had elements of the kind of punishment said to hurt the giver more than the receiver though I do not know what they were punishing her for, unless it was for being female to a degree unprecedented among them' (p. 181). Later, when the centaurs understand that Albertina is Desiderio's mate, 'and therefore [his] property' (p. 182), they apologise to him for their 'punishment' of Albertina's 'crime'. To put the finishing touches on this construction of femininity, Carter has Albertina suggest that the centaurs were an emanation of her desire, not Desiderio's, and that the gang rape was 'dredged up and objectively reified from the dark abysses of [her] unconscious' (p. 186).

The quest plot that structures *The Infernal Desire Machines of Doctor Hoffman* is a contorted version of Oedipal narrative that Carter uses to foreground the ideological stakes in this kind of story. Because Desiderio's adventures represent a direct expression of his desire – both conscious and unconscious – the text serves as a commentary on the gendering of that desire as masculine. This novel is an in-depth exploration of male subjectivity in narrative, and the construction of sexual difference along binary and often violent lines; as such, it foregrounds the problematics in reading as a woman. Yet Carter systematically disrupts the pleasure of the text by foregrounding the enunciative apparatus behind its inscriptions of desire. If the pleasure of the text is dependent on identification with Desiderio who, after all, has been produced as a 'war hero' by History, that pleasure is continuously disrupted by Carter's insistence on what that official History leaves unspoken: the complicities between desire and domination. Desire, in this text, ultimately destroys both its subject and its object. For, although Desiderio emerges intact from his adventures, Carter deprives him, at the last minutes, of his 'climax': he fails, after all, to find either a worthy master–father, since Hoffman turns out to be a 'hypocrite', a 'totalitarian of the unconscious'; or the object of desire, since Albertina must be killed in order for Desiderio to fulfil his mission and become a 'hero'. Desiderio, in turn, deprives his imagined reader of that climax, as well, breaking the pattern of narrative dénouement which would ensure the pleasure of the text through the release of tension, modelled, as Peter Brooks and others seem to assume, on male sexuality: 'See, I have ruined all the suspense. I have quite spoiled my climax. But why do you deserve a climax, anyway?' (p. 208). But the pleasure of this text resides elsewhere, an 'alternative thrill', as Laura Mulvey would say, 'that comes from leaving the past behind without rejecting it ... or daring to break with normal pleasurable expectations in order to conceive a new language of desire' ('Visual Pleasure', p. 8). That thrill, in Carter's text, comes from the negotiation of seduction by and resistance to narrative forms and their production of gender.

In Linda Hutcheon's terms, the text 'seduces' its readers into certain constructions of Woman, through its use of traditional conventions of first-person quest narrative. These conventions ensure that Man's self-representation is achieved through his objectification, appropriation, and exploitation of feminine figures: Self can only be realised in opposition to others. But Carter's exaggeration and literalisation of these conventions serves to deconstruct the processes by which narrative engenders the subject as male through a violent negation of female subjectivity. Unlike Hutcheon, who implies that construction and deconstruction cancel each other out, and thus, leaves postmodern parody floundering in 'political ambidexterity', I have argued that this double strategy in Carter's text carries a sharp ideological critique that is not neutralised by the fact that the text does, in fact, represent Woman in all too traditional ways.[22] On the contrary, it is through Carter's strategic engagement with various master narratives of Western culture that her critique of the politics of representation emerges. While this text presents many difficulties for a feminist reading, those difficulties foreground the stakes in pursuing such a reading. Carter is no idealist, not one to take a utopian leap beyond normative representations of Woman to some uncontaminated representation of women; rather, her text inscribes, in order to subvert, representations that produce women as Woman. ...

From Sally Robinson, *Engendering the Subject: Gender and Self-Representation in Contemporary Women's Fiction* (Albany, NY, 1991), pp. 77–9, 97–108, 111–17.

NOTES

[With the author's permission, this essay has been made up from several extracts from Chapter 2, 'Angela Carter and the Circus of Theory: Writing Woman and Women Writing', of her book-length study of Doris Lessing, Carter and Gayle Jones, *Engendering the Subject,* with some notes cut. This book explores certain issues concerning poststructuralist conceptions of subjectivity in relation to gender (subjectivity denoting the experience of being a subject, those identities structured by larger systems of power and signification such as patriarchy, racism, heterosexuality and international capitalism). Robinson asks whether it is possible to theorise another subject, one which is still gendered but not within the old systems of meaning, and whether writers can ever create other places from which women may speak. Reading theory alongside fiction to create a dialogue between them, Robinson in her original chapter uses Derrida's *Spurs* (seen as a persistently masculinist deconstruction of the humanist subject), and Irigaray's 'Veiled Lips' (a reading of Derrida's reading of Nietzsche) as a way of exploring the political implications of poststructuralism for women, in particular questions of whether women have agency within actual relations of domination and subordination. Also in the original essay is a discussion of *Nights of the Circus* as a parody of postmodern valorising of the 'ex-centric'. Printed here is her discussion of *The Infernal Desire Machines of Doctor Hoffman* which explores Carter's appropriation of a man's subjectivity in this novel in order to describe the fictions of masculine sexuality. Through a consideration of how the text positions the reader, Robinson investigates the problems of how a writer can subvert, rather than simply reinforce, these master narratives. Ed.]

1. The new explorations of the place of woman in theory have taken a number of different forms. Alice Jardine, *Gynesis: Configurations of Woman and Modernity* (Ithaca, NY, 1985), is an excellent introduction to, and critique of, the place of woman in 'high' French theory. See also Jonathan Culler's remarks on 'reading as a woman' in *On Deconstruction: Theory and Criticism After Structuralism* (Ithaca, NY,

1982), and Terry Eagleton's comments on feminist strategies of reading in *Literary Theory: An Introduction* (Minneapolis, 1983). Jean-François Lyotard, 'One of the Things at Stake in Women's Struggles', *SubStance*, 20 (1978), 9–17, also links feminism up with the larger 'postmodern condition', and the essays collected in *Men in Feminism*, ed. Alice Jardine and Paul Smith (New York, 1987), provide a vigorous and interesting sampling of the debates around these theoretical issues and what is at stake in them. Tania Modleski, 'Feminism and the Power of Interpretation: Some Critical Readings', in *Feminist Studies/Critical Studies*, ed. Teresa de Lauretis (Bloomington, 1984), pp. 121–38, comments on the (male) desire to read as a woman, and Diana Fuss, *Essentially Speaking: Feminism, Nature and Difference* (New York, 1989), in turn, comments on Modleski's readings.

2. Linda Hutcheon, *A Poetics of Postmodernism: History, Theory, Fiction* (New York, 1988), pp. 57–73.

3. Teresa de Lauretis, *Alice Doesn't: Feminism, Semiotics, Cinema* (Bloomington, 1984), p. 159.

4. In both of Hutcheon's books, *A Poetics of Postmodernism* and *The Politics of Postmodernism* (London, 1989), she insists, repetitively, that postmodernism's 'complicitous critique' can only question; it paradoxically 'both legitimises and subverts that which it parodies' (*Politics*, p. 101). I will question Hutcheon's certainty about the political ambidexterity of postmodernism later in this chapter.

5. Angela Carter, *The Infernal Desire Machines of Doctor Hoffman* (1972, reprinted New York, 1985), p. 22. All subsequent references are to this edition.

6. Brian McHale, *Postmodernist Fiction* (New York, 1987), points to the text's Manichean opposition between the Apollonian Minister of Justice and the Dionysian Hoffman. But, in describing Hoffman as the 'agent of fantasy and pleasure' (p. 143), he banishes gender from this scene, and elides the question that is central to the text: *whose* fantasy, and *whose* pleasure?

7. See Peter Brooks, *Reading for the Plot: Design and Intention in Narrative* (New York, 1984) for an analysis of desire as the (phallic) 'piston' of narrative, its 'motor force'.

8. Jacques Derrida, *Spurs/Eperons*, trans. Barbara Harlow (Chicago, 1979).

9. Laura Mulvey, 'Afterthoughts on "Visual Pleasure and Narrative Cinema" Inspired by "Duel in the Sun" (King Vidor, 1946)', *Framework*, 15, 16, 17 (1981), 15–17. de Lauretis, *Alice Doesn't*, explores the reversal of Mulvey's claim. See particularly, pp. 103 and 109.

10. Carter, *The Sadeian Woman and the Ideology of Pornography* (1978, reprinted New York, 1988). All subsequent references are to this edition.

11. For other, interesting, feminist discussions of *The Story of 0*, see Kaja Silverman, 'Histoire d'O: The Construction of a Female Subject', in *Pleasure and Danger: Exploring Female Sexuality*, ed. Carole Vance (Boston, 1984), pp. 320–49; and Nancy K. Miller, 'The Text's Heroine: A Feminist Critic and Her Fictions', *Diacritics*, 12 (1982), 48–53.

12. I wish to thank the students in my seminar on 'Gender, Desire and Contemporary Fiction' at Case Western Reserve University for prompting me to consider these difficult questions.

13. Interestingly, when Hutcheon focuses explicitly on feminist postmodernist practice, her certainty about postmodernism's operations breaks down, particularly in her reading of Hannah Wilke's nude self-portrait (*The Politics of Postmodernism*, p. 159).

14. See Mulvey, 'Afterthoughts'; and Mary Ann Doane, 'Film and the Masquerade: Theorizing the Female Spectator', *Screen*, 23 (September/ October 1982), 74–87.

15. According to Carter, pornography is 'art with work to do' – its chief function being the arousal of sexual desire (*The Sadeian Woman*, p. 12). Carter disdains the opposition between pornography and erotica on the grounds of a class analysis, noting that erotica is 'the pornography of the elite' (p. 17).

16. Luce Irigaray, 'Veiled Lips', in *Amante marine: de Frederich Nietsche*, trans. Sara Speidel, *Mississippi Review* (Winter/Spring 1983), 93–131.

17. Irigaray, 'Veiled Lips'.

18. Jardine, *Gynesis*, never explicitly makes this point, but implies it in her discussions of fictional fantasies of (female) dismemberments and the like.

19. Gayle Rubin, 'The Traffic in Women: Notes on the "Political Economy" of Sex', in *Toward an Anthropology of Women*, ed. Reiter Raynor (New York, 1978), p. 192.

20. Linda Hutcheon notes that this episode 'reveals the extreme of ... ex-centric ethnicity' and that Carter 'uses this society to ironic and satiric ends' (*Poetics*, p. 71).

21. Carter here is mimicking a scene from Sade, in which a woman sports her 'flexible clitoris-cum-prick' (*The Sadeian Woman*, p. 112).

22. Robert Clark comes to an opposite conclusion in his reading in 'Angela Carter's Desire Machine', *Women's Studies*, 14:2 (1987), 147–61. For Clark, Carter's work, in general, fails to include 'within

its own critical representation an understanding of the complicity of that representation with the social forces it appears to reject' (p. 154). Further, according to Clark, 'Carter's insight into the patriarchal construction of femininity has a way of being her blindness: her writing is often a feminism in a male chauvinist drag, a transvestite style, and this may be because her primary allegiance is to a postmodern aesthetics that emphasises the non-referential emptiness of definitions. Such a commitment precludes an affirmative feminism founded in referential commitment to women's historical and organic being. Only in patriarchal eyes is femininity an empty category, the negation of masculinity' (p. 158). Apart from the fact that the second statement seems to contradict the first, underlying these comments is an assumption of an essential femininity – an 'organic being' – that Carter's 'transvestite' style, in fact, works to deconstruct. Clark would have Carter leave behind what I am reading as her radical critique and focus, instead, on some affirmation that would place women *outside* patriarchal eyes.

6

Textualising the Double-gendered Body: Forms of the Grotesque in *The Passion of New Eve*

HEATHER JOHNSON

The world of Angela Carter's fiction is inhabited by fabulous, monstrous creations: she-wolves, bird women, drag queens. The composite nature of these mythic figures often becomes the point of textual fascination in several of her novels and short stories. In order to examine the treatment of such composite images more closely, this article will focus on two characters of compound identity in *The Passion of New Eve*: Eve(lyn) and Tristessa. Specifically, I wish to argue that Carter's text reclaims the figure of the double-gendered body through the shifting values of the term *grotesque* that can be charted in the development of the narrative. This use of the grotesque also intersects and informs the parody of gender norms in the novel. In a reading of these figures as grotesque, one can discover here the two distinctive forms of this term as proposed by Bakhtin and the corresponding values generally associated with the term itself. It is possible to recognise one of these as positive and the other as negative.

A definition of the term *grotesque realism* is located in Bakhtin's reading of Rabelais and is dependent on a set of images that describe a transgressive body – one which emphasises the lower stratum, which takes pleasure in bodily functions, and which embraces an interrelation of death and birth. He describes this grotesque body as open, protruding, secreting, a body of becoming: 'In grotesque realism ... the bodily element is deeply positive.' The material body is shown to be 'festive' and 'utopian'.[1] Bakhtin also delineates a second meaning of the term *grotesque* as 'post-Romantic'. This refers to the grotesque in its modern sense as it furnishes descriptions of alienation, hostility, and inhumanity. To this form it is possible to assign a negative value since its meaning is preoccupied with issues of rejection and revulsion. Its use in common speech is clearly derogatory.

Both these forms of the grotesque are inscribed in the bodies of the two central figures. Carter's protagonist begins the novel as the male Evelyn but is transformed physically and then mentally into a woman – Eve. Captured in the desert by the women of Beulah, Evelyn is taken to meet the self-designed goddess 'Mother', whose body seems to fill the captive's visual frame: 'She was so big she seemed, almost, to fill the round, red-painted, over-heated, red-lit cell.'[2] Her arms are 'like girders', her vagina is 'like the crater of a volcano', and Evelyn imagines 'the sun in her mouth' (p. 64). In the manner of Artemis, Mother has required the sacrifice of one breast from each of her followers and has 'flung a patchwork quilt stitched from her daughters' breasts over the cathedral of her interior' (p. 60). Thus she presents an imposing figure of physical amplitude and abundant fertility. Here we can see some aspects of the Rabelaisian grotesque – the bodily form exaggerated to excess, the symbol of fertility, and the focus on the lower stratum. This focus is obviously emphasised further by the subsequent construction of Eve's womb and the location of Beulah's uterine rooms beneath the desert floor. The image is not without humour, of course – 'Her nipples leaped about like the bobbles on the fringe of an old-fashioned, red plush curtain' (p. 64) – and here it coincides, in its celebration of excess, with the notion of carnivalesque laughter, a significant feature of the Rabelaisian mode.

Carter uses the figure of Mother to disrupt patriarchal conceptions of the female body, as the grotesque body irrupts into the conventional presentation of that body. The description of Mother is filtered through the male sensibility of Evelyn as narrator and as such enacts a parody of the conventional maternal image through physical exaggeration, excess, and distortion. Evelyn responds to Mother as a monster: 'the bull-like pillar of her neck, ... false beard of crisp, black curls', and the obvious result of the programme of grafting fill him with 'squeamish horror' (p. 59). In the context of Carter's novel this reaction is significant since Evelyn is responding as a male to an exaggerated female body. The figure of Mother can be regarded as pivotal here in accounting for the shift in meaning of the grotesque. Evelyn's interpretation of her body as disgusting rather than life-affirming is soon transferred onto his own new body. Evelyn is castrated and then transformed by two months of plastic surgery into a biological woman. Once completed, the new Eve finds that she is 'as mythic and monstrous as Mother herself' (p. 83). This neatly illustrates Mary Russo's criticism of Bakhtin's definition of the bodily grotesque. Russo notes that he 'fails to acknowledge or incorporate the social relations of gender in his semiotic model of the body politic, and thus his notion of the Female Grotesque remains ... repressed and undeveloped'.[3] Her point is that the female body is already displaced and marginalised within social relations since it is often a body which must either conform to a set of regulated norms or be dismissed as Other. Therefore, the body which is female and grotesque must be recovered from a place of double exile. The post-Romantic definition of the grotesque as the described experience of alienation, isolation, and marginalised irregularity corresponds to the kind of physical difference featured in Carter's novel.[4] This difference is dependent on the composite nature of Eve and her counterpart, Tristessa – both acquire the identity of the hermaphrodite. A hint of Evelyn's future shape comes early in the novel, when he is browsing through the attic of his neighbour the alchemist: 'There was a seventeenth century print, tinted by hand, of a hermaphrodite carrying a golden egg that exercised a curious fascination upon me' (p. 13). Any sense of fascination that might have been occasioned by a real androgynous body is expressed as revulsion and derision when the hermaphroditic nature of Tristessa is brutally revealed. The reclusive film star's glamour is world renowned and based on the construction of her femininity. So when it is discovered that under her gowns and fragile appearance she is actually a man, the very basis of the constitution of femininity is brought into question. The group which captures Tristessa subjects her to various forms of torture, treating her as a grotesque because of her dual nature: 'They made ropes from twisted strips of his own négligé and tied him by his wrists from a steel beam, so there he dangled, naked, revealed' (p. 129). The image of Tristessa's exposed body suggests a reading of the grotesque as wholly negative – this androgyne is a 'freak' to its captors and is spared no form of ridicule or humiliation. When Eve is seen to be sympathetic towards their victim, she is treated with the same cruelty.

This interpretation of the grotesque body is also confirmed by the experience of the abject, which we can read across the bodies of Eve(lyn) and Tristessa. Kristeva's category of the abject locates the source of alienation in the subject's body and in the moment when one being emerges from or merges into another. This corresponds to Evelyn's repulsion at the sight of Mother whose likeness is then stamped onto his own body. In Kristeva's definition of the abject it is possible to comprehend fully its traumatic effects: it is 'what disturbs identity, system, order. What does not respect borders, positions, rules. The in-between, the ambiguous, the composite.'[5] In Carter's novel experience of the abject occurs when each body is forced to transgress socially established boundaries of gender as written on the body. We have seen that Evelyn reacts with horror at the moment of her biological transformation, the form of her own body provoking a sense of disgust. When his own transformation into a biological woman is complete, the sense of disgust is articulated through a direct comparison to Mother's: 'I would wince a little at such gross modulation of a flesh that had once been the ... twin of my new flesh' (p. 77). The rearrangement of the body's borders means that Evelyn responds to himself as if he had been modelled after a monster as hideously devised as Frankenstein's.

Similarly, a transgressive act is inscribed in the removal of Tristessa's gown. This marks a significant textual shift in meaning that is enacted in the violently forced reconsideration of her sexual status. Made to acknowledge the presence of her hidden genitalia, Tristessa experiences a shift in identity to which he responds with 'wailing [which] echoed round the gallery of glass' (p. 128). Both characters are forced to recognise their own formation, and it is at the moment of change in ontological certainty that they too participate in the abjection of their bodies. Beyond this subjective view of the grotesque body, the image of a composite being, unnatural and constructed out of seemingly disparate parts, is clearly the body experienced as grotesque by the other characters. The Gothic setting of Tristessa's glass house, where she is abused by the intruders, contains bodily images that further accentuate the theme of self-invention and physical reconstruction. In Tristessa's waxwork mausoleum, 'The Hall of the Immortals', exquisitely fashioned corpses are dismembered by Tristessa's attackers, and when they decide that a mock wedding is to take place between Eve and Tristessa,

they gather the scattered limbs together in order to construct witnesses for the event. Yet in doing this, 'they put the figures together
haphazardly, so Ramon Navarro's head was perched on Jean
Harlow's torso and had one arm from John Barrymore Junior, the
other from Marilyn Monroe and legs from yet other donors – all
assembled in haste, so they looked like picture-puzzles' (p. 134).

This simile of the picture-puzzle brings us to the heart of our understanding of the modern or post-Romantic grotesque. This composite image has the appearance of something that is unresolved
and provokes a reaction in the viewer that strives to unify the
obvious disparities, thereby rescuing it for the realm of the normal,
the familiar. Through ridicule and objectification of the Other,
people attempt to reassure themselves of their own normality, their
regularity. In his introduction to the memoirs of a nineteenth-
century French hermaphrodite, Michel Foucault has shown that
from the Middle Ages through to the last century, anyone whose
sexual status was open to question was required to choose one
sexual identity for life and usually it was a doctor's task to decipher
which was the 'true' sex of the body. And now, in the twentieth
century, the idea of one sex being close to 'the truth' has not been
completely dispelled. It is still widely believed that homosexuality
and the swapping of gender characteristics are somehow 'errors' –
that is, Foucault says, 'a manner of acting that is not adequate to
reality' and, further, that 'sexual irregularity is seen as belonging
more or less to the realm of chimera'.[6]

As we have seen, the image of the chimera, that fabulous mythical creature of mixed forms, is at the centre of Carter's novel. The
fantastic element in her fiction is often treated by the narrative voice
with the banal tone of acceptance characteristic of writing in the
vein of magical realism. And here, any scenario or person that
might at first seem unusual, including the figures of Eve, Tristessa,
and even Mother, are treated in the text as factual, not as frightening aberrations. And so it is that the central figure of this novel sets
out on a journey of discovery and, through the reading of his/her
own body, embraces the full spectrum of gender identities, some of
which were once alien to him – most notably those of the female.
Evelyn, then, begins his trip with this intent:

> I would go to the desert, to the waste heart of that vast country, the
> desert on which they turned their backs for fear it would remind
> them of emptiness – the desert, the arid zone, there to find, chimera

of chimeras, there, in the ocean of sand, among the bleached rocks of the untenanted part of the world, I thought I might find that most elusive of all chimeras, myself.

(p. 38)

In our reading of the bodies of this central character and its companion, it is possible to discover more than one meaning of the grotesque. When Eve and Tristeassa embrace, once they are alone, Eve is aware that 'we had made the great Platonic hermaphrodite together' (p. 148). In Plato the hermaphrodite is the original human form which was then split into two, thus accounting for the two sexes and the human desire to rejoin with an original mate. In *The Passion of New Eve*, the reaction to the hermaphroditic subject first appears to belong to a reading of the grotesque similar to the image of the grotesque often found in southern American writing – Carson McCullers, for example, has used this image to explore the lives of those regarded as freakish and marginalised by society. However, if we return to Rabelais, we may discover an interesting connection between that bodily grotesque of carnival, which Bakhtin finds in his work, and the post-Romantic grotesque in which the irregular body reflects a modern condition of alienation. These two possible renderings of the grotesque meet in the central character of Rabelais's *Gargantua and Pantagruel*. For here is the description of the emblem on the hat that Gargantua wears: 'Against a base of gold weighing over forty pounds was an enamel figure very much in keeping. It portrayed a man's body with two heads facing one another, four arms, four feet, a pair of arses and a brace of sexual organs male and female. Such, according to Plato's *Symposium*, was human nature in its mystical origins' (qtd in Bakhtin, p. 323).

So what do we make of this image of the epitomic form of the positive grotesque wearing an emblem of the negative grotesque? They are both situated outside the official culture, but the first is celebratory, disruptive, redemptive. The grotesque of the modern period, as our use of the word as a term of derision attests, represents rejection, exile, and abnormality. When Gargantua champions the hermaphrodite as the symbol of the grotesque, he celebrates the fact that all humans once had that form, that we all share the origins of the grotesque. The fact that the hermaphroditic figure is rejected as alien in modern times suggests a denial of this condition, not out of respect for scientific fact but due to the social pressures towards visual conformity. And this sense of denial is applied to any body which displays chimerical characteristics.

Thus it is significant that New Eve is ultimately reconciled to her changed body. New Eve's body has been designed by Mother to reflect an ideal of perfect femininity as determined by social norms. Yet it is clear that Eve herself regards the process by which this appearance of normality has been achieved as grotesque in itself. She cannot forget that her present body is a manufactured one: 'I had been born out of discarded flesh, induced to a new life by means of cunning hypodermics, ... my pretty face had been constructed out of a painful fabric of skin from my old inner thighs' (p. 143). When Eve looks into the face of Tristessa she is instantly reminded that they are 'mysteriously twinned by [their] synthetic life' (p. 125).

In transcending this view of her body, overcoming the resistant feelings about her condition, Eve(lyn) participates in a celebration of her chimerical nature when she is united with Tristessa after the destruction of the glass house. The moment of sexual congress between the two hermaphroditic figures may be dismissed by some as a heterosexual fantasy of recaptured unity. Yet the celebration of the body and its transgression of gender boundaries is, I think, intended to espouse a positive reading of this image.

The relocation of the chimerical, the hermaphroditic, within the realm of possibility, as a source of origin and a site for pleasure, is written in the bodies of these two characters. Carter playfully recentres the figure of chimerical form in this novel. In her use of the grotesque Carter parodies those characters, such as Mother and Zero, who impose a myopic perspective on the constitution of gender identity, while challenging traditional perspectives on gender and its boundaries. As Eve(lyn) and Tristessa embrace, they form a single bodily image in which these boundaries are temporarily lost. It is tempting to read this image as an example of Bakhtin's positive grotesque in which the death of one and the birth of another can be seen in the one body: 'two bodies in one, the budding and the division of the cell' (Bakhtin, p. 52). As Eve begins to grow into her newly grafted identity and Tristessa enters into the final hours of his life, they share this climactic dissolution of identity, making the shape of this one fabulous, mythic creature together.

From *Review of Contemporary Fiction*, 14:3 (1994), 43–8.

NOTES

[Heather Johnson's essay is the first of three essays included in this collection which draw on aspects of Mikhail Bakhtin's work on carnival and the grotesque to explore relations of social power and their historical contexts in Carter's work. (Carter herself did not read Bakhtin's work until after the publication of *Nights at the Circus*, a novel for which his ideas also provide a useful lens – see essay 7.) *The Passion of New Eve*, the subject of Johnson's essay, charts the journey of the male, English narrator, Evelyn, through a futuristic United States where by surgical means he is forced to become female (his/her body made the patriarchal idealisation of woman). Renamed Eve, she eventually meets with and makes love with the ageing film star, Tristessa, revealed to be biologically male. These two transgressive bodies thus demonstrate, indeed recognise the constructiveness of the gendered body; normality in Eve is made to seem grotesque. Bakhtin's ideas of the grotesque, based on his reading on Rabelais, are central to an understanding of the literature of the body in political terms – the grotesque body is excessive, monstrous and revolting, with the power to disrupt limits fixed by present powers. Mary Russo (see also essay 7 in this volume) reads the grotesque specifically as a female form – woman's existence, and in particular her body, as monstrous in patriarchal eyes. Johnson also refers to Foucault (whose work on sexuality and the power of social institutions was important to Carter) to establish how normality and abnormality in gender roles are constructed by those who police sexuality in society. Kristeva's psychoanalytic but politically charged ideas of abjection – a horror at and attempted expulsion of things which disturb established identity, system, order – are also used to describe the characters' subjectitivity in recognising their own formation. The essay finally asks whether the grotesque can still be read positively. Ed.]

1. Mikhail Bakhtin, *Rabelais and His World* (Bloomington, 1984), p. 19; hereafter cited parenthetically.

2. Angela Carter, *The Passion of New Eve* (London, 1986), p. 63; hereafter cited parenthetically.

3. Mary Russo, 'Female Grotesques: Carnival and Theory', in *Feminist Studies/Critical Studies*, ed. Teresa de Lauretis (Basingstoke, 1988), p. 219.

4. My use of the term *post-Romantic* is taken from Bakhtin who has chosen it to distinguish between a modern understanding of the term *grotesque* and the much earlier meaning grounded in the social reality of the Middle Ages. I realise that this distinction is by no means an absolute one and exceptions do exist in the post-Romantic period.

5. Julia Kristeva, *Powers of Horror: An Essay on Abjection* (New York, 1982), p. 4.

6. *Herculine Barbin: Being the Recently Discovered Memoirs of a Nineteenth-Century French Hermaphrodite*, trans. Richard McDougall, introd. Michel Foucault (Brighton, 1980), p. x.

7

Revamping Spectacle: Angela Carter's *Nights at the Circus*

MARY RUSSO

I begin with the description of a fictional poster depicting a young woman with wings shooting through the air like a rocket, a French circus poster hanging in the London dressing room of a famous aerialiste, 'the most famous aerialiste of her day' – her day being the end, 'the fag-end, the smouldering cigar-butt, of a nineteenth century which is just about to be ground out in the ashtray of history'[1] – a day, in other words, not unlike our own. In large letters, advertising her engagement in Paris, is her slogan: 'Is she fact, or is she fiction?' The poster's sensational image of female flight is marked by a rather unusual angle of viewing:

> The artist had chosen to depict her ascent from behind, bums aloft, you might say; up she goes, in a steatopygous perspective, shaking out about her those tremendous red and purple pinions, pinions large enough, powerful enough to bear such a big girl as she. And she was a *big* girl. Evidently this Helen took after her putative father, the swan, around the shoulder parts.
>
> (p. 7)

The Helen in question, 'Helen of the High-wire', sometimes called 'the Cockney Venus', is the fabulous 'Fevvers', the central character of Angela Carter's 1984 novel, *Nights at the Circus*.[2] As her stage names indicate (and all her names are stage names),

Fevvers straddles high and low culture. A woman with wings, she is no ordinary angel – if there could be such a thing – but rather an exhilarating example of the ambivalent, awkward, and sometimes painfully conflictual configuration of the female grotesque. Everything about this creature is sublime excess: her size, of course, and those wings which strain and bulge beneath her 'baby-blue satin dressing gown'; her six-inch-long eyelashes which she rips off gleefully one eye at a time, suggesting not only her deliberate production of unnaturalness, but also the prosthetic grotesque (a question of give and take); her taste for immense quantities of champagne with eel-pie and a bit of mash; and her overwhelming rancid smell ('something fishy about the Cockney Venus') (p. 8). 'Heroine of the hour, object of learned discussion and profane surmise, this Helen launched a thousand quips, mostly on the lewd side' (p. 8):

> Fevvers begins her act under a heap of brightly coloured feather behind tinsel bars while the orchestra plays 'I'm only a bird in a gilded cage'. Vamping, she strains at the bar and mews 'part-lion and part-pussy cat'.
>
> (p. 14)

Walser, the sceptical young American reporter who is assigned to cover her for a paper in the United States, smugly identifies this opening bit as 'kitsch'. With great self-satisfaction, he notes that 'the song pointed up the element of the meretricious in the spectacle, reminded you that the girl was rumoured to have started her career in freak shows' (p. 14). In fact, Fevvers has performed in meretricious spectacles her entire life, beginning with the *tableaux* staged in Ma Nelson's whorehouse and moving on to a less hospitable institution, the Museum of Female Monsters, directed by the gruesome Madame Schreck, who kept her anatomical performers in niches in an underground cave, stacked like wine bottles, for private viewings.[3]

In fact, it is debatable whether any performance site is not meretricious in this novel for Carter, who described herself as both a feminist and a socialist writer, and who seems to have gone beyond the more individualistic, psychic model of spectacularity which characterises her short stories, such as 'The Flesh and the Mirror', to map an historical and even global notion of spectacle similar to that described by Guy Debord in *Society of the Spectacle*. For Debord, 'the spectacle is not a collection of images, but a social relation among people, mediated by images'.[4] Spectacle in this sense is not an immaterial world apart, but rather the condition, divided, and producing division, of late capitalism:

> the spectacle, grasped in its totality, is both the result and the project of the existing mode of production. It is not a supplement to the real world, an additional decoration ... it is the omnipresent affirmation of the choice *already made* in production and its corollary consumption.
>
> (Debord, p. 6)

In a different though not incompatible sense, the concept of the 'already made' is central to postmodernist discourse,[5] where it refers to the characteristic mode of cultural reprise or intertextuality of which Angela Carter's work is often taken to be an example.[6] Linda Hutcheon, for instance, in an essay on the politics of parody, cites the production of Fevvers as a feminist parody of Leda and the Swan as an example of subversive repetition. Describing *Nights at the Circus*, she writes:

> The novel's parodic echoes of *Pericles, Hamlet,* and *Gulliver's Travels* all function as do those of Yeats' poetry when describing a whorehouse full of bizarre women as 'this lumber room of femininity, this rag-and-bone shop of the heart'; they are all ironic feminisations of traditional or canonic male representations of the so-called generic human-Man. This is the kind of politics of representation that parody calls to our attention.[7]

In *Nights at the Circus* alone, dozens of other examples of intertexts from high and low culture might be cited, and not all of them by any means as central to the European canon as Shakespeare, Swift, or Yeats.[8] Allusions abound to the twentieth-century artistic and political avant-gardes, to Andrei Bely's *Petersburg*, to Freud, Poe, Bakhtin, and to the Marquis de Sade who remains perhaps the most striking influence throughout Carter's work.[9] Equally important, popular culture, which had once produced its own version of critical parody in carnival, reappears and is transformed in modes of display, performance, and reproduction which characterise its institutionalisation in the European circus, museums, journalism, and advertising. Nor does Carter limit herself to male producers and performers. In what may be my favourite bit of intertexual play, Fevvers looks into the mirror as she prepares to go on stage in

St Petersburg and delivers Mae West's famous line, 'Suckers', from *I'm No Angel* (1933), which features the great female impersonator dressed in circus garb as a lion tamer in an imposture of dominance and control.[10] This Hollywood image of Mae West as a 'double-bluff' dominatrix is refigured in the excesses and obvious artifice of Fevvers' body and her act.[11] The cinematic frame is transposed to the frame of the mirror, an historical backward slide from high technology to the artisanal production of the female body 'making-up'.

Female narcissism itself as a canonical representation of the feminine is parodied and revised in the frames, mirrors, and circus rings which accompany the hyperbole of self-consciousness that is female masquerade. Carter returns again and again in her writing to female narcissism as a scene of failed transcendence. ...

The heroine of *Nights at the Circus* begins in some ways where the heroine of 'Flesh and the Mirror' leaves off,[12] trying to act natural which, in her case, will mean acting flamboyantly artificial. Like all of Carter's creations she loops and somersaults backward as well as forward in the plot, expanding the spatial dimensions of female spectacularity but never leaving the mirror entirely behind. Female narcissism is still a dilemma in this book, but Fevvers, without reading Simone de Beauvoir, knows at least that she is not born a 'natural' woman. In fact, she is not even born, but hatched. The lack of human origins confounds the expectations of Walser, who wonders why all of London isn't searching, as he is, for her belly button. But Fevvers 'does not bear the scar of loss': 'Whatever her wings were, her nakedness was certainly a stage illusion.'[13] Her body is not lacking but her trajectory, as I will describe it in relation to her act, is out of sync with the conventions of what is called human development. She starts and stops in the intervals between points, hovering on the brink of possibility, instead of going forward.[14]

WINGS OF CHANGE

A Klee painting named *Angelus Novus* shows an angel looking as though he is about to move away from something he is fixedly contemplating. His eyes are staring, his mouth is open, his wings are spread. This is how one pictures the angel of history. His face is turned toward the past.[15]

> *Never mind the diabolical explanations of air-foil you get in Pan-*
> *Am's multilingual INFORMATION TO PASSENGERS, I happen*
> *to be convinced that only my own concentration (and that of my*
> *mother – who always expects her children to die in a plane crash)*
> *keeps this bird aloft.*
>
> (Amanda Wing in Erica Jong's *Fear of Flying*)

In an interview,[16] Carter identifies a crucial intertext which I would
like to follow up in discussing Fevvers as a female grotesque, a
passage written by the poet Guillaume Apollinaire which she had
previously quoted in her controversial non-fiction work, *The
Sadeian Woman:*

> 'It was no accident that the Marquis de Sade chose heroines and not
> heroes', said Guillaume Apollinaire. Justine is woman as she has been
> until now, enslaved, miserable, and less than human; her opposite,
> Juliette, represents the woman whose advent he anticipated, *a figure*
> *of whom minds have as yet no conception, who is rising out of*
> *mankind, and will have wings and who will renew the world*
> (emphasis mine).[17]

Although Carter's critics have sometimes confused her own views
of the 'praxis of femininity'[18] with Sade or Sade's heroine, Juliette,
who wraps herself in the flags of male tyranny to avoid victimisation, Carter is quite explicit about Juliette's limits as a model of the
future for women.[19] 'She is, just as her sister is, a description of a
type of female behaviour rather than a model of female behaviour
and her triumph is just as ambivalent as is Justine's disaster.' If
Juliette is a New Woman, 'she is a New Woman in the model of
irony'.[20] What Juliette gains in the way of freedom is the ability to
occupy space, 'transforming herself from pawn to queen ... and
henceforth goes wherever she pleases on the chess board.
Nevertheless, there remains the question of the presence of the king,
who remains the lord of the game.' Juliette masters the destructive
techniques of power, inflicting suffering rather than suffering
herself; yet although she seeks to avoid the fate of her sister at all
costs, the two figures of femininity are inversely connected to pain,
pleasure, and death. The difference may be that Justine's narrative
of female suffering and submission may seem more representative
of an essentialistic formulation of feminine identity and the 'condition of women', whereas Juliette's behaviour is far in excess of any
possible identification with other women because disavowal of any

shared 'femininity' is a condition of her dominance and her freedom.[21]

Nights at the Circus is unique in its depiction of relationships between women *as* spectacle, *and* women as producers *of* spectacle. To the extent that female countercultures are depicted in the novel, they are placed within larger social and economic histories and fictions. The point I want to make here is simply that to the extent that value is contested in the production of images of women in this novel, it is contested socially. One body as production or performance leads to another, draws upon another, establishes hierarchies, complicities, and dependencies between representations and between women. Conflict is everywhere. Female figures such as Madame Schreck, 'the scarecrow of desire', organise and distribute images of other women for the visual market. Her disembodied presence suggests the extreme of immateriality and genderless politics; she may, as the narrator suggests, be only a hollow puppet, the body as performance *in extremis*.[22]

It is with great irony that Carter reproduces aspects of Juliette and the libertarian tradition in *Nights at the Circus*. In a series of critical counterproductions of the affirmative woman 'who will have wings and who will renew the world', Fevvers is born and born again, as an act (in the theatrical sense) of serial transgression. I have described Fevvers as the figure of ultimate spectacularity, a compendium of accumulated cultural clichés, worn and soiled from circulation. Yet, poised as she is on the threshold of a new century, her marvellous anatomy seems to offer endless possibility for change. Seeing her wings for the first time, Ma Nelson, whose whorehouse gives Fevvers a comfortable girlhood, identifies in 'the pure child of the century that just now is waiting in the wings, the New Age in which no woman will be bound down to the ground' (p. 25).

Ironically, in the context of the whorehouse, this means only that Fevvers will no longer pose as Cupid with a bow and arrow, but will now act as the Winged Victory, a static performance of her femininity 'on the grand scale', but hardly a pure or transformative vision. The magnificent Nike of Samothrace from the second century BC, long thought to be the greatest example of Hellenistic sculpture, is deservedly famous for its activation of the space around it. Standing eight feet tall, the figure of the victorious goddess leans out into the spatial illusion of onrushing air, still in motion, barely touching the ground. This icon of classical culture was much reproduced as a collectible souvenir and model of classicism. Through the techniques of miniaturisation and reproduction, Nike re-emerged in the late nineteenth century as Victorian bric-a-brac. It is in this guise that she is reproduced and re-enlarged by the young Fevvers, whose domestic portrayal (on the whorehouse mantel) of this art object-souvenir in the *tableau vivant* for male visitors would seem merely to set the terms for their accession to, and repeatable acquisition of, the other women who service them. Like Trilby,[23] Fevvers poses as the advertisement and model for similar commodities; not exactly a prostitute herself, she nonetheless instals the myth of femininity as virgin space in the displaced aura of the art work, while suggesting the comfort of the already-used, the 'sloppy seconds' of womanhood waiting, for a price, in the upper chambers.

THE POSE

The redundancy of such posing, its mimetic charge, is always already excessive, as Craig Owens has pointed out in one of the most interesting essays on contemporary mimesis and the pose.[24] Owens tentatively isolates two different perspectives on the question of the pose: the social and the psychosexual. As an example of the social perspective, he cites the work of Homi Bhabha on the mimetic rivalry of colonial discourse as an 'ironic compromise' between what Bhabha describes as 'the synchronic *panoptical* vision of domination – the demand for identity, status – and the counter-pressure of the diachrony of history – change, difference'. From the social perspective, Fevvers' first pose looks down (here, from a domestic perch) as if reversing the power relations of the panoptical gaze with the power of aerial surveillance. The compromised circumstances of her pose within the topography of the 'house' (already a mock family space, headed by a Madame) contributes further to the irony of the *tableau*.

From the psychosexual perspective, this pose reveals the constraints of the masquerade of femininity, as described and analysed by Mary Ann Doane.[25] Although Doane's first essay on masquerade had focused on female spectatorship rather than female spectacle, it would appear, as she acknowledges in her second essay on the topic, that the concept of masquerade is more promising as a way to understand femininity as spectacular production:

To claim that femininity is a function of the mask is to dismantle the question of essentialism before it can even be posed. In a theory which stipulates the claustrophobic closeness of the woman in relation to her own body, the concept of masquerade suggests a 'glitch' in the system ... Masquerade seems to provide that contradiction insofar as it attributes to the woman the distance, alienation, and divisiveness of self (which is constitutive of subjectivity in psychoanalysis) rather than the closeness and excessive presence which are the logical outcome of the psychoanalytic drama of sexualised linguistic difference. The theorisation of femininity as masquerade is a way of appropriating this necessary distance or gap, in the operation of semiotic systems, of deploying it for women, of reading femininity differently.

('Masquerade Reconsidered', p. 37)

But this shift leaves some problems unsolved. The theoretical drawbacks of appropriating the psychoanalytical model of masquerade as if it were the definitive feminist answer to the constraints of gender (or worse, as if the dismantling of essentialist models of femininity could *tout court* dispel the effects of the imposition of gender, making feminism unnecessary) are, in my view, increasingly evident in the disavowal of the female body as a site of political activism.

In the case of Fevvers as Winged Victory, there is redoubled irony in her grotesque body (already redundant with wings *and* arms) in exposure and retreat as her arms are released to represent the complete 'original' of a dismembered female figure, an ideal of Beauty, while her feathery humps are spread out to the viewer only to be taken as useless, arty, attachments:

Well, Ma Nelson put it out that I was the perfection of, the original of, the very model for that statue which, in its broken and incomplete state, has teased the imagination of a brace of millennia with its promise of perfect, active beauty that has, as it were, been mutilated by history.

(p. 37)

To the redundancy of arms and wings, Ma Nelson (alias Admiral Nelson) adds even more; to complete the picture, she places a sword in the hands of Victory ('as if a virgin with a sword was the fittest guardian angel for a houseful of whores'). This finally is too much for the clients: 'Yet it may be that a *large* woman with a sword is not the best advertisement for a brothel. For slow, but sure, trade fell off from my fourteenth birthday on' (p. 32). Although blame for the demise of the whorehouse falls, in the last analysis, on the bad influence of Baudelaire ('a poor fellow who loved whores not for the pleasure of it but, as he perceived it, the *horror* of it'), business falls off when young men become impotent at the sight of the big girl becoming a big woman with too many appendages and a phallus – a Medusa with her own sword. And, of course, she has received the sword from a symbolic mother who is giving her best part, in the theatrical sense, to complete the pose of the living statue. Ma Nelson, a cross-dresser·and a Madame, is also (not surprisingly) a feminist:

> 'Yet we were all suffragists in that house; oh, Nelson was "Votes for Women", I can tell you!'
>
> 'Does that seem strange to you? That the caged bird should want to see the end of cages, sir?' queried Lizzie, with an edge of steel in her voice.

Lizzie's questions and commentary, which repeatedly interrupt the autobiographical narrative that Walser hopes will pin down the truth about Fevvers, suggest an interrogation of female biography modelled on the stories of Cinderella or Snow White, filled with evil mothers and sisters and a Prince. Fevvers herself describes her coming of age as an apprenticeship in being looked at: 'Is it not to the mercies of the eyes of others that we commit ourselves on our voyage through the world?' And she does not wait for a Prince to take her away; on the contrary, her greatest fear is that his kiss would harden the white powder on her face and 'seal me up in my *appearance* forever!' (p. 39). Her way out, as it were, is in the company of the other women who, if Fevvers is to be believed, were, when not working, learning to read and play instruments. Lizzie describes a world of female sociality set in a liminal time when, as with the French clock she carries with her, it is always noon or midnight – the time of change and of revolution. The portrait of the artist as a young mannequin ends with the Winged Victory keen on learning how to fly:

> We all engaged in our intellectual, artistic or political – Here Lizzie coughed – pursuits and, as for myself, those long hours of leisure I devoted to the study of aerodynamics and the physiology of flight.
>
> (p. 40)

FLYING: LESSONS OF CLASS, GENDER, AND SEXUALITY

How did Fevvers really learn to fly? The Oedipal Walser, always searching for origins and empirical certainties, can only assume that a male impresario, some Svengali or other, has created Fevvers and her act. He cannot fathom the collaboration of Fevvers and her inseparable companion and foster mother, Lizzie, and it is this disbelief that leads him to wonder whether, after all, underneath the layers of masquerade, Fevvers may not be a man, throwing all questions of identity, authenticity, and origins onto the axis of gender:

> 'Don't excite yourself, gel,' said Lizzie gently. Fevvers' chin jerked up almost pettishly.
> 'Oh, Lizzie, the gentleman must know the truth!'
> And she fixed Walser with a piercing, judging regard, as if to ascertain just how far she could go with him. Her face, in its Brobdingnagian symmetry, might have been hacked from wood and brightly painted up by those artists who build carnival ladies for fairgrounds or figureheads for sailing ships. It flickered through his mind: Is she really a man?
>
> (p. 35)

The figure of the aerialist has repeatedly produced the question of gender for the male viewer. The female aerialist as masculinised or ambiguous in relation to gender appears in historical sources, as well as fiction and visual representation. Arthur Munby's famous photographs and diaries of Victorian working girls includes female gymnasts and acrobats whose masculine qualities he never fails to note. Although, as Stallybrass and White have noted, Munby's voyeurism is usually characterised by the 'conjunction of the maid kneeling in the dirt and the standing voyeur' (from high to low), and gaze upward (from low to high) can produce a similar effect: on the one hand, a reinforcement of male power and social standing and on the other a temporary reversal so that the male viewer appears childlike or at least diminished.[26] From Huysmans' Miss Urania to Cleopatra, the 'big woman' in Tod Browning's *Freaks*, the aerialist and the female acrobat have been women represented through the eyes of a dwarfed, clownish, or infantilised man. In an unusual reversal, George Grosz's *Seiltänzerin* (1914), an aerial drawing of a female tightrope walker, shows a demonic clown looking up from far below at the large, muscular figure straddling the rope between her thighs as she strains to raise herself up onto one leg. This grotesque caricature of the Romantic ideal of ethereal Womanhood suggests, as well, an altered masculinity in the balance.

Carter's production of Fevvers as the aerial diva, enigmatic regarding gender, is only the latest version of this image, produced typically by male artists but occasionally and with surprising results by twentieth-century women artists and writers. The figure of the trapeze artist Frau Mann (alias the Duchess of Broadback) who appears in the first chapter of Djuna Barnes' *Nightwood*, is the repressed, lesbian prefiguration of a Fevvers – a possible body.[27] Her body is strong and muscular, and in the air, it appears 'much heavier than that of women who stay on the ground'. It is a body shaped through her work and the technology of aerial performance. Her legs, for instance, 'had the specialised tension common to aerial workers; some of the bar was in her wrists, the tan bark in her walk'. Like Fevvers, her very flesh seems sewn into her performance costume, making an artifice of nudity; Frau Mann, however, goes a bit further in this regard than Fevvers, in that her costume reweaves the crotch in a textual rezoning of the body as off-limits to men:

> The stuff of her tights was no longer a covering, it was herself; the span of the tightly stitched crotch was so much her own flesh that she was as unsexed as a doll. The needle that had made one the property of the child made the other the property of no man.
>
> (p. 13)

Nudity and clothing are a continuous surface, flattening the image of Frau Mann's body, and in a reversal of the usual fetishistic practice as described by Freud, redesigning the 'phantasmagoric division between an inside and an outside' which characterises the representation of the female body as invested with mystery or threat.[28] Whether this feminine surface sufficiently interferes with the (male) fetishist's desire to know and therefore have, or whether 'the needle' in question is the projection of a lesbian morphology, there is definitely a *different* line of viewing and a different spectatorship suggested than that represented by Walser's suggestion that Fevvers really needs a tail: 'Physical ungainliness in flight caused, perhaps, by the absence of a *tail* – I wonder why she doesn't tack a tail on the back of her cache-sexe; it would add verisimilitude and, perhaps, improve the performance.'

The comparison of *Nights at the Circus* with Barnes' *Nightwood*, written in 1936, reveals a commonality of surrealist techniques and themes, as well as a mutual interest in the dispersion of carnivalesque materials in new social formations. *Nightwood* was introduced in the thirties by an extremely anxious T. S. Eliot, who feared that the characters in the novel would be regarded 'as a horrid sideshow of freaks'.[29] His evocation of the freak show as the trope to be shunned would seem to substantiate Allon White's claim that the remnants of carnival as cultural history re-emerge as 'phobic alienation' in bourgeois neurosis, since 'bourgeois carnival is a contradiction in terms'.[30] The metaphor of the freak show in Eliot's introduction (clearly a reference to the lesbian and transsexual themes of the novel) resonates oddly with the first chapter, 'Bow Down', in which Felix (Baron Volkbein) is introduced as a dévoté of the circus and popular theatre. The high/low dichotomies of class and gender give way as the 'carnival of the night' temporarily subsumes difference. Volkbein's attachment to 'that great disquiet called entertainment' mirrors his own aristocratic yearnings: 'In some way they linked his emotions to the high and unattainable pageantry of kings and queens' (p. 11). The entertainers, of course, in the carnivalesque tradition, mimic the pomp and titles of the upper classes. Felix's pleasure in the mock ritual of the 'blow down' to the demimonde is palpable. At once degrading and liberatory, his social and sexual dissolution amidst the carnival of *Nightwood* recalls Aschenbach's encounters with the grotesque figures in *Death in Venice*:

> He moved with a humble hysteria among the decaying brocades and laces of the *Carnavalet*; he loved that old and documented splendour with something of the love of the lion for its tamer – that sweat-tarnished spangled enigma that, in bringing the beast to heel, had somehow turned toward him a face like his own.
>
> (p. 11)

> The emotional spiral of the circus, taking its flight from the immense disqualification of the public, rebounding from its illimitable hope, produced in Felix longing and disquiet. The circus was a loved thing he could never touch.
>
> (p. 12)

In contrast, Walser is a male spectator oblivious to the transcendent powers of the circus. Though Carter's deeply historic novel is set at the end of the nineteenth century, Walser is much younger than the Baron, as a representative of the bourgeoisie. Of course, he is first of all an American on the brink of the 'American Century', filled with all the common sense and the imperialistic instincts required to make him an ideal employee for Colonel Kearney (a P. T. Barnum clone). Secondly, he is a journalist and a professional debunker, sent to reveal the secrets of the trade, to sort, discard, and exploit the travesties of the circus as he will later plunder ethnographic materials in his ethnocentric exploration of other cultures. No aesthete or modernist intent on looking up to women or lamenting old myths, he tries instead, in what to him is the most effective democratic mode, to bring Fevvers down to his scale.

As model spectator, Walser is continuously in the dark when it comes to issues of gender and generation, especially the aspects of female homosociality which dominate the London section of the book. He cannot tolerate sexual ambiguity and he cannot recognise or place 'older' women, particularly in foreign national contexts. The dialogical narrative of Lizzie and Fevvers, with its dissonant tonality, silences, and contradictions makes him increasingly anxious to place Fevvers and to illuminate those aspects of her anatomy and her story which are extraneous or implausible. The story of her first flight, which is simultaneously the story of her surrogate mother, Lizzie, and her 'natural' mother, London ('London, with one breast, the Amazon queen') is told as a night fable (p. 36). The nocturnal carnival which occasions intimations of the sublime for Felix borders on the terrifying for Walser, whose imagination is easily overwhelmed: 'Although he was not an imaginative man, even he was sensitive to that aghast time of night when the dark dwarfs us' (p. 37). Fevvers, if she is (and she certainly is in some sense) a bird, is not a natural flier:

> Like Lucifer, I fell. Down, down, down I tumbled, bang with a bump on the Persian rug below me, flat on my face amongst those blooms and beasts that never graced no natural forest, those creatures of dreams and abstraction not unlike myself, Mr Walser. Then I knew I was not ready to bear on my back the great burden of my unnaturalness.
>
> (p. 30)

She learns to fly through cultural imitation (a fake Titian of Leda and the Swan), some library books, risks and falls, a momentary sense of hovering ('that sensation that comes to us, sometimes on the edge of sleep') (p. 31), and finally, through the help of Lizzie's knowledge gleaned from observing pigeons learning to use their 'aerial arms', she lets Lizzie push her into the air, risking not only death but the 'terror of irreparable *difference*' (p. 34). She flies for the first time through the dark, into a liminal space in the hours before dawn on Midsummer's Night, and then back to work, posing as Winged Victory.[31]

The elevation of the grotesque body to the nocturnal sublimity of a midsummer's night is accomplished with great effort, and, like the narrative itself, it works as a collaborative effort between Fevvers and Lizzie. The model for flight is a lowly pigeon but the experience and its description are meant nonetheless to be sublime. Fevvers' flying style is as eclectic, grand, and ungainly as her voice and as indeterminate with regard to its origins. Walser's description of her voice reflects his own scepticism regarding the narrative of her first flight:

> Her voice ... her cavernous, sombre voice, a voice made for shouting about the tempest, her voice of a celestial fishwife. Musical as it strangely was, yet not a voice for singing with; it comprised discords, her scale contained twelve tones. Her voice with its warped, homely Cockney vowels and random aspirates ... Yet such a voice could almost have had its source, not within her throat but in some ingenious mechanism or other behind the canvas screen, voice of a fake medium at a seance.
>
> (p. 43)

This 'throwing' of the female voice is an extremely telling acoustical image. It is reminiscent of *Trilby* and of the seemingly disembodied telephone voice of Claire Niveau in Cronenberg's *Dead Ringers*. Located at the site of 'perhaps, the most radical of all subject divisions – the division between meaning and materiality', the voice is that place of excess which precedes and follows the organisation of meaning.[32] The spatial image of the *thrown voice* further stretches the gaps or intervals between the body and language, like one of Fevvers' long, antisocial yawns. The body which produces this voice is not identical with it, any more than the sounds produced are identical in any positive sense with meaning. In relation to music as organised sound, 'this voice is not for singing', meaning that it is 'noisy' in the technical sense and exceeds the regimes of canonical Western music. As an instance of cultural noise, this voice, which is the voice of the novel as well as the voice of Fevvers, contains within it a particularly resonant blend of modernist scales, class and regionally inflected vowels and aspirates, and the 'rough music' of carnival.[33] The 'grain' of this voice, to use Roland Barthes' expression, suggests a different cultural as well as a different musical history in which, as he suggested, 'we would attach less importance to the formidable break in tonality accomplished by modernity'.[34] Deeply historical as well as radically modernist in its trajectory, the voice of the 'celestial fishwife' – the sonic female grotesque *par excellence*[35] – flies from the cavern, above the tempest, and to the heavens and down again to Cockney London, sombre, full, and in its own way sublime.

To recapitulate briefly the relationship between the aerial sublime and the female grotesque, I want to return to Fevvers in the midst of her circus act. By way of reference, I turn to the paradigm of the trapeze act as analysed by Paul Bouissac in his work on the semiotics of the circus. Once in the air, the act is a negotiation, with interruptions, between two stations, with a certain expenditure of energy by the velocity of flight (up to 60 mph), permitting the human body to offer a certain illusion of suspension. Bouissac fails to note that in the case of the female performer, her negotiation of space is often interrupted by a male performer who catches her. Fevvers in the air, however, travels alone.

An additional model of normativity for the flying act is provided by Thomas Aquinas who notes, writing of 'real' angels, 'their motion can be as continuous or as discontinuous as it wishes. And thus an angel can be in one instant in one place and at another instant in another place, not existing at any intermediate time.' I am assuming that in relation to identity, Fevvers has equal claim to either of these models yet no full claim at all to either, since her act seems to dissimulate failure to occupy either time or space in these modes. Quoting the novel, from the point of view of the informed male spectator:

> When the hack *aerialiste*, the everyday wingless variety, performs the triple somersault, he or she travels through the air at a cool sixty miles an hour; Fevvers, however, contrived a contemplative and leisurely twenty-five, so that the packed theatre could enjoy the spectacle, as in slow motion, of every tense muscle straining in her Rubenesque form. The music went much faster than she did; she dawdled. Indeed, she did defy the laws of projectiles, because a projectile cannot *mooch* along its trajectory; if it slackens its speed in mid-air, down it falls. But Fevvers, apparently, pottered along the invisible gangway between her trapezes with the portly dignity of a

Trafalgar Square pigeon flapping from one proffered handful of corn to another, and then she turned head over heels three times, lazily enough to show off the crack in her bum.

(p. 17)

For Walser, semiotician and connoisseur of the hoax, it is precisely the limitations of her act which allow him momentarily to suspend disbelief and grant her a supernatural identity, for no mere mortal could effect such incompetence in the air without dire consequences. Walser observes:

For, in order to earn a living, might not a genuine bird-woman – in the implausible event that such a thing existed – have to pretend she was an artificial one?

(p. 17)

What is more interesting to me than this sophisticated insight which, after all, only goes so far as to permit him the pleasure of a naïve spectator's night at the circus, is that Fevvers reveals what angels and circus stars normally conceal: *labour* and its bodily effects in the midst of simulated play and the creation of illusion. Her body dawdles lazily (the hardest work of all in the air) and yet, unlike her angelic sisters, she never seems to occupy discrete spots on her trajectory; she does not rest. She vamps in the musical sense, filling in the intervals with somersaults. The one time she is static in the air, perched on the swing, the rope breaks and she is stranded. What is revealed in her routine is at one level economic: the Victorian working girl is not the angel (in the house), and the novel is in many ways about working girls.[36] This is not to say that here finally a materiality has emerged from underneath an illusion, that with the appearance of work, we have a ground, that we are no longer, so to speak, in the air. Rather, I would read Fevvers' act as a reminder that the spectacle which conceals work is itself produced, and revamping spectacle shows up and diverts this cultural production.

THE INTERGENERATIONAL BODY (POLITIC)

Carter herself has remarked that 'the creation of Fevvers necessitated the creation of her foster mother, Lizzie, a gnarled old leftist'. Throughout the novel, Lizzie undercuts the high-flying rhetoric of the new age woman while working behind the scenes to effect a revolution. Her own body is unfetishised. She exists unadorned as a kind of maid or sidekick in the drama of the star performer, but her work is nonetheless indispensable. As a couple, Lizzie and Fevvers produce a real challenge to the male and heterosexual gaze of Walser, who is confused both by their narrative mode and by their apparent physical incompatibility, which he can only articulate as a question of scale, measured in height. From a distance, he sees them as 'a blond, heroic mother taking her daughter home from some ill-fated expedition up west, their ages obscured, their relationship inverted'.

Together, they figure an intergenerational grotesque of the kind which Mikhail Bakhtin evokes in his paradigm of the grotesque terracotta images of senile, pregnant hags. When Lizzie first sees that her young ward has wings, she does not uncritically welcome the new in the guise of youth, as Ma Nelson does; rather, she historicises *herself*, and sees in Fevvers the 'Annunciation of my own Menopause'. When the figurative biological clock is communal, birth and rebirth are dialectical. This parody of the annunciation is of the critical variety which Linda Hutcheon has described in her work on postmodernism as signalling 'how present representations come from past ones, and what ideological consequences derive from both continuity and difference'.[37] The consequence of such an intergenerational conception is that the new is not immediately and transparently identified with the young. This interrupts the logic of what Debord describes as 'false choice in spectacular abundance', the creation of arbitrary contrasts and competitions which seem natural or self-evident. Among these false choices is a certain commodification of generational difference:

> Wherever there is abundant consumption, a major spectacular opposition between youth and adults comes to the fore among the false roles – false because the adult, master of his life, does not exist and because youth, the transformation of what exists, is in no way the property of those who are now young, but of the economic system, of the dynamism of capitalism. *Things* rule and are young.[38]

Again, my point is not to deny that there are such things as ageing and generational difference; rather, the spectacle of the new is produced and can therefore be counterproduced. As Fevvers and Lizzie together reconfigure 'the pure child of the new century', the 'new' becomes a possibility that already existed, a part of the ageing body in process rather than the property (like virginity) of a discrete and static place or identity. What appeals to me about this vamping onto the body (to use the word in a slightly archaic sense) is that it not only grotesquely de-forms the female body as a cultural construction in order to reclaim it, but that it may suggest new political aggregates – provisional, uncomfortable, even conflictual, coalitions of bodies which both respect the concept of 'situated knowledges' and refuse to keep every body in its place.

It is tempting to read this novel and even Carter's entire *oeuvre* as a progression, as one critic sees it, from the alienation of the femininity of the 'coded mannequin' to the liberatory prospects of the woman with wings.[39] Indeed, towards the end of the novel, Fevvers looks forward to the day when 'all the women will have wings, the same as I':

> The dolls' house doors will open, the brothels will spill forth their prisoners, the cages, gilded or otherwise, all over the world, in every land, will let forth their inmates singing together the dawn chorus of the new, the transformed.
>
> (p. 285)

But Carter never lets this optimistic progressivism stand unchallenged:

> 'It's going to be more complicated than that,' interpolated Lizzie. 'This old witch sees storms ahead, my girl. When I look at the future, I see through a glass, darkly. You improve your analysis, girl, and *then* we'll discuss it.'
>
> (pp. 285–6)

Lizzie's view of the future is not forward-looking but rather – like the angel of history in a powerful and much-quoted passage from Walter Benjamin – a look backwards to see the future in the past, not as a 'sequence of events' but as 'a catastrophe which keeps piling wreckage upon wreckage' (Benjamin, p. 257). To Lizzie and to the angel of history, 'a storm is blowing from Paradise' (p. 257). And there is no going back. In Benjamin's image, borrowed from Klee's painting *Angelus Novus*, the angel is caught by the storm with his wings blown open; the storm 'propels him into the future to which his back is turned, while the pile of debris before him grows skyward. *This storm is what we call progress*' (emphasis mine)(Benjamin, p. 258).

Only if Lizzie's stormy comments are read as merely cynical or extraneous can the exchange be made to stand for a developmental antithesis in Carter's writing rather than an apocalyptic intersection of incommensurate discourses, resulting in a 'blow-up' of the narrative and a breakup of two women's narrative partnership. To side provisionally with Lizzie, who represents an ever-present but minority voice in the novel, it is more complicated than that.

I would prefer to read their differences as part of an ongoing dialogue, filled with conflict and repetition – to a difficult friendship and an improbable but necessary political alliance.[40] At this point in the novel, the conversation is about losses and making do. Fevvers has 'mislaid her magnificence on the road from London; one wing is bandaged and the other has faded to drab. She is no longer commercially viable. God knows if she will ever fly again.' Lizzie's anarchic power, 'her knack for wreaking domestic havoc', is lost. As the designated heroine of the novel, Fevvers is trading in her wings for marriage with what she hopes will be a transformed Jack Walser ('I'll sit on him, I'll hatch him out. I'll make him into the New Man, in fact, a fitting mate for the New Woman'). And Lizzie, of course, is sceptical: '"Perhaps so, perhaps not", she said, putting a damper on things.'[41] For Lizzie, it is necessary to think twice 'about turning from a freak into a woman' (p. 283).[42]

This exchange between Lizzie and Fevvers is, like everything in the novel, inconclusive. As Susan Suleiman has written, Carter's strategy '*multiplies* the possibilities of linear narrative and of "story", producing a dizzying accumulation that undermines the narrative logic by its very excessiveness'.[43] There is always something left over, something as untimely as subjectivity itself, that forms the basis of a new plan, perhaps another flight.

Like Fevers' excessive body itself, the meaning of any possible flight lies in part in the very interstices of the narrative, as the many-vectored space of the here and now, rather than a utopian hereafter. The end of flight in this sense is not a freedom from bodily existence but a recharting of aeriality as a bodily space of possibility and repetition:

> *There is a feeling of absolute finality about the end of a flight through darkness. The dream of flight is suddenly gone before the mundane realities of growing grass and swirling dust ... Freedom escapes you again, and the wings which were a moment ago no less than an eagle's and swifter, are metal and wood once more, inert and heavy.*[44]

From Mary Russo, *The Female Grotesque: Risk, Excess, and Modernity* (New York and London, 1994), pp. 159–62, 164–81.

NOTES

[This essay was originally published as the closing chapter of Mary Russo's *The Female Grotesque*; one short section on Carter's short story, 'Flesh and the Mirror' has been omitted and some notes cut with the author's permission. Using a wide array of theoretical, visual, literary, autobiographical and performance texts, Russo's book is a materialist reading of the ambivalent figure of the grotesque female body in relation to the 'body politic', the realm of what is commonly thought of as the political. The chapter reprinted here explores spectacle as a historical and global socio-economic relation among people and part of the condition of late capitalism. To do this Russo draws on several theorists of spectacle: Bakhtin's ideas of carnival; the anarchist, post-Marxist Guy Debord; Mary Ann Doane on masquerade (drawn from film studies) as a way of understanding femininity; and Walter Benjamin on history. Russo's historicism (finding many references and parallels) and her materialist analysis (for example, spectacle as work) both demonstrate how deeply historical Carter's text is, and how it is possible to rethink certain postmodern elements of the novel, for example, intertextuality, in terms of capitalist production and consumption. Finally, Russo interrogates the view that Carter's *oeuvre* evolves towards a successfully realised feminist vision. Ed.]

1. Angela Carter, *Nights at the Circus* (London, 1984). All subsequent references are to this edition.

2. I am indebted to three extraordinary students who worked with me on senior theses which focused on the work of Angela Carter: Linda McDaniel and Jennifer Hendricks of Hampshire College, and Meg O'Rourke of Mt Holyoke.

3. The topography of the Madame Schreck episode owes much to Edgar A. Poe, but there are historical precedents for the anatomical museum. See, for instance, Christiane Py and Cecile Vedart, 'Les Musées d'anatomie sur les champs de foire', *Actes de la recherche en sciences sociales*, no. 60 (November 1985), 3–10.

4. Guy Debord, *Society of the Spectacle* (Detroit, 1983), p. 1.

5. Fevvers construes her own primal scene from a possibly fake and certainly filthy ('as though through a glass darkly') painting of the Leda and the Swan by Titian (p. 30).

6. For an extremely important discussion of feminist writing in relation to the historical avant-garde in general and Dada/Surrealist parody in

particular, see Susan Rubin Suleiman, *Subversive Intent: Gender, Politics, and the Avant-Garde* (Cambridge, MA, 1990).

7. Linda Hutcheon, *The Politics of Postmodernism* (London, 1983), p. 98.

8. For a discussion of intertextuality and politics in her work, see Angela Carter, 'Notes From the Front Line', in *On Gender and Writing*, ed. Michelene Wandor (London, 1983), p. 71.

9. In her interview with Helen Cagney Watts, Carter herself says that Sade was a primary influence. Helen Cagney Watts, 'Angela Carter: An Interview with Helen Cagney Watts', in *Bête Noire* (August 1985), 162. In relation to Sade, see also David Punter, 'Angela Carter: Supersessions of the Masculine', in his *The Hidden Script: Writing and the Unconcious* (London, 1985), pp. 28–42.

10. Carter writes about Mae West, in *Nothing Sacred* (London, 1982). This impersonation of the impersonator is Fevvers' (and Carter's) stock-in-trade.

11. The 'double bluff' was not only sexual (a woman playing a man playing a woman playing a man), but also existential: she plays on the 'freedom' given to older women. As Carter points out, Mae West started her Hollywood career in middle age. Her self-display played on the masquerade of youthfulness, the freedom of the discard who has nothing left to lose, and the impersonation of male power. 'She made of her own predatoriness a joke that concealed its power, whilst simultaneously exploiting it. Yet she represented a sardonic disregard of convention rather than a heroic overthrow of taboo' (*The Sadeian Woman and the Ideology of Pornography* [New York, 1978], p. 62).

12. Carter, 'The Flesh and the Mirror', in *Fireworks: Nine Profane Pieces* (London, 1987).

13. This question is posed first to Walser by an Indian fakir. Walser sees his journalistic quest as a compilation of 'Great Humbugs of the World' (p. 11).

14. As a male and heterosexual witness to Fevvers' naked artificiality, it is Walser's impossible task to 'cover Fevvers' story' which means to expose her fiction.

15. Walter Benjamin, 'Thesis on the Philosophy of History', in *Illuminations*, trans. Harry Zohn (New York, 1969), p. 257.

16. See Watts, 'Interview', pp. 161–75.

17. Carter, *The Sadeian Woman*, p. 79.

18. See, for instance, Andrea Dworkin, *Pornography: Men Possessing Women* (New York, 1979.), pp. 84–5. The phrase 'praxis of femininity' is Carter's (*The Sadeian Woman*, p. 78).

19. For an excellent discussion of Justine and Juliette in relation to criticism of Carter, see Elaine Jordan, 'The Dangers of Angela Carter', in *New Feminist Discourses: Critical Essays on Theories and Texts*, ed. Isobel Armstrong (London, 1991), pp. 119–31. 1 am in agreement with Jordan's 'defence' of Carter (not, as she says, that Carter needs defending). For another view of Carter on Sade, see Susanne Kappeler, *The Pornography of Representation* (London, 1986), pp. 133–7. See also Andrea Dworkin cited in previous note. For a critical overview of the pornography debates within feminism, see B. Ruby Rich, 'Feminism and Sexuality in the 1980s', *Feminist Studies*, 12 (1986), 525–61.

20. Carter, *The Sadeian Woman*, p. 79. For another influential and provocative account of the interests and pitfalls of Sade for contemporary feminists, see Jane Gallop, *Thinking Through the Body* (New York, 1988); see also her *Intersections: A Reading of Sade with Bataille, Blanchot, and Klossowski* (Lincoln, NA, 1981).

21. In relation to Juliette's character, Carter is quite unambiguous: 'A free woman in an unfree society is a monster' *(The Sadeian Woman*, p. 27; also quoted in Jordan, p. 121). Jordan makes the excellent point that both figures of antithetical femininity point towards something else in Carter and are meant to show up the limitations of these types as models of resistance.

22. For a very different use of the iconography of the emaciated female in the context of body, see for instance the puppetry of Lotte Prinzel, or in the context of feminist art, see Valic Export's performance work described in 'Persona, Proto-Performance, Politics', *Discourse*, 14:2 (Spring 1992), 6–35.

23. [Trilby, the eponymous heroine of George du Maurier's novel (1894) is transformed by the spellbinding musician, Svengali, from a model into a virtuoso singer. Ed.]

24. Craig Owens, 'Posing', in *Difference: On Representation and Sexuality Catalog* (New York, 1985), pp. 7–17. Owens identifies the pose as both an 'imposition' and an 'imposture'. Since, in his view, sexuality is imposed (culturally) we might characterise Fevver's installation of femininity as a reimposition.

25. See Mary Ann Doane, *Femmes Fatales: Feminism, Film Theory, Psychoanalysis* (New York, 1991), especially pp. 17–43. Doane's influential 1982 essay, 'Film and Masquerade: Theorizing the Female Spectator', is reprinted in this collection along with the recent 'Masquerade Reconsidered'. The first essay represents an attempt to dislodge the psychoanalytic discussion of masquerade as the norm of femininity and to see it, rather, as a defamiliarisation and a 'way out'. Her second essay emphasises the theoretical constraints and the sociopolitical implications of the concept of sexuality as masquerade in

Riviere and Lacan. In relation to feminist theory and theories of the feminine, see especially her reply to Tania Modleski (pp. 40–3). Modleski's critique of Doane is contained in *The Women Who Knew Too Much: Hitchcock and Feminist Theory* (New York, 1988), pp. 25–8.

26. Munby indicated in his diary that he intended to write a paper on female gymnasts. His interest in their sexuality is evident in most entries. See Michael Hiley, *Victorian Working Women, Portraits from Life* (Boston, 1980), p. 116. See also D. Hudson, *Munby: Man of Two Worlds: The Life and Diaries of Arthur Munby* (London, 1972). Stallybrass and White point out that the contradiction between the high social standing of the upper-class male and the low class standing of the maid is complicated by the physical comparisons of his weakness and her strength, and his childishness in relation to her role as nurse. Of course, a point to be made here is that Munby is controlling both the sight-lines and the social configuration. See *The Politics and Poetics Of Transgression,* (Ithaca, NY, 1986), pp. 155–6. See also L. Davidoff, 'Class and Gender in Victorian England: The Diaries of Arthur J. Munby and Hannah Cullwick', *Feminist Studies,* 5:1 (1979), 89–141.

27. Djuna Barnes, *Nightwood,* with an introduction by T. S. Eliot (New York, 1961). All subsequent references are to this edition.

28. For an important, recent consideration of fetishism and the depth model of the female body in relation to curiosity, see Laura Mulvey, 'Pandora: Topographies of the Mask and Curiosity', in *Sexuality and Space,* ed. Beatriz Colomina (New York, 1992), pp. 58–9.

29. Barnes, *Nightwood,* p. xvi. Although Eliot does not mention the lesbian texts and in his plea that the book not be read as a 'psychopathic study', his insistence that the 'miseries that people suffer through their particular abnormalities of temperament' be understood not on the surface but in light of 'the deeper designs ... of the human misery which is universal'.

30. Allon White, 'Hysteria and the End of Carnival: Festivity and Bourgeois Neurosis', in *The Violence of Representation: Literature and the History of Violence,* ed. Nancy Armstrong and Leonard Tennenhouse (New York, 1989), pp. 156–70.

31. Fevvers herself interrupts the sublime narrative of night flight with the ongoing account of her working life (p. 37).

32. See Kaja Silverman, *The Acoustic Mirror: The Female Voice in Psychoanalysis and Cinema* (Bloomington, IN, 1988), p. 44.

33. For a study of noise and cultural production in relation to carnival and twentieth-century music, see Mary Russo and Daniel Warner, 'Rough Music', *Discourse,* 10:1 (1987–88), 55–76. See also

Jacques Attali, *Noise: The Political Economy of Music* (Minneapolis, 1985).

34. Roland Barthes, *Image–Music–Text*, trans. Stephen Heath (New York, 1977), p. 189.

35. The figure of the fishwife suggests the marketplace speech of carnival, the revolutionary power of the women of the French Revolution, and the 'fishwives' of Marx's *Eighteenth Brumaire*. Carter also elicits the olfactory image of fishy women in descriptions of Fevvers' 'perfume' in the first chapter.

36. For an account of the female circus performer as Victorian working girl, see Hiley, *Victorian Working Women*. The figure of the female acrobat raises the predictable questions of gender and propriety: 'Ought we forbid her to do these things? ... And, though it is not well to see a nude man fling a nude girl about as she is flung, or to see her grip his body in midair between her seemingly bare thighs, I think that an unreflecting audience takes no note ... and looks upon these things and looks at him and her only as two performers. Still, the familiar interlacing of male and female bodies in sight of the public, is gross and corrupting, though its purpose be mere athletics' (p. 119).

37. Hutcheon, *The Politics of Postmodernism*, p. 93.

38. Debord, *Society of the Spectacle*, p. 27.

39. Paulina Palmer's 'From "Coded Mannequin" to Bird Woman: Angela Carter's Magic Flight', in *Women Reading Women's Writing* (New York, 1987), pp. 179–205.

40. The claim that 'an emergence of a female counter-culture is celebrated' in the novel (Palmer, p. 180) is, in my view, true only as a prefigurative *possibility*. And many female types and institutional contexts are represented in the novel, implicating any definition of female counter-culture in the histories and metahistories of violence and oppression by and of women. Fevvers herself eats caviar in a grand hotel, at the expense of the peasant woman, Baboushka. Countess P., Olga Alexandrovna, and Madame Schreck all partake in criminality and destruction.

41. The prospects for life with Walser, the New Man, have seemed dim for most of my students. Although I have suggested alternative readings, on the numerous occasions when we have discussed his transformations as successively a brash American journalist, a fellow traveller with the clowns, a surrealistic anthropologist who 'goes native', and a new age man, students tend to see him in all these roles as a 'jerk' – something closer to the bad alternatives in Tanya Modleski's *Feminism Without Women* than to the non-dominant types in Kaja Silverman's *Male Subjectivity at the Margins*.

42. Lizzie's greatest fear is that Fevvers will become the 'tableau' of 'a woman in bondage to her reproductive system, a woman tied hand and foot to that Nature which your physiology denies' (p. 283). Carter never accedes to a definition of even motherhood as the 'natural'; throughout the novel mothers are secondhand representations within fictions, images, and tableaux.

43. Suleiman, *Subversive Intent*, p. 137.

44. Beryl Markham, *West with the Night* (Boston, 1942), p. 17.

8

Blonde, Black and Hottentot Venus: Context and Critique in Angela Carter's 'Black Venus'

JILL MATUS

Angela Carter's 'Black Venus' takes Jeanne Duval, the Eurafrican mistress of Charles Baudelaire, as the subject of its subversive narrative. Baudelaire's letters and poems, as well as the accounts of Jeanne Duval offered by his biographers, provide Carter with material for this short narrative fiction. Engaging the 'Black Venus' cycle of poems from *Les Fleurs du Mal* in a series of ironic allusions, Carter's text alternates imaginative, dramatic scenes of Jeanne and Baudelaire (and the cat) in his gloomy apartment with speculative commentary on such diverse matters as Jeanne's native land, the state of the colonies under Napoleon, Manet's representation of female nudity, and the evidence provided by Nadar (alias Felix Tournachon, photographer and friend of Baudelaire) about the fate of Jeanne as an old woman. Does Carter's story claim to be a substituting or superseding version, presenting a new and improved Jeanne Duval? The concerns raised in this question are perhaps allayed by the narrator's awareness of the problem, for the narrative voice continually dissolves the illusions it creates and disputes its own authority (along with that of Baudelaire, Nadar or anyone else) to tell the real story about this woman.[1]

Yet even as it disclaims the truth of its own representations, and teases out the racist and colonialist assumptions that inform traditional versions of Jeanne Duval, Carter's fiction appropriates and reconstructs Jeanne in its own politically-interested image. 'Black Venus' is engaged and interested in challenging the politics of assumptions about the sexualised woman as dark, diseased and corrupting. The title of the story refers, therefore, not only to a cluster of poems Baudelaire wrote, and to the woman who inspired them, but to a wider context – the ironised discourse of Venus in nineteenth-century constructions of female sexuality. What informs and underscores Carter's story is a network of associations from nineteenth-century comparative anthropology, physiology and anatomy, as well as from art and literature, in which blackness, primitive sexuality, prostitution and disease are closely linked. This essay approaches the contexts in which such associations develop by considering, for example, how Baudelaire's poem on the anthropologist Cuvier relates to Cuvier's verdict on the Hottentot Venus; what derogratory connotations the term 'steatopygia' has in nineteenth-century constructions of female sexuality, and how Angela Carter uses this term in celebratory description; what connection the Hottentot Venus may have with Zola's Nana and Manet's painting 'Nana'; and what Carter's Jeanne has to do with Manet's portrait of Jeanne Duval or, strangely, Courbet's effacement of her from his painting 'L'Atelier du Peintre'.

Venus, goddess of love, has a long history as the signifier of feminine beauty and purity. Mythology, visual representation and literature show, however, that the figure of Venus has also been used to suggest whorish seductiveness and voluptuousness, narcissistic female self-absorption, and a variety of other denigrating versions of woman. The context for the label 'Black Venus' is frequently colonial, where it reveals much about colonial perceptions of race and gender. Its range of associations is wide, from the virulence of Jef Geeraert's *Gangrene*, subtitled *Black Venus*, to the benign paternalism of Stephen Gray's poem 'Black Venus', in which the speaker implores an island beauty not to yearn for the white man's world, sure to spoil her charms.[2] Both idealisation and denigration may be suggested by the term 'Black Venus' – Baudelaire's friend Banville captures its quality when he describes Jeanne as both bestial and divine.[3] But like 'Hottentot Venus', the term is often employed in a bitterly ironic or oxymoronic way – as if to say, 'How can what is black also be Venus-like?'

In a discussion of Zola's *Nana*, Roland Barthes uses the term 'Hottentot Venus' in this way when he suggests that it would be ludicrous to imagine a woman like the Hottentot Venus possessing seductive power.[4] Writing of Zola's capacity to objectify, he points out how the men and women of the Second Empire become a 'piece of anthropology as strange as the life of the Papuans' (p. 92). Barthes likens Zola to an ethnologist studying a Kwakiutl tribe, so awesome is his detachment. We have an overwhelming sense of difference between ourselves and the people of whom he writes – we may even find it 'difficult to understand the wholesale devastation that Nana brings about; affectively, it seems to us almost as improbable as the seductive power of the Venus of the Hottentots'. Barthes' implication is that, as unbelievable as the seductive power of the Hottentot Venus may be, so improbable seems Nana's capacity for devastation. Just as Papuans and the Kwakiutl tribe are other, so are the Hottentot Venus as a seductive power, and Nana as man-eater. (*Mangeuses d'hommes* is a common term for prostitutes in nineteenth-century France.[5]) But what Barthes's analogy does not make clear is that 'the historically particular version of the eternal Man-eater', the Hottentot Venus, and a remote 'primitive' tribe, have a specific kind of sexual otherness in common. To explore this further, we need to know more about the historically particular version of the Hottentot Venus.

In the second decade of the nineteenth century, a young African woman called Saartjie Baartman was exhibited in London and then Paris to show the peculiar and 'typical' physiognomy of the African woman. She was known as the Hottentot Venus.[6] About five years later she died in Paris and the renowned Georges Cuvier wrote up his observations on her cadaver.[7] Cuvier's paper drew attention to the similarity of woman and ape and noted the distortions and anomalies of her 'organ of generation'. According to Cuvier, the highest form of ape – the orangutan – was comparable to the lowest form of man/woman, and more particularly, black woman. The Hottentot Venus was exhibited not as an incidental freak in a cheap circus, but as a type – the essence of woman's low position on the evolutionary ladder and the irrefutable evidence of her bestial and degenerate associations.

Sander Gilman's detailed study of the Hottentot Venus suggests that Cuvier was responsible for constituting the Hottentot Venus as the major signifier for the image of the Hottentot as sexual primitive in the nineteenth century (pp. 83–9). According to Gilman, the idea of primitive sexuality is also signified in images of size and grossness, particularly the steatopygia of the Hottentot woman. So, for example, Gilman argues that in a painting like Manet's 'Nana', the line of the exaggerated buttocks in the prostitute associates her with the Hottentot Venus and signifies her internal blackness and atavistic sexuality. (In nineteenth-century iconographies of the prostitute, steatopygia is a recurrent characteristic.) But the nineteenth-century association of the prostitute with the black was most readily compounded by the belief that prostitutes differed physiologically from ordinary women, that they were sexually primitive, even degenerate. Since the prostitute was also associated with disease, the link between blackness, primitive sexuality and corruption was further determined. In a complex variety of combinations, these characteristics could signal the grotesque and degenerate, as well as the exotic, forbidden and exciting. So, for example, Carter has Baudelaire, poet of decadence, look with fascination upon his dark mistress as 'an ambulant fetish, savage, obscene, terrifying'.[8]

Baudelaire wrote a poem called 'Cuvier's Verdict', in which Cuvier, questioned about where he would situate the Belgian on the chain of being, replies that this is indeed a problem since there is quite a gap between ape and mollusk. Another Belgian poem deals with the unsanitary habits of Belgian women, who surely use black soap since they always appear to be dirty. (Carter's Jeanne complains that Baudelaire will not pay for hot water for her bath and adds caustically that he probably thinks she does not need to bathe because her dark skin doesn't show the dirt.) Baudelaire's disparagement of Belgians, especially Belgian women, draws on the two categories that inform Cuvier's remarks about the Hottentot Venus – degeneration and blackness. Although Baudelaire did not write a poem about Cuvier's verdict on the Hottentot Venus, Carter's implication is that he nevertheless inscribed that verdict in the 'Black Venus' poems.

Degeneration and blackness also define the white prostitute, such as Zola's Nana, celebrated in the novel as 'la Blonde Vénus'. In the opening scenes of *Nana* she takes part in an operetta called *La Blonde Vénus* at the Théâtre des Variétés. Although she is not able to move members of the audience with her artistic talents, she can certainly move its male members with the sight of her naked body. Zola describes her as a Venus in the true sense of the word, and as a force of nature. Although at first sight, La Blonde Vénus and the Hottentot Venus do not appear to have much in common, their association is closer and more complex than Barthes' analogy suggests. Though the former may arouse and seduce while the latter provokes curiosity and derision, they are both versions of female sexuality characterised as primitive and other, black and degenerate. It is, however, only when Zola's Blonde Vénus is dying, having contracted smallpox from her son, that her concealed inner blackness and rot are revealed. Smallpox, in this sense, is not so much small as it is merely pox – syphilis. Nana's demise is instructive in that her putrefaction is described as the rotting and decomposition of Venus. Since her son's contagion is the cause of her death, the text suggests that it is, of course, the produce of her thighs that eventually contaminates her. Those 'snowy thighs' that corrupted Paris mock the association of snow and whiteness with purity, demonstrating that white as they are, hers are no different from the black ones overtly associated with corruption and disease. Nana reminds us of Nanahuatzin, the Aztec goddess, whom Carter mentions in 'Black Venus' as the one blamed by Europeans for sending venereal disease from the New World to the Old – an erotic vengeance for imperialist plunder. Carter, however, mines the irony that Baudelaire's 'black-thighed witch' (as his poem 'Sed Non Satiata' styles her) may have contracted syphilis from him.

Carter's 'Black Venus' situates itself squarely within the contexts of Venus mythology that I have been discussing, and confronts stereotypes with iconoclastic wit. The story displays qualities of much of Carter's work, which has been described by various critics as shocking, intoxicating, revisionist, abrasive. A characteristic procedure of Carter's is to seize upon some image, icon or bit of mythology and draw out its implications, making gorgeous what is denigrated or scorned, blaspheming against what is held sacred, and exposing what is usually kept covert. Carter's fiction relishes the so-called freaks excluded from the Western pantheon of Venuses and relegated to circuses and sideshows. Carter is interested in women larger than life, the giantesses of myth and history and fiction – Helen, Venus, Josephine Baker, Jeanne Duval and Sophia Fevvers, the birdwoman in *Nights at the Circus*, in whom the association of gross size, deformity and sexual licentiousness, for example, are brought gloriously together. A poster advertises the attractions of the bewinged aerialiste Fevvers thus:

> The artist had chosen to depict her ascent from behind – bums aloft, you might say; up she goes, in a steatopygous perspective, shaking

out about her those tremendous ... pinions ... powerful enough to bear up such a big girl as she.[9]

Celebratory emphasis on the rear of this 'Cockney Venus' seems to mock the association of grossness with female sexuality.

Although not specific about Jeanne in the way that she is about the 'Cockney Venus', Carter emphasises Jeanne's size, describes her as a 'woman of immense height', and imagines Jeanne thinking of herself as a 'great gawk of an ignorant black girl, good for nothing' (p. 18). In opposition to Jeanne's self-deprecation, Carter regards her as one of 'those beautiful giantesses who, a hundred years later, would grace the stages of the Crazy Horse or the Casino de Paris in sequin cache-sexe and tinsel pasties, divinely tall, the colour and texture of suede. Josephine Baker!' (p. 12). In contrast to the Hottentot Venus, exhibited in Paris as the butt of racist and misogynist humour, Josephine Baker exhibited herself at the Revue Nègre, commanding awe and capitalising on her 'savage' and 'primitive' blackness. A recent biography, *Jazz Cleopatra*, describes how the dancer marketed herself in Paris by emphasising her black animality, symbolised by the extraordinary life and power of her undulating buttocks. 'The rear end exists,' said Baker. 'I see no reason to be ashamed of it. It's true that there are rear ends so stupid, so pretentious, so insignificant, that they're only good for sitting on.'[10]

Biographers of Baudelaire who write about Jeanne Duval concede her beauty, but in such a way as to suggest that she is an aesthetic object rather than a beautiful woman. She had that 'enigmatic stylised black beauty which combines line and patina to produce an aesthetic effect, like a work of art in bronze or dark stone' writes Baudelaire's biographer, A. E. Carter.[11] But he also says she was 'a common slut, totally uncultivated and extremely stupid; and like most whores she lied with a deliberate compulsive mendacity which is close to paranoia' (p. 37). Rather than an exotic and fetishised *objet d'art*, she is, for Carter, a means to unsettle and parody canonical Western art. Carter asks us to imagine 'The Birth of Black Venus', describing her (in terms of Botticelli's painting) aloft her scallop-shell, 'clutching an enormous handful of dreadlocks to her pubic mound' while 'wee black cherubs' blow her across the Atlantic (p. 18). Artistic representations of Jeanne Duval by Manet and Courbet provide an interesting gloss on Carter's representation of Duval in the story. Courbet originally painted her next to Baudelaire himself in the 'Atelier' but later removed her at

Baudelaire's request.[12] A close scrutiny of the painting reveals the ghostly traces of her effacement, which underscores Carter's suggestion in the story that Jeanne exists for Baudelaire as something on which he may feast his eyes, or that he may remove from sight, according to his whim. Carter mentions Manet's 'Le Déjeuner sur l'Herbe' in relation to a scene where Baudelaire sits impeccably dressed while Jeanne must be naked, clothed only in her skin, but she does not mention Manet's portrait of Jeanne (1862) in which she is positioned half-reclining, but very much clothed in full crinoline. Like Zola's Nana, Jeanne was reputed to be a bad actress and a good courtesan; however, Manet paints her very differently from the young and seductive Nana, in whom signs of degeneration are covert (see Gilman, p. 102). In Manet's portrait of Duval, such signs are (at least in the eyes of some critics) more obvious. She is described as suffering the wages of her pathological sexuality: 'stiff and half-paralysed, and her face ... stupid and bestial from alcoholism and vice'.[13]

In 'Black Venus' one of the problems confronting Carter is how to represent Jeanne without presuming to speak for her or know her mind. Bakhtin's notion of dialogic interchange may help to explain Carter's sense of Jeanne, since Bakhtin emphasises how the word in language is always half someone else's, 'exists in other people's mouths'. It becomes one's own only when the speaker populates it with intention and 'expropriates' the word, adapting it to his or her own semantic and expressive needs.[14] Jeanne's words, Carter suggests, have been more than half someone else's. A Francophone whose Creole patois made her feel in France as if 'her tongue had been cut out and another one sewn in that did not fit well', Carter's Jeanne is without words, without country, without history (p. 18). Noting that Baudelaire's eloquence has denied Jeanne her language, the narrator is concerned to make the silences of Jeanne's own narrative speak. Since her sugar daddy does not hear her, we should. As she dances for her 'Daddy', Jeanne hums 'a Creole melody ... but Daddy paid no attention to what song his siren sang' (p. 12). As she does with other mythic ideas, Carter uses the notion of the irresistible song of the sirens to ironic effect. Baudelaire may call his mistress his siren, pose her as a seductress, but he is far too self-absorbed to hear any song but his own as irresistible.

Though Jeanne has been, in effect, silenced by Baudelaire's words and eclipsed by his shadow, Carter does not presume to appropriate

Jeanne's story by knowing her mind; rather, she draws attention to other possible representations of her than those we already have by persistently imagining her as an ordinary down-to-earth woman concerned with her own immediate material conditions. Her language cannot speak for Jeanne, but it can compete with and challenge the languages that have sought to possess and exploit her. She attempts to formulate an alternative vocabulary to Baudelaire's and to expose the contingencies of his vocabulary. Carter's habit of unsettling ascriptions and projections manifests itself in making the reader scrutinise language closely and attend to the nuances of apparent tautology and the connotations that make a crucial difference. A good example hinges on how we understand 'promiscuous': 'Her lover assumed she was promiscuous because she *was* promiscuous' (p. 13). But Jeanne has her own code of honour. To her

> prostitution was a question of number; of being paid by more than one person at a time. That was bad. She was not a bad girl. When she slept with anyone else but Daddy, she never let them pay. It was a matter of honour. It was a question of fidelity.
>
> (p. 12)

The passage draws attention to the misconstruction of Jeanne's actions from the point of view of the onlooker. Because she was promiscuous – took many sexual partners – does not mean in her terms that she was promiscuous (unable to discriminate among them).

One way in which Carter questions distorting versions of Jeanne is by challenging the poet's metaphoric power: 'My monkey, my pussy cat, my pet' he croons as he imagines taking her back to the island where the 'jewelled parrot rocks on the enamel branch' and where she can crunch sugar-cane between her teeth (p. 10). 'But, on these days', the narrator counters, 'no pet nor pussy she; she looks more like an old crow with rusty feathers in a miserable huddle by the smoky fire' (p. 10). Nor is there any romanticising of her as the dispossessed child of the islands, yearning for her heritage: she doesn't know that she has a heritage, let alone that she has been deprived of it. Since the colony – white and imperious – fathered her, she is a child without history. The narrative suggests that traditional poetic tropes are inadequate and appropriating when they underscore Western constructions of motivation and desire.

As the poet's 'agonised romanticism' transforms the homely Caribbean smell of coconut oil into the perfume of the air of tropical islands, his imagination performs an 'alchemical alteration on the healthy tang of her sweat' (p. 19). 'He thinks her sweat smells of cinnamon because she has spices in her pores.' In place of the poet's 'weird goddess, dusky as the night', 'vase of darkness', – a 'black Helen' to his tortured Faust – the narrative shows us a woman who lights the smelly cheroots she smokes with his manuscripts, who tells him to let the cat out before it craps on the Bokhara, and who fears the syphilis she has contracted from her 'first white protector' – Baudelaire.

Another strategy Carter uses is to challenge the mythical constructs that allow Jeanne to be represented as the exotic Eve, black temptress and queen of sin. The poet might like to believe she has come from an island paradise, but the narrator describes it as a 'stinking Eden'. Her fall, after she bites 'a custard apple', is presented as a fall into the European – civilised – world. Later, however, the narrator offers another interpretation: if Jeanne is to occupy any position in the Genesis story, she would have to be the forbidden fruit – and Baudelaire has consumed her. (Felix Nadar once described her as a special dish for the ultrarefined palate.)

Baudelaire's biographers agree that Jeanne was a 'mulatto' from the French Caribbean.[15] Angela Carter writes:

> Where she came from is a problem; books suggest Mauritius, in the Indian ocean, or Santo Domingo, in the Caribbean, take your pick of two different sides of the world. (Her *pays d'origine* of less importance than it would have been had she been a wine.)
>
> (p. 16)

What is important to Carter's story, whose ending envisages Jeanne's return to Martinique, is that her origins are colonial. Insofar as Jeanne's story is ever told it usually ends with Nadar's description of her hobbling on crutches, her teeth and hair gone. Carter, however, constructs a possible resurrection for her in the last pages of the story: 'You can buy teeth, you know; you can buy hair.' While Carter's narrator points out that the poet near death is so estranged from himself he is said to have bowed politely to his reflection in the mirror, Jeanne is pictured as having found herself. 'She had come down to earth, and, with the aid of her cane, she walked perfectly well on it' (p. 23). A number of sources mention Duval's brother – a man she claimed was her brother – who lived off her and absconded with her possessions while she was in hospital.[16] In Carter's closure this 'high-yellow, demi-sibling' takes over her finances and, 'a born entrepreneur', sets her back on her feet. She makes for Martinique and starts up a brothel.

The inclusion of this putative brother figure in the story preserves a bit of the biographical data, but what is the significance of this managing male? A self-directed female avenger might be thought more appropriate to the text's feminist politics, but Carter's text, besides challenging Western sexual stereotypes, is also a fable from a postcolonial perspective. Carter uses the brother figure to make a point about pimping, capitalist enterprise and colonial trade. Earlier the narrator tells us: 'Seller and commodity in one, a whore is her own investment in the world and so she must take care of herself' (p. 20). Jeanne has not taken care of herself in this way, but under the management of this possibly demonic brother (we are told that for all Jeanne cares he could be Mephistopheles), who seems to be out for a cut of the profits, she gets a new lease on life dispensing pleasure and death to the colonial administrators of her native land. The last sentence of the story imagines her keeping in circulation the 'gift' that Baudelaire had given her:

> Until at last, in extreme old age, she succumbs to the ache in her bones and a cortege of grieving girls takes her to the churchyard, she will continue to dispense, to the most privileged of the colonial administration, at a not excessive price, the veritable, the authentic, the true Baudelairean syphilis.

(p. 23)

What goes around comes around. If Baudelaire's poems about Jeanne are often called the 'Black Venus cycle', the name is apt, not least because they recycle a cluster of attitudes that govern the representation of sexualised woman, be she a Blonde, Black or Hottentot Venus. Angela Carter has, however, given that cycle a new turn.

From *Studies in Shorter Fiction*, 28:4 (1991), 467–76.

NOTES

[Jill Matus's discussion of the title story from Carter's 1985 collection, *Black Venus*, takes up a well-established critical topic, Carter's rewriting of established texts and myths, in Matus's case with a meticulous, detailed and wide-ranging historicist approach to Carter's appropriations which serves to reveal the importance and validity of her project. Given Carter's wariness of imperialist complicities (see interviews, *Nights at the Circus* and *Wise Children*), postcolonial criticism is an appropriate tool to assist Matus in her consideration of the perennial question of what Carter's end result is – here a realisation that the narrator does not have the authority to tell the 'real' story, and indeed dispelling the illusion that one could. Matus's use of Bakhtin's idea of dialogic interchange helps to explain Carter's approach to her protagonist, challenging the languages that have been used to possess or exploit her. Ed.]

1. Charles Baudelaire, *Oevres Complètes*, 2 vols, ed. Claude Pichois (Paris, 1975–76); Baudelaire, *Correspondance*, ed. Claude Pichois and Jean Ziegler (Paris, 1973); Baudelaire, *Flowers of Evil*, trans. George Dillon and Edna St.Vincent Millais (New York, 1936); Felix Nadar, *Charles Baudelaire Intime: Le Poète Vierge* (Paris, 1911).

2. Jef Geeraerts, *Gangrene*, trans. Jon Swan (New York, 1975); Stephen Gray (ed), *A World of Their Own: Southern African Poets of the Seventies* (Johannesburg, 1976), p. 56.

3. Enid Starkie, *Baudelaire* (London, 1957), p. 87.

4. Roland Barthes, 'Man-Eater', in *Critical Essays on Emile Zola*, ed. David Baguley (Boston, 1986), pp. 90–3.

5. Charles Bernheimer, *Figures of Ill Repute: Representing Prostitution in Nineteenth-Century France* (Cambridge, MA, 1989), p. 96.

6. Stephen Gray's poem, 'Hottentot Venus' (*Hottentot Venus and Other Poems* [Cape Town, 1979]) begins:

   My name is Saartjie Baartman and I come from Kat Rivier
       they call me the Hottentot Venus
   they rang up the curtains on a classy peepshow two pennies
       two pennies in the slot and I'd wind up
   shift a fan and roll my rolypoly bum
       and rock the capitals of Europe into mirth.

7. Sander Gilman, *Difference and Pathology: Stereotypes of Sexuality, Race and Madness* (Ithaca, NY, 1985), pp. 76–108.

8. Angela Carter, 'Black Venus', in *Black Venus* (London, 1985), p. 20. All subsequent references are to this edition.

9. Carter, *Nights at the Circus* (London, 1984), p. 7.

10. Phyllis Rose, *Jazz Cleopatra* (New York, 1989), p. 24.

11. A. E. Carter, *Charles Baudelaire* (Boston, 1977), p. 37.

12. I am grateful to my student Mary Kavoukis for bringing this painting to my attention.

13. Henri Perruchot, *Manet*, trans. Humphry Hare, ed. Jean Ellsmoor (London, 1962), p. 98.

14. M. M. Bakhtin, *The Dialogic Imagination: Four Essays*, trans. Caryl Emerson and Michael Holquist, ed. Michael Holquist (Austin, TX, 1981), p. 294.

15. See F. W. J. Hemmings, *Baudelaire the Damned: A Biography* (London, 1982), p. 50, who suggests that her grandmother was a black woman shipped to Nantes to become a prostitute there, her mother was most probably a mulatto, and Jeanne herself was a quadroon.

16. See Starkie, *Baudelaire*, p. 404, and Hemmings, *Baudelaire the Damned*, p. 184.

9

Angela Carter's Fetishism

CHRISTINA BRITZOLAKIS

> Like so many girls, I passionately wanted to be an actress when I was in my early teens and I turn this (balked, unachieved and now totally unregretted) ambition over in my mind from time to time. Why did it seem so pressing, the need to demonstrate in public a total control and transformation of roles other people had conceived? Rum, that.[1]

> It is understandable, I suppose, that someone could approach the fantastic and exotic surface of your fictions and not be able to bridge the gap to the central point that your theatricality is meant to heighten real social attitudes and myths of femininity.[2]

> Her two favourite periodical publications were *Vogue* and *The New Statesman*.[3]

If there is a single theme that appears central to criticism of Carter's writing, that theme must surely be theatricality. This is not surprising, since dramatic performance in all its varieties – masquerade, carnival, burlesque, travesty, cross-dressing, drag – leaps out at the reader from the pages of Carter's texts as both style and subject. In *Nights at the Circus* (1984), she writes of 'the freedom that lies behind the mask, within dissimulation, the freedom to juggle with being, and, indeed, with the language which is vital to our being, that lies at the heart of burlesque'.[4] The current interest in Carter's writing is not unconnected with the fact that such metaphors also govern areas of contemporary feminist theory, where the concept of 'gender performance', based on a history of appropriations of Joan Riviere's 1929 essay 'Womanliness as masquerade', has become *de rigueur*.[5] For many of Carter's most recent critics, her theatricalism, which dates back to her earliest work, has emerged, often by way of this body of 'gender performance' theory, as synonymous with her self-proclaimed, 'demythologising' project, the project of 'investigating' femininity as one of 'the social fictions that regulate our lives'.[6]

If Carter's texts seem to lend themselves in an exemplary manner to the ongoing dialogue between psychoanalysis and feminism, this is in part because they increasingly and self-consciously engage with a wide range of post-1968 theoretical debates, and with a distinctively semiological conception of culture. Carter consistently inscribes herself as an intellectual, a 'culture-worker',[7] and marks her texts with associations from both high and low culture. If she is, as she states, 'in the demythologising business', she also describes herself, elsewhere, as 'in the entertainment business'.[8] She sees herself, moreover, as an allegorist: 'I do put everything in a novel to be *read* – read the way allegory was intended to be read, the way you are supposed to read *Sir Gawayne and the Grene Knight* – on as many levels as you can comfortably cope with at the time.'[9] Political enlightenment and entertainment – to bring these two roles together in fiction is a difficult act to pull off, and Carter's claims have not always met with a sympathetic reception. For a certain purist tradition of Marxism, as much as for liberal humanist criticism, Carter is a deeply embarrassing figure, adopting as she does a postmodern aesthetic which, it has been argued, privileges style over substance, eroticises the fragment and parasitically colludes with consumer capitalism.[10] Feminist criticism has, however, with few exceptions, embraced Carter's postmodern aesthetics as inseparable from her commitment to socialism and to feminism. A rift between politics and pleasure, between allegory and fantasy, thus comes to inhabit Carter criticism, as indeed, I will argue, it inhabits Carter's writing. Although I am far from wishing to discount the usefulness of poststructuralist theory in reading her texts, or to deny their fruitful engagement with poststructuralism, I would like to ask some questions about the function of spectacle in these texts, and about its relation to fashion, questions with complicate the celebratory symbiosis between fiction and theory in much Carter criticism. Can the staging of femininity as spectacle indeed be linked with a liberatory feminist project, and why does this particular formation emerge as the code for Carter's identity as a writer?

Carter's abiding fascination with femininity as spectacle has hitherto been understood predominantly in terms of a feminist critical

project which identifies and rejects male-constructed images of
women as a form of false consciousness. The early novels represent
women who are in danger of being turned into fetishised, puppet-
like objects by a male master – what Carter calls the mad scientist/
shaman/toymaker figure.[11] These women tend to seek out or actively embrace the role of the spectacularly suffering victim of male
cruelty. The earliest example is Ghislaine in *Shadow Dance* (1966),
who is mutilated and finally murdered by Honeybuzzard. In the
later novels, the seductions of self-immolating femininity are rejected, or at least qualified. Paulina Palmer notes the shift from
'coded mannequin' to 'bird-woman' as marking a shift from a de-
terminist to a more utopian, celebratory vision of femininity.[12]
Fevvers in *Nights at the Circus* (1984) and the Chances in *Wise
Children* (1991) are exemplary postmodern heroines who take
control of their own performances and manipulate their self-
stagings for their own advantage. But the celebration of femininity
remains, in both cases, linked to what Lizzie in *Nights at the Circus*
calls 'the discipline of an audience' (p. 280). It seems to me far from
clear whether these characters, in exploiting the creative possibilities of illusion, do indeed escape objectification or whether they end
up colluding in their own objectification. Is the spectacle of femininity a form of freedom or necessity? Moreover, how does it inflect
the language of Carter's novels, which is saturated with sensuous
detail, with coruscating surfaces and ornate facades?

MAD GIRLS AND REVOLUTIONS

I would like to begin by examining what could be described as an
iconic moment in one of Carter's early novels, *Love* (1970), a
moment in which the spectacle of femininity is still clearly linked
with self-immolation. The passage turns on a brief moment of confrontation, between Lee Collins and his wife Annabel, who has
prepared herself for suicide by having an elaborate 'makeover':

> He was so struck by the newly adamantine brilliance of her eyes he
> did not see they no longer reflected anything. With her glittering hair
> and unfathomable face, streaked with synthetic red, white and black,
> she looked like nothing so much as one of those strange and splendid
> figures with which the connoisseurs of the baroque loved to decorate
> their artificial caves, those *atalantes composés* fabricated from rare
> marbles and semi-precious stones. She had become a marvellous

crystallisation, retaining nothing of the remembered woman but her form, for all the elements of which this new structure were composed had suffered a change, the eyes put out by zircons or spinels, the hair respun from threads of gold and the mouth enamelled scarlet. No longer vulnerable flesh and blood, she was altered to inflexible material. She could have stepped up into the jungle on the walls and looked not out of place beside the tree with the breasts or the carnivorous flowers for now she was her own, omnipotent white queen and could move to any position on the board.

'Go away,' she said to Lee. 'Leave me alone.'

'Dear God,' said Lee, '*Le jour de gloire est arrivé.*'

Inevitably, he began to laugh at such a reversal for the revolution which he both feared and longed for had arrived at last and he was reduced to bankruptcy for there was nothing left to love for him in this magnificent creature. All would not, now, continue in the old style for she dismissed him without a blessing.[13]

The apparition of Annabel provides the occasion for a *tour de force* of metaphoric display; this is the kind of virtuoso passage, characteristic of Carter's writing, which foregrounds its own spectacular stylistic effects. The transformation of woman into *objet d'art* is enacted as a phantasmagoria which, like much of the action of *Love*, tilts unstably between mimesis and hallucination. In an echo of Ariel's song in *The Tempest*, Annabel has 'suffered a change', in which 'vulnerable flesh and blood' has been 'altered to inflexible material'. This process is coded, for both Annabel and for the reader, as a symbolic anticipation of the 'perfection' which death will visit upon her. The fabrication of the masquerade of femininity is seen as an aesthetic process which *exchanges* the organic for the inorganic or 'adamantine', exemplified by precious and semiprecious gemstones and metals: 'gold', 'zircons' and 'spinels'. It is both an addition of value and a subtraction of life, at once idealising and death-dealing. The logic of this exchange is completed by the last mention of her in the novel as 'a painted doll, bluish at the extremities' and a 'bedizened corpse' (p. 112).

An intensely specular figurative energy turns language into a matter of collecting, hoarding, displaying, fondling, possessing and continually looking, an activity at once clinical and museological. In this poetics of specularity, the narrator is at least partially identified with those 'connoisseurs of the baroque' who 'loved to decorate their artificial caves' with 'strange and splendid figures'. The sumptuous materiality and theatricality of the narrator's 'bejewelled' language therefore mimes Annabel's 'marvellous crystallisation' and turns in upon itself. Words are flaunted as objects; discrete images are isolated from their context. Although Carter describes herself as an allegorist, here, as elsewhere, she writes as an unabashed female fetishist; and it is the conjunction, as well as the disjunction, between these two terms, fetishism and allegory, which requires closer scrutiny.

Carter's description of Annabel as 'a marvellous crystallisation, retaining nothing of the remembered woman but her form' recalls Marx's famous analysis at the beginning of *Capital* of the commodity form as fetish. In commodity fetishism, Marx argues, the social character of the product of labour assumes, through the abstraction of exchange, an 'enigmatical' or 'mystical' character which masks its use-value.[14] Annabel has turned herself into an idol or *eidolon*, an act presented as the culmination of her superstitious and obsessional behaviour throughout the narrative. At the same time, her act is enmeshed in a network of images of prostitution and signals a prevailing (and perverse) economic rationality. In her transformation, Annabel is linked with Lee's mother, who in an apocalyptic access of insanity painted her body with cabbalistic signs and transformed herself into 'the whore of Babylon'. She is also emulating the 'photographic whore' who features in the pictures given to her by Buzz in the first part of the novel, and whose 'bland, white, motionless face' (also 'painted') she desires for herself.

The work of Walter Benjamin, who explored the links between Marx's conceptualisation of the commodity form and the status of the aesthetic within commodity culture, is of foundational importance for this area of study. Benjamin writes that fashion 'prostitutes the living body to the inorganic world. In relation to the living it represents the rights of the corpse. Fetishism, which succumbs to the sex-appeal of the inorganic, is its vital nerve; and the cult of the commodity recruits this to its service.'[15] Benjamin arrived, by way of a Marxist appropriation of Freud, at the key concept of the phantasmagoria. The commodified environment of nineteenth-century Paris becomes a spectral theatre, where commodities disport themselves as fetishes on display. The chief emblem and embodiment of this phantasmagoric landscape, which appears as allegory in the poetry of Baudelaire, is the prostitute. In the prostitute, Benjamin argues, the female body has lost its aura of natural femininity and has become a commodity, made up of dead and petrified fragments, while its beauty has become a matter of cosmetic disguise (make-up and fashion). *Love* follows the precedent of Baudelaire (and of Surrealism, an equally important model for Benjamin) in making a fetishised femininity serve as the figure for, and displacement of, socio-historical crisis, at the level both of figurative language and of narrative perspective.

In an afterword to the 1987 edition of the novel, Carter criticises *Love* for its 'almost sinister feat of male impersonation', 'icy treatment of the mad girl' and 'ornate formalism of style', and describes the text as 'Annabel's coffin' (p.113). Annabel is indeed less of a desiring and acting subject than an object in plots constructed for her by others. As one corner of the erotic triangle whose other points are formed by Lee and Buzz, she intrudes into their homo-erotic dyad and is finally sacrificed to it. What Carter refers to as the novel's 'ornate formalism of style', and what I would describe as a fetishism of the signifier, or disjunction of the signifier from the signified, is accompanied by an insistent allegorical overdetermination at the level of the overall narrative. Settings, events and characters serve as emblems of larger social and cultural narratives. Despite its claustrophobic concentration on the erotic triangle, the novel is concerned with the 1960s, and with the failure of the emancipatory hopes which Carter associated with that decade. The characters, Carter writes, are 'not quite the children of Marx and Coca-Cola, more the children of Nescafé and the Welfare state', and 'the pure, perfect products of those days of social mobility and sexual licence' (p. 113). When Lee hails Annabel's transformation as a *revolutionary* denouement (*'Le jour de gloire est arrivé'*) he makes explicit the status of Annabel's suicide as a parodic pseudo-solution to a plot riven by social and sexual contradiction.

The Gothic staging of the mad girl as spectacle in *Love* is the corollary of a certain kind of narrative stance – the psychiatric stance of the clinical 'case-study', beloved of late nineteenth-century French novelists.[16] Carter incorporates a parodic version of this narrative perspective into the text through the figure of a female psychiatrist with whom Lee discusses Annabel's illness. In this episode, Lee 'found himself confronted by the woman's high, brown boots in such unnatural perspective that the feet were enormous and the uppers soared above him like mill chimneys. The boots were so beautifully polished they appeared irradiated from within' (p. 55). The hallucinatory vision of the shiny boots inaugurates a (possibly fantasised) sexual approach to the woman psychiatrist. The whole episode, suspended between fantasy and allegory, reads as a send-up of the more comical aspects of Freud's 1927 account of fetishism.[17] But at the same time it thematises the text's own processes. The fetish-object – standing in metonymically for the desired but absent maternal phallus – is associated with a particular style, an 'unnatural perspective' which deviates from realism, and which Lee calls 'a kind of Expressionist effect' (p. 55).

In *Love*, the clinical stance of the female psychiatrist is constantly infected by the alternative narrative logic represented by Annabel's tendency to attribute magical powers to inanimate objects. The autistic private language of the 'mad girl' marks the absence from the novel of a feminist analysis which cannot yet be articulated (though class, which sets the bourgeois Annabel apart from the proletarian Collinses, evidently enters into the equation). At the same time the text is preoccupied with representations, fantasies and icons of female madness, a point underscored when Lee buys Annabel a print of Millais's 'Ophelia'. But the script of the numb and passionless 'beautiful hysteric' who haunts male subjectivity with the spectre of disorder cannot contain Annabel's complaint without a great deal of mess.[18] Carter's later novels leave behind the Ophelia plot (though it is worth noticing that *Wise Children* resurrects it in the figure of Tiffany). The death of the mad girl announces the need for a mutation of style, from a residual of Gothicised social realism into full-blown metafiction and the playful deconstruction of narrative conventions; a mutation which, at least for Carter's hostile critics, involves a transmutation of politics into style.

What connects *Love* with the later novels is a preoccupation with the power of images. If the 1960s was the moment of the counter-culture, it was also, as Marc O'Day has argued in his essay on Carter's 'Bristol Trilogy', the period in which the rapid turnover in ideas, images, and styles 'became fully institutionalised as an objective feature of social and economic life'.[19] While the other characters see themselves in terms of manipulable self-representations, Annabel literalises the deadly logic of the fetish and becomes embodied masquerade. It is possible to argue that Carter practises not merely an aesthetic but also an analytic of fetishism, which links the ideas of Marx and Freud in a politically ambiguous, perpetually self-cancelling allegorical loop of image and idea. Can one write as a demythologiser, in the Enlightenment tradition which attacks the 'idols of the mind' (an outstanding example of which is Marx's analysis of commodity fetishism) and at the same time embrace the verbal fetish at the level of style? As a category of cultural analysis, fetishism, as various analysts of Marx's essay have argued, has an uncanny ability to turn against those who deploy it, turning iconoclasts into their obverse, idolaters.[20]

Carter's work, then, raises the question of the role of fetishism in both a feminist and in a broader socialist praxis. One of a number of recent attempts to draw parallels between the Marxist and the Freudian theories of the fetish by Laura Mulvey points out that 'for Freud, the body that is the source of fetishism is the mother's body, uncanny and archaic. For Marx, the source of fetishism is in the erasure of the worker's labour as value. Both become the unspeakable, and the unrepresentable, in commodity culture.'[21] Carter's fiction generates homologies and substitutions between these two different (and possibly irreconcilable) scenarios of fetishism. The major evaluative problem which faces her interpreters is that of separating critique from the logic of consumerism; a problem which, in the wake of 1968, it could be argued, comes to define the field of left cultural politics in general.

DECADENT ICONOGRAPHY

Carter has characterised her stylistic excesses as a species of decadence: 'It's mannerist, you see: closing time in the gardens of the West.'[22] This comment sits uneasily with her oft-expressed belief in her fiction as an instrument of social change and intervention.[23] But it does resonate with the attraction in her work towards the rhetoric and iconography of a prominent, largely male-authored strand of European literary history, which runs from the mid-nineteenth century through Baudelaire, Poe, Sade, much of French Symbolism, the Decadent writing of the *fin de siècle* and Surrealism. Carter's readings of these texts unerringly focus on their metaphorisation of femininity in its most fetishised and spectacular forms.

The image of the female performer, for example, is a staple of male-authored *fin de siècle* literature, where it is often aligned with the figure of the prostitute and that of the mechanical woman. These figures crystallise an ambivalent response to the rationalising, technological forces of capitalism, and figure the crisis-ridden birth of modernity.[24] It is in the context of this weight of prior symbolisations of femininity that I believe Carter's texual masquerades need to be placed. Her attraction to the male-authored texts of the

Decadence suggests a distinctively magpie-like relation to literary history, and one which frequently involves a cross-dressed or masculine narrative perspective: witness Lee's vision of Annabel. Carter characteristically writes in the postmodern mode of pastiche, mixing high and low culture. She produces a reworking of myth and literature which treats Western European culture as 'a great scrap-yard from which you can assemble all sorts of new vehicles ...'.[25] The period of her apprenticeship, during the 1960s, coincides with the canonisation and institutionalisation of Modernism within the academy. The voracious and often dizzying intertextuality of her writing needs to be seen as not only a reaction against this development but also as its product. Unlike some of the Decadent or proto-Decadent authors (Poe, Baudelaire, Huysmans) who fascinate her, Carter is no enemy of the forces of technology and progress, which she celebrates for having liberated women from the bondage of reproduction. Her attempts to imagine 'a new kind of being, unburdened by the past',[26] in the absence of any contemporary realisation of this vision, have to work upon the prefeminist myths, allegories and iconographies of the past.

Nowhere is this more clearly illustrated than in *The Passion of New Eve* (1977), apparently Carter's most anti-essentialist text, which sets out, in her words, 'to say some quite specific things about the production of femininity ... there is quite a careful and elaborate discussion of femininity as a commodity, of Hollywood producing illusions as tangible commodities'.[27] The book is an early example of what Elaine Jordan calls Carter's 'speculative fictions'.[28] As Jordan points out, 'Excitement about demythologising was historically specific, a thing of the 70s.'[29] *The Passion of New Eve* is informed by Barthes' analysis of myth as the coded product of history, made not found, and perhaps not a little by his essay on Garbo in *Mythologies* (1972). Fetishism and the masquerade were also part of the excitement about demythologising. They were key concepts within the film theory of the 1970s, which arose from a confluence of semiotics, psychoanalysis and Althusserian 'ideology critique'. Tristessa is recognisably a spectacle in the sense identified by film theorists: herself a commodity, she is also a phantasmatic space which sustains the cinematic production of commodities. Her shadowy, enigmatic, suffering femininity is revealed as 'a piece of pure mystification' (p. 6) when she turns out to be a transvestite. But if *Passion* alludes to the cinematic fetishisation of the female body, the extent to which it can be aligned with a 'demythologising' cultural analysis is uncertain. This figure of Tristessa resolves itself, when Tristessa and Eve are united, into the mythic figure of the Platonic androgyne.

The Passion of New Eve is, at the same time, locked into a regressive circulation of literary metaphors of fatal, apparitional and mechanical femininity, from Poe and Baudelaire to the Symbolists (the technological creation of Eve alludes to Villiers de L'Isle Adam's *L'Eve Future*, 1886). The figure upon which I wish to focus is Leilah the naked dancer, who is transformed into Lilith, the revolutionary guerilla leader. The representation of Leilah in the novel parodies the 'Jeanne Duval' cycle of poems in the *Fleurs du mal*. She first appears as a hallucinatory embodiment of the city and its labyrinthine corruptions; her femininity is seen as the expression of a decadent, narcotic culture. Leilah, of whom Evelyn claims, 'I never knew a girl more a slave to style', is part prostitute, part female performer, obligingly transforming herself every evening under his gaze into an exotic and fetishised *objet d'art*. Lilith, her *alter ego*, explains to Evelyn near the end of the novel that his seduction formed part of an apocalyptic purging. Are we, then, to read Lilith the activist as the revelation of Leilah's true self? Leilah and Lilith represent the sundered halves of Carter's project – her baroque, eclectic appropriation of the Western cultural heritage and her commitment to demythologising it in the cause of political transformation. Carter's attempt to bridge the gap between these two projects in the later novels leads her to create heroines who are no longer the puppets of male-controlled scripts but who use theatricality and masquerade to invent and advance themselves. I wonder, however, whether the shift from the one to the other is as clear-cut or as decisive as has sometimes been assumed.

It is instructive to compare the treatment of Leilah/Lilith in *Passion* with the later reworking of Baudelaire's so-called 'Black Venus' cycle in Carter's short story of that name (1980). This text enacts with great skill the ambiguities of Carter's relation to one of her major literary models, Baudelaire, and to the fetishistic economy of the feminine which forms the very substance of his aesthetic. In a mixture of parody, translation, interpretation and historical reconstruction, Carter borrows metaphors and phrases from the poems to summon up in loving detail the vaporous, nostalgic and melancholy atmospherics of the *Fleurs du mal*:

Sad, so sad, those smoky-rose, smoky-mauve evenings of late Autumn, sad enough to pierce the heart. The sun departs the sky in winding sheets of gaudy cloud; anguish enters the city, a sense of the bitterest regret, a nostalgia for things we never knew, anguish of the turn of the year, the time of impotent yearning, the inconsolable season.[30]

Carter's language turns Baudelaire into a décor, a gesture which is part tribute to 'the greatest poet of alienation' (p. 18), and part critique of the 'exoticism' with which he invests the figure of Jeanne Duval, described as 'an ambulant fetish, savage, obscene, terrifying' (p. 20). Baudelaire's nostalgia is seen as one aspect of a broader Western colonial imaginary which linked blackness, degeneration and prostituted female sexuality in a multitude of late nineteenth- and early twentieth-century representations.[31]

Style presents Carter with a problem here: the problem of re-representing Baudelaire's icon without colluding with the Baudelairean eloquence which denies her language. Her stratagem is to construct a narrative voice which moves in and out of Jeanne Duval's subjectivity, and which moves between documentary and figurative registers. Sometimes this narratorial perspective identifies with the poet and embraces the fetishistic imaginary in which Jeanne figures; at others it identifies with Jeanne and exposes the banal character of the poet's fantasies. Carter's narrative perspective enacts an oscillation of identification and desire in which the permeability of fantasy (including its literary, male-authored inscriptions) across the boundaries of gender plays a large part.

In Carter's fictional completion of the known facts of Jeanne's life, she not only survives Baudelaire but returns to the West Indies to become a successful businesswoman in her own right. Yet Carter's stylistic investment in Baudelaire's text cannot help but reinscribe her, at least partially, within the iconic framework of the *Fleurs du mal*. Carter's reading of symbolism-modernism involves her in a double drag, since, as she shows, it turns on an imaginary identification with or impersonation of femininity. At the same time, Carter's story shows how Baudelaire's fetishising of Jeanne marks the limits of modernist subversion. The albatross, the aerialiste who 'dares death upon the high trapeze', before an audience of 'phlegmatic, monochrome, flightless birds' (p. 19), figures the self-lacerating irony generated by an oppositional yet independent relation to the bourgeoisie, a theme which, as I shall now argue, is of keen interest to Carter.

PROFESSIONALISM AND MASQUERADE

To assimilate Carter's work, through the mediation of poststructuralist semiology, to a revisionary feminist aesthetic, runs the risk of hypostatising, indeed of 'fetishising', a complex trajectory. For these formations of spectacular femininity trace Carter's ambiguous relation to the literary climate of 1960s and 1970s Britain, and her self-conscious invention of herself as a professional woman writer and woman of letters within it. In 'Notes from the Front Line' (1983), where Carter attempts to summarise the importance of feminism to her as a writer, she writes of her sense of herself as 'a new kind of being, unburdened with a past'. This new woman, Carter argues, has been freed by contraception to combine a career as a professional writer with a life as a sexually active woman. At the same time, running through the essay is an autobiographical reflection on the difficulty of acquiring this affirmative (not to say Utopian) political self-consciousness. Carter recurs more than once to her early propensity to use charm as a defensive strategy, 'especially when, however unconsciously, I was going straight for the testicles'.[32] One might note that the audience is gendered as male.

The founding text of 'gender performance', Joan Riviere's famous essay 'Womanliness as Masquerade' (1929), argues that the woman with professional ambitions often uses an exaggerated femininity in order to mask her identification with a supposedly masculine intellectual or creative power. Exaggeratedly feminine behaviour is a display of guiltlessness, an act of restitution to the father whose phallic power the woman desires, and a defence against the threat of symbolic castration. The transgressive wish or fantasy enacted behind the screen of placatory womanliness is the theft of the paternal phallus; thus the masquerade is a strategy for survival in a man's world. The spectre of this regressive tactic haunts even Carter's most avowedly and joyfully affirmative feminist texts.

As John Fletcher points out, 'The masquerade generates images and stories of a doubled female subject which may be retold from the position of the curious, suspicious, fascinated, masculine subject. The masquerade tells the story of the fetish from the other side of the screen.'[33] 'Gender performance' is therefore, I would argue, a double-edged sword in the analysis of Carter's work. It enables us to argue that Carter deploys masquerade-like tactics in order to expose the fictional and inessential character of femininity. But it also enables us to argue that she is at least equally engaged by the male scenario of fetishism which lies behind, and is required by, the female scenario of the masquerade.

The facts of social and intellectual mobility can give some historical content to the role of masquerade in Carter's work. In a recent collection of essays on Carter's work, Marina Warner refers to 'a specifically proletarian strategy of advancing, through the construction of self in image and language'.[34] Although I agree that Carter's style answers to a pattern of social and intellectual mobility, her strategy is surely not so much proletarian as petit-bourgeois, the mode of the newly enfranchised, post-war intellectual, whom Carter links, in her essay on the 1960s, with the post-war expansion of educational opportunities within the welfare state.[35] Theatricalism is the language of the female 'parvenue' whose critique of the establishment must always be conducted in the mode of a greedy and more or less fetishistic taking possession of its cultural properties, and which remains partly mortgaged to the heritage which it travesties. The psychoanalytical scenario of fetishism, like the Marxist scenario of commodity fetishism, opens up the problem of complicity with the structures of domination against which these texts are often ranged.

THE LIMITS OF CARNIVAL

Carter continuously reinvented herself as a writer. The 'sinister feats of male impersonation' give way to the cocky, carnivalesque and Cockney female impersonations of the last two novels. In *Nights at the Circus*, published in 1984 but set in 1899, the *fin de siècle* heroine, Fevvers, is a circus artiste, and a figure for the deployment of a self-conscious fictionality which also dares to attempt the suspension of disbelief. Fevvers's byline – 'Is she fact or is she fiction?' – suggests that, as John Stokes points out, 'Carter's thoroughgoing intertextuality turns the structuring of history into a confidence trick.'[36] Fevvers's larger-than-life music-hall persona as the Cockney Venus also allegorises the 'vulgarity' of Carter's writing – not only the 'overwriting', or stylistic excess, the agitated baroque display of the surface of the texts, but their self-consciously allegorical quality, the use of the narrative as a device for the patent exposition and exploration of ideas (such as the reworking of Foucault's *Discipline and Punish* in Part Three of the novel). Fevvers makes a virtue out of her specular objectification and positively demands to be looked at:

> Look at me! With a grand, proud, ironic grace, she exhibited herself before the eyes of the audience as if she were a marvellous present too good to be played with. Look, not touch.
>
> She was twice as large as life and as succinctly finite as any object that is intended to be seen, not handled. Look! Hands off! LOOK AT ME![37]

If the deployment of female spectacle/masquerade/transvestism starts out as part of Carter's demythologising project – to demonstrate that femininity is culturally produced – how does Carter arrive at a point, in her later career, where she can be read by contemporary feminist critics as celebrating spectacle as a viable means of self-empowerment for women? Carter stressed the allegorical nature of Fevvers, but the multiple overdeterminations of her heroine sit uneasily with one another, even by Carter's own account. Fevvers starts out as 'a metaphor come to life ... the Winged Victory' but she is also 'Mae West with wings' and emulates 'the way Mae West controls the audience response towards herself in her movies'.[38] Like Leilah in *Passion*, Fevvers has a revolutionary antitype in the shape of her foster mother Lizzie, who provides a severe Marxist and Foucauldian counterpoint and corrective to Fevvers's dreams of having it all – freedom, heterosexual love and money. For Lizzie, Fevvers is the New Woman heralding a New Century in which women will no longer be shackled by the bondage of nature and reproduction; but Fevvers is both more sentimental and more mercenary than her foster mother; for her, self-display is a means of power, and especially financial power. When the Circus is derailed and the performances are halted, Fevvers loses her looks and becomes the Feathered Frump; her vitality is seen to be dependent on the presence of an audience (*Nights*, p. 280), and in particular of her lover, Jack Walser. Fevvers may be the avatar of the 1890s New Woman but she is also a construct that reveals the ambivalent alignments of women with both consumer and commodity, a pressing theme in Thatcher's Britain.

Carnivalesque is Carter's way of puncturing the commodifying link between the spectator and the specular female object; Fevvers is a farting, lumbering, down-to-earth creature. It also dominates the representation of the Chance sisters, spectacular crones for whom 'The habit of applying warpaint outlasts the battle' (p. 6). In *Wise Children* (1990) music-hall is the carnivalesque deflator of the bombast of 'high culture', epitomised in the myth of Shakespeare's genius as 'national treasure' (p. 38). Music-hall is the illegitimate and unacknowledged child of the Shakespearian stage. But it could be argued that the novel ends up reinforcing this myth, notably in the scene at the end of the novel, in which Dora and Nora achieve their heart's desire when they are publicly reconciled with Melchior Hazard. A self-conscious and camp sentimentality licenses a reconstitution of the family under the sign of Shakespeare.

The Cockney comedy of the last two novels, and particularly of *Wise Children*, can be read in two very different ways: either in terms of evolutionary metaphors which see these novels as announcing reconciliation, maturity, synthesis or, in a quite different way, as a strategy for making the best of a bad job – namely, the failed millennial hopes of the 1960s.[39] The vernacular, salt-of-the-earth idiom of *Wise Children* seems to me as fabricated, as much of an impersonation, as anything else in Carter's writing. It is worth noting that both of the last novels find their inspiration and point of reference in pre-electronic forms of entertainment – the circus, the music-hall – a celebration which in some ways sidesteps the more troubling implications of the way in which subjectivity might be inflected by spectacle in a culture of consumption.

The carnivalesque philosophy of *Wise Children*, of 'Let's face the music and dance', seems profoundly inadequate to meet the challenges of the 1990s. Carter's astute comment on the vogue for Bakhtin and carnival as a sign for the defeated political hopes associated with other kinds of revolution provides a timely counterbalance to the tendency to celebrate the carnivalesque energies of her work under the banner of 'gender performance' theory, without examining the ambivalences and tensions which these energies mediate.[40] One of the reasons why Carter seems such a significant figure for women's writing is because her career is so clearly a map of the disappointments as well as the triumphs of feminism.

From *Textual Practice*, 9:3 (1995), 459–75.

NOTES

[Christina Britzolakis begins by dissenting from recent interest shown by some of Carter's commentators in using ideas about gender identity as something performed rather than given, fixed and permanent (see note 5 on Judith Butler in this essay). Britzolakis approaches both issues of postmodernity and the central theme of theatricality in Carter's work (involving spectacle, mimicry, masquerade, carnival) from a different perspective. Commodity fetishism as a category of economic analysis originates with Marx, and is used by Walter Benjamin to appropriate other psychoanalytic ideas of the fetish for his analysis of culture. (Carter had read Benjamin's work with admiration.) Using these concepts Britzolakis is able to approach from a different standpoint the recurrent critical question of the relationship between pleasure and politics in Carter's work and the issue of her possible, if unwitting collusion with that which she ostensibly wishes to demolish. Ed.]

1. Angela Carter, 'Notes from the Front Line', in *Gender and Writing*, ed. Michelene Wandor (London, 1983), p. 74.

2. John Haffenden, 'Angela Carter', in John Haffenden, *Novelists in Interview* (London, 1985), p. 91.

3. This comment on Angela Carter was made by Lorna Sage at a recent conference on Carter's work, 'Fireworks: Angela Carter and the Futures of Writing', at the University of York, 1994. I would like to thank the conference organiser, Joseph Bristow, for his insight and encouragement.

4. Carter, *Nights at the Circus* (London, 1984), p. 103.

5. Joan Riviere, 'Womanliness as Masquerade', *International Journal of Psychoanalysis*, 10 (1929), rpt. in *Formations of Fantasy*, ed. Victor Burgin, James Donald and Cora Kaplan (London, 1989), pp. 35–44. The contemporary influence of Riviere has been heavily mediated through the work of Jacques Lacan and Luce Irigaray, especially Lacan's essay, 'The Significance of the Phallus', in *Ecrits: A Selection*, trans. Alan Sheridan (London, 1977), pp. 281–91, and Irigaray, *This Sex Which Is Not One*, trans. Carolyn Porter (Ithaca, NY, 1985), pp. 132–4. One of the most influential contemporary appropriations is that of Judith Butler, who argues in *Gender Trouble: Feminism and the Subversion of Identity* (London, 1990) that gender is a matter not of 'core' identity but of discursively constrained performative acts. At the 'Fireworks' conference on Carter's work, a large number of the papers drew on psychoanalytical conceptions of masquerade and mimicry.

6. Carter, 'Notes', p. 70.

7. Ibid., p. 71.

8. Haffenden, 'Angela Carter', p. 82.

9. Ibid., p. 86.

10. For representative examples of these two positions, see Robert Clark, 'Angela Carter's Desire Machine', *Women's Studies*, 14 (1987), 147–61, and John Bayley, 'Fighting for the Crown', *The New York Review of Books*, 23 April 1992, 9–11.

11. Haffenden, 'Angela Carter', p. 88.

12. Paulina Palmer, 'From "Coded Manniquin" to "Bird Woman": Angela Carter's Magic Flight', in *Women Reading Women's Writing*, ed. Sue Roe (Brighton, 1987), pp. 179–205.

13. Carter, *Love* (London, 1987), p. 104.

14. Karl Marx, 'The Fetishism of Commodities and the Secret Thereof', in *Karl Marx: A Reader* (Cambridge, 1986), ed. John Elster, pp. 63–75.

15. Walter Benjamin, 'Paris – The Capital of the Nineteenth Century', in *Charles Baudelaire: A Lyric Poet in the Era of High Capitalism*, trans. Harry Zohin (London, 1983), p. 166.

16. For a suggestive discussion of the 'medicalised literariness' of the *fin de siècle* 'pathography' as a fetishistic discourse, see Emily Apter, *Feminizing the Fetish: Psychoanalysis and Narrative Obsession in Turn-of-the-Century France* (Ithaca, NY, 1991).

17. Sigmund Freud, 'Fetishism', in *Pelican Freud Library*, ed. Angela Richards and Albert Dickson (Harmondsworth, 1953–77), vol. 7, pp. 345–57. Freud adduces the foot or shoe as a prime example of the fetish, which is 'a substitute for the woman's (the mother's) penis that the little boy once believed in ... and does not want to give' (p. 352). The fetish is a memorial of the male castration complex as articulated around a primal act of looking: the boy-child's traumatic discovery of a phallic lack in the opposite sex.

18. Carter hints at Annabel's genealogy as a phantasm of the Romantic imagination when she refers in the Preface to Benjamin Constant's novel of sensibility, *Adolphe*, as a model. See also Sue Roe, 'The Disorder of *Love*: Angela Carter's Surrealist Collage', in *Flesh and the Mirror: Essays on the Art of Angela Carter*, ed. Lorna Sage (London, 1994), pp. 60–97.

19. Marc O'Day, ' "Mutability is Having a Field Day": The Sixties Aura of Angela Carter's Bristol Trilogy', in Sage, *Flesh and the Mirror*, pp. 24–59.

20. See, for example, Jean Baudrillard, *For a Critique of the Political Economy of the Sign*, trans. Charlers Levin (St Louis, 1981), and W. J. T. Mitchell, *Iconology: Image, Text, Ideology* (Chicago, 1986), pp. 151–208.

21. Laura Mulvey, 'Some Thoughts on Theories of Fetishism in the Context of Contemporary Culture', *October*, 65 (Summer 1993), 19. For Freud, fetishism is a paradigmatically male perversion, the normal component of which structures sexual difference around the castration complex. Recently, a number of feminist critics have attempted to appropriate Freudian fetishism for feminism. See Naomi Schor, 'Female Fetishism: The Case of George Sand', in *The Female Body in Western Culture*, ed. Susan Rubin Suleiman (Cambridge, MA, 1986), pp. 363–72; Apter, *Feminizing the Fetish*; and Lorraine Gamman and Merja Makinen, *Female Fetishism: A New Look* (London, 1994). For an argument against such appropriations as collusive with the norms of heterosexuality, see Marjorie Garber, 'Fetish Envy', *October*, 54 (Fall 1990), 45–56, rpt. in *Vested Interests: Cross-Dressing and Cultural Anxiety*, ed. Marjorie B. Garber (London, 1992), pp. 118–27.

22. Haffenden, 'Angela Carter', p. 91.

23. See, for example, Carter, 'Notes', p. 71; Haffenden, 'Angela Carter', p. 86.

24. See Rita Felski, 'The Counter-Discourse of the Feminine in Three Texts by Wilde, Huysmans and Sacher-Masoch', *PMLA*, 106:5 (1991), 1094–105, and 'The Gender of Modernity', in *Political Gender: Texts and Contexts*, ed. Sally Ledger, Josephine McDonagh and Jane Spencer (Hemel Hempsted, 1994), pp. 144–55.

25. Haffenden, 'Angela Carter', p. 92.

26. Carter, 'Notes', p. 73.

27. Haffenden, 'Angela Carter', p. 86.

28. Elaine Jordan, 'Enthralment: Angela Carter's Speculative Fictions', in *Plotting Change: Contemporary Women's Fiction*, ed. Linda Anderson (London, 1990), pp. 19–40.

29. Jordan, 'Fictions', p. 23.

30. Angela Carter, *Black Venus* (London, 1985), p. 9.

31. See Jill Matus, 'Blonde, Black and Hottentot Venus: Context and Critique in Angela Carter's "Black Venus"', *Studies in Short Fiction*, 8:4 (Fall, 1991), 467–76. [Reprinted in this volume, pp. 161–72 – Ed.]

32. Carter, 'Notes', pp. 75, 71.

33. John Fletcher, 'Versions of Masquerade', *Screen*, 29:3 (Summer 1988), 43–70. Fletcher argues that the specificity of Riviere's concept of the masquerade, along with its potential for critique, is lost in its frequent conflation with the Lacanian formula of 'woman as phallus' and with the Freudian concept of fetishism. My reading of Carter's texts supports this argument, although an exegesis of the theoretical literature

on fetishism and masquerade, much of which has been produced in the context of film theory, is outside the scope of my discussion.

34. Marina Warner, 'Angela Carter: Bottle Blonde, Double Drag', in Sage, *Flesh and the Mirror*, p. 248.

35. Angela Carter, 'Truly, It Felt Like Year One', in *Very Heaven: Looking Back on the Sixties*, ed. Sara Maitland (London, 1988), pp. 209–16.

36. John Stokes, 'Introduction', in *Fin-de-Siècle, Fin du Globe: Fears and Fantasies of the Late Nineteenth Century*, ed. John Stokes (New York, 1992), p. 7.

37. Carter, *Nights*, p. 15.

38. Haffenden, 'Angela Carter', pp. 92–3, 88.

39. Marina Warner also makes this point. See Sage, *Flesh and the Mirror*, p. 253.

40. Angela Carter, interview with Lorna Sage, cited by Marina Warner, in *Flesh and the Mirror*, p. 254.

10

Seriously Funny: *Wise Children*

KATE WEBB

I INTRODUCTION: CRISSCROSS

I'm sure Angela Carter would have been pleased to hear that the hottest thing in pop music these days[1] are two young mixed-race American rappers who wear their trousers back to front and call themselves 'CrissCross'. Carter's last work of fiction, *Wise Children* – in the spirit of the novel one could call it, perhaps, an old bird's-eye/I view of the social, cultural, imperial and sartorial history of the century now ending – is itself patterned with intersecting tracks and grooves that are made by her characters 'crossing, crisscrossing'[2] the globe; by the zigzagging lines of familial and artistic descent that reach across and into their lives; and by the writing itself, which passes through – often parodying – many genres and styles, yet remains something completely authentic and her own.

II FAMILY AND CULTURE: TWIN PEAKS

Wise Children is the story of 'the imperial Hazard dynasty that bestrode the British theatre like a colossus for a century and a half', and its bastard progeny, Dora and Nora Chance, identical twin girls who are illegitimate twice over: by birth, because their father, Melchior Hazard, denies his paternity of them time after time; and by profession, where, as a novelty act, they dance the boards in music hall, appear briefly as extras in an ill-fated Hollywood

192

musical, and finally undress (though never beyond the G-string) in seedy postwar strip shows like 'Nudes Ahoy!' and 'Nudes of the World!'.

The story is told by one of these lovely bastards, Dora, the wise-cracking, left-handed, southside twin sister who rakes over more than a century of family romance and history. As in all the best modern fiction, the action of the novel takes place in just one day. A special day, however: it is the anniversary of Shakespeare's birth-day, which happens also to be Dora's and Nora's own – this year their seventy-fifth. It's the birthday and centenary, too, of another set of twins, Melchior and Peregrine Hazard, father and uncle (but which is which?) of these performing sisters, 'The Lucky Chances'. The double-faced Hazard/Chance family is served up to the reader as a model for Britain and Britishness, obsessively dividing itself into upper and working class, high and low culture. And just as Dora proves these strict lines of demarcation to be false within her own family, so, too, her story shows the reader how badly they fit the complexity and hybridity of British society and culture.[3]

If it is relatively easy (and Carter has a lot of fun doing this) to show how we foster and exploit binary oppositions in culture in order to justify the domination and exclusion of others, and to sustain elite privilege in society, it is a much more complicated thing to respond to the fictions, the romances – family and otherwise – which we have built upon the idea of legitimacy and illegitimacy. Master of this dialectic is William Shakespeare, whose 'huge overar-ching intellectual glory'[4] dominates the English literary canon and whose work, like Carter's own, is brimful with ideas of doubleness, artificiality and parody. In *Wise Children*, Carter not only weaves Shakespeare's stories in and out of her own, she also reminds us of the extent to which his words and ideas impregnate English culture and life: his face is on the £20 note that Dora doles out to the fallen comic, Gorgeous George; and contemporary television programmes that poach their names from him, like *The Darling Buds of May*, *May to September* and *To the Manor Born*, all make pointed, if somewhat disguised, appearances in the novel.

Part of what attracts Carter to Shakespeare is his playing out of the magnetic relationship of attraction and repulsion that exists between the legitimate and the illegitimate, between energy and order. This occurs most famously, perhaps, in the sliding friendship of Prince Hal and Falstaff. Near the close of her story, Dora tries to reimagine one of Shakespeare's cruellest moments: what if Hal, on becoming king, had not rejected Falstaff, but dug him in the ribs and offered him a job instead? What if order was permanently rejected, and we lived life as a perpetual carnival? These questions are not answered directly (and I will return to her implied answers later), but this challenge to order, to the legitimate world, is made throughout the novel.

Dora, illegitimate as she is, may sympathise with some of Falstaff's bastard qualities, but her story is not one of martyrdom or victimhood. She knows that as outsiders she and her sister Nora are given freedoms for which their legitimate twin sisters, Imogen and Saskia, could never hope. When Dora describes Nora's first sexual experience, she warns her reader not to:

> run away with the idea that it was a squalid, furtive miserable thing, to make love for the first time on a cold night in a back alley with a married man with strong drink on his breath. He was the one she wanted, warts and all, she *would* have him, by hook or by crook. She had a passion to know about life, all its dirty corners, and this is how she started.
>
> (p. 81)

Wise Children, then, not only challenges legitimacy, it is also a celebration of the vitality of otherness. Paradoxically, though, because the legitimate and illegitimate worlds rely upon one another's mirror-image of difference through which to define themselves, such a celebration of illegitimacy necessarily implies a valorisation of the system which produces outcasts. Knowing this, one of the questions Carter asks us in the novel is: What, then, should a wise child do? Revel in wrong-sidedness and, therefore, the system that produces it, or jettison the culture of dualism altogether? In answer, Carter's wise – though by now somewhat wizened – child, Dora, pulls off the sort of conjuring trick that her Falstaffian Uncle Perry is famous for: she manages both to have her cake and eat it, to revel in her wrong-sidedness, to sustain her opposition to authority, and yet to show that the culture and society she inhabits is not one of rigid demarcation, but has always been mixed up and hybrid: Shakespeare may have become the very symbol of legitimate culture, but his work is characterised by bastardy, multiplicity and incest; the Hazard dynasty may represent propriety and tradition, but they, too, are an endlessly orphaned, errant, and promiscuous bunch.

III CULTURE AND IMPERIALISM

'High' Culture: William's Word

The Hazard family is a patriarchal institution, but its father figures (Ranulph and later his son, Melchior) find their authority deriving not from God, but from a Shakespeare who has come to seem omnipotent in the hegemony of British culture, to embody not only artistic feeling but religious and national spirit too: for Ranulph, 'Shakespeare was a kind of God. ... It was as good as idolatry. He thought the whole of human life was there.' By becoming, each in his generation, the 'greatest living Shakespearian', Ranulph and then Melchior assume a kingly status themselves. Having so often rehearsed the role of Shakespearian prince or king, these actors take on the mantle of royalty itself: 'the Hazards belonged to everyone. They were a national treasure.'

At a late stage in the family's history, mirroring the collapse both of empire and of royalty, the imbrications of 'The Royal Family of the theatre' make them appear as vulgar and commercialised as our latter-day House of Windsor. Like them, the Hazard dynasty becomes national sport, soap opera masquerading as news. But in earlier times this regal troupe of players are not only commodities for the country ('national treasure'), they are agents of Britain's colonial ambition. Before the fall of the House of Hazard, Ranulph's evangelical zeal for spreading the Word of Shakespeare is so great that he 'crosses, crisscrosses' the globe, travelling 'to the ends of the empire' in his efforts to sell the religion of Shakespeare and the English values he represents:

> Ranulph. He was half mad and thought he had a Call. Now he saw the entire world as his mission field ... [in] the family tradition of proselytising zeal ... the old man was seized with the most imperative desire, to go on spreading the Word overseas.
>
> (p. 17)

In Tasmania, Shanghai, Hong Kong, Singapore, Montreal, Toronto, Alberta and even Gun Barrel, North Dakota, Ranulph Hazard's travelling theatre troupe meet in their audience a passion for self-fashioning as great as Shakespeare's own. As a consequence, they leave in their wake around the globe a string of towns called Hazard.

Throughout *Wise Children* Carter celebrates the vital and carnivalesque in life. 'What a joy it is to dance and sing!' is Dora's refrain, but she is aware of the effect that the enthusiasm and self-absorption of carnival can have upon others: aware, too, of the ways in which this power can be harnessed by a dominant group and brought to bear upon a weaker one. So she celebrates the craziness, 'a kind of madness', that drives old Ranulph to travel the world taking Englishness to foreigners, yet deftly shows how intimately connected are Shakespeare's cultural domination and British imperialism.

Carter's connecting of art and religion reinforces this idea: Ranulph sees it as his 'mission' in life to perform Shakespeare throughout the world in order to persuade other people of the greatness of the Bard's words, just as missionaries took the Bible and tried to persuade 'natives' of the truth of God's Word. Ranulph Hazard's theatre troupe literally follow in the steps of religious evangelicalism – his 'patched and ravaged tent went up in the spaces vacated by the travelling evangelicals'. They perform in 'wild, strange and various places', and their costumes are 'begged or improvised or patched and darned'. Cultural hegemony may have been an important part of the imperial vision, but acting, Carter reminds us, has always been an illegitimate profession: peripatetic, thrown-together, made-up and sexually ambivalent (in Central park, Estella plays Hamlet in drag). Theatre, and particularly the theatre of Shakespeare, has played its role in colonising the minds of other countries, but it is also a potentially destabilising and subversive force.

'Low' Culture: Gorgeous George

'Tragedy, eternally more class than comedy,' sighs Dora, meaning both that it has a classier pedigree than comedy and that it is associated with the classes rather than the masses. Carter's qualification, however, points to her conviction that, like everything else in life, art form (choosing to write comedy rather than tragedy) is a question of politics.[5] 'Comedy is tragedy that happens to other people,' she says (taking in the process, perhaps, a swipe at Martin Amis,[6] whose comedies often are).

Dora first encounters the comic Gorgeous George when she is thirteen, entertaining the masses on Brighton pier. Uncle Perry arrives unexpectedly in Brixton with a carload of good things to eat and drink, and packs the ersatz Chance family (Dora and Nora, Grandma and one of Perry's many foundlings, 'our Cyn') off to Brighton for the day. There they find George; a combination of

Frankie Howerd ('*Filthy* minds, some of you have') and Larry Grayson ('Say no more'), he comes in the tradition of the holiday *camp* entertainer and his jokes are endlessly insinuating, every phrase or object carrying with it some double, sexual meaning. Sex is everywhere and with it, therefore, the possibility of incest. Reflecting England's fallen status, George's jokes mock ideas of strength and purity, and fuel paternal anxiety about redundancy and impotency. His comedy is parodic and slippery and perfectly timed, and his punchline, when it's finally delivered, is a withering attack on a foolishly deluded old patriarch who thinks himself the greatest stud around: the son, taken in by his father's boasts of promiscuity, becomes worried about committing incest with some unknown bastard offspring, but his mother tells him not to worry because, after all: '*E*'s not your father.' *B-bum!*

George's final *coup de grâce*, after singing 'Rose of England', 'Land of Hope and Glory', 'God Save the King' *and* 'Rule Britannia', is to strip off before his dazzled audience and reveal a torso tattooed with a map of the world: 'George was not a comic at all but an enormous statement.' But even a statement as blatant as the pink- (for British colonies) dominated world (Dora smartly picks out Ireland, South Africa and the Falkland Islands) emblazoned across the body of this latter-day St George is fraught with ambiguity. Unlike St George of old, Gorgeous George no longer wins battles and rules the waves; he merely represents the idea of conquest. He is a walking metaphor, an effete mirror-image. George shows us an empire falling: having once dominated the world, this Englishman can now be master of only one space: his own body.

George's decline, like the British Empire's, continues apace. Dora encounters him once more as an anachronistic Bottom (his kind of peculiarly English comedy doesn't travel) in the Hollywood production of *A Midsummer Night's Dream*, a débâcle over which Melchior presides, and in which she and Nora have bit parts (they play Mustardseed and Peaseblossom). Finally, back in London, George ends up hitting rock bottom: Dora, catching a glimpse of his pink tattoo, recognises him in the pathetic street beggar who approaches her for the price of a cup of tea.

Fallen

If Shakespeare provides English literary culture with a model for plurality, it is in Milton, particularly in *Paradise Lost*, that we find a model for dualism in the world, a dualism resulting from the patriarchal and monistic vision of Christianity. One of Dora's refrains (she has a few up her sleeve) is the Miltonic phrase 'Lo, how the mighty are fallen', which is both a silly semantic joke and a serious intimation of the world she inhabits. Many of the descriptions of fallenness in *Wise Children* are specifically Miltonic or Christian: for instance, both Melchior and Peregrine are figured as Godlike *and* Satanic. Peregrine lands into the lives of the naked, innocent, unselfconscious and therefore Eve-like Nora and Dora as Adam arrived on earth: out of nowhere. And it is of Adam that Dora thinks when she sees him, because this is to be her First Man, the man who, like the fallen angel Lucifer, will first seduce her. In the same way, Melchior, 'our father' who 'did not live in heaven' but who, God-like, is worshipped by the girls from afar, is also given a Satanic side: he appears 'tall, dark and handsome' with 'knicker shifting' eyes, dressed in 'a black evening cape with a scarlet lining'. Later he is Count Dracula (a late-nineteenth-century Satanic pretender), ordering Dora and Nora to carry dirt over from Stratford – as Dracula had carried it from Transylvania – to scatter on the Hollywood set of his film of *A Midsummer Night's Dream*.

In Hollywood, the English colony represents a parody version of the once great Empire, playing Disraeli, Queen Victoria and Florence Nightingale. Just as in Ranulph's generation English theatre was shown to embody the nation's imperial strength, so now the film industry in Hollywood symbolises America's new role as a world power. Melchior's attempt to produce a film version of *A Midsummer Night's Dream* is his way of trying to conquer Hollywood, 'his chance to take North America back for England, Shakespeare and St George'. But the trip to Hollywood is presaged by the burning down of Melchior's manor house, and with the English theatre symbolically erased in the fire, 'the final degeneration of the House of Hazard' ensues. Ultimately we find Melchior's son, Tristram, the 'weak but charming, game-show presenter and television personality, last gasp of the imperial Hazard dynasty', presiding over an S/M game.

The End

The sense of limitless freedom that I, as a woman, sometimes feel *is* that of a new kind of being. Because I simply could not have existed, as I am, in any other preceding time or place. I am the pure product of an advanced industrialised, post-imperialist country in decline.[7]

It is typical of Carter that unlike many modernist writers she sees in the decline of empire – to adapt Brecht – not the death of bad old things but the birth of good new ones – her own liberation, for instance. Symbolising the newness that the death of the old might now bring into being, *Wise Children* is secreted with what Salman Rushdie, in a short story, called 'the eggs of love':[8] Dora's and Nora's bottoms jiggle like hard-boiled eggs; there are dried eggs during the war and smuggled black-market ones; Scotch eggs that landladies put out for supper; and in the snow, Dora sees egg-shaped depressions.

This is a cuspy, millennial novel, and 'millennia', Carter believes, 'always get strange towards the end'.[9] Part of *Wise Children*'s strangeness is due, perhaps, to the disconcerting sense of beginnings and possibility at the moment of ending, of death. The story's finale has a riotous celebration for the now-centenarian Melchior and Peregrine, after which Dora (who, at seventy-five, has herself been thinking about calling it a day), finds that she and Nora have suddenly had motherhood thrust upon them. They toddle home – these unmarried, non-biological and overage mothers – 'Drunk in charge of a baby carriage'.

Death has a strong presence in this book – not just the end of empire or the death of the patriarch, which Dora is happy to let go, but a sense of the presence of death in the midst of life. Dora is someone who wrestles with this, a spirited fighter who refuses to grieve for long, or give in to defeat. 'Let other pens dwell on guilt and misery', our autodidact narrator recites from Jane Austen. Dora's optimism derives from both a moral and a political sense of duty learned at her grandma's knee, whose often-recited maxim 'Hope for the best, expect the worst' lies on the map somewhere between Gramsci's 'Pessimism of the intellect, optimism of the will' and St Augustine's 'Don't presume, don't despair'. Neither she nor Nora sheds a tear at the news of their beloved Tiffany's death, though both are heartbroken by it. 'Life must go on,' says Nora, refusing to be engulfed by despair.

One of *Wise Children*'s characteristic inversions of the supposed order of life is that no one dies of old age, all are 'untimely' deaths – the only 'true tragedy', Dora says wisely: Grandma, hit by a flying bomb on her way to the off-licence; Cyn's husband, killed in North Africa in the war, and Cyn herself succumbing to the Asian flu of '49 (the cat to the cat flu of '51); Dora's lover, Irish, makes his last exit in Hollywood, caused by too much booze and a 'dicky-ticker'; finally, there is the apparent suicide of their godchild, the young, mixed-race

Tiff, who, Ophelia-like, seems to have made her suicide a watery one, into the bosom of Old Father Thames. But this is just one of the instances in which – to use Edward Said's[10] phrase – Carter 'writes back'. Her Ophelia does not give in to patriarchal abuse (by committing suicide in Father Thames): like Carter she, too, imagines herself as 'a new kind of being', and in the end it is she (the illegitimate outsider) who lays down the new rules of play for the Hazard dynasty.

IV   A LOOKING-GLASS WORLD

Pluralism and Difference

In *Wise Children*, Carter is able to suggest a jumbled, impure multi-culture, while showing clearly that class, racial and sexual elites which seek to exclude otherness are still a powerful and conditioning force. A reader of Foucault, Carter fully understood the way in which the dualistic structures that belong to the dying past – to Christianity, patriarchy and empire – are still extant in the present.[11] By showing Shakespeare at the heart of English culture, as the 'author of our being', father to both the Hazards and the Chances (legitimate and illegitimate share his birthday), Carter is arguing that plurality and hybridity are not simply conditions of modernity, products of its wreckage, but have always existed and are characteristic of life itself. From this it follows that she does not see in plurality, as many postmodernists do, a nihilistic loss of value; rather, an existential acceptance of the facts of life and death in which contradictions are a sign of hope, and difference has to be negotiated rather than fought over as if there were only one place of rightness, one correct way of living that must be identically reproduced the whole world over. This is something that Dora's grandma knows innately – feels it, as Dora does, 'in her ancient water'. When, in wartime, she waves her stick in the air at the bombers overhead, she recognises that war is a result of patriarchal insistence upon monism: men fight to wipe out women and children (whom 'she knew they hated ... worst of all' – because they are most other); but forever locked in some recidivist oedipal struggle, they fight, as well, to stop younger men stealing their thunder, to stop them taking away their distinguished mantles of poet or god.

Glasshouse Fun

But while men continue to fight wars, to battle for absolute control of land or language, Carter tells us we live now in a world of endless refraction. The days when a looking-glass reflected just one wicked witch, one absolute image of otherness, are gone. Now we have cinema, television, radio and video splintering the world 'in a gallery of mirrors',[12] a glasshouse of perpetual reproduction. Our relationship to these multiple, often contradictory reflections, especially for women, is as important and as determining as our relationship to other people. It is this awareness, critics like Lorna Sage[13] have argued, that defines much of Carter's work, and makes it unique.

In *Wise Children*, however, the glasshouse is not the house of horror, the bloody chamber we have peered into with Carter so often in the past. These characters are not the glassy, fragile forms of some of her reworked fairy stories, eternally caged by images not of their own making. Dora's narrative is a much freer, bouncier one, with a resilience that comes from a new kind of resourcefulness. Perhaps we have now lived long enough with our shadow selves, Carter seems to be suggesting, that we are at last learning how to gain some control over them. Dora is a toughie, a survivor and a canny self-observer, and is not imprisoned by her female sexuality or the multitude of images of femininity that surround her. Rather, she seems like one of Shakespeare's bastards, Edmund, determined not to let the Dionysian wheel of fate[14] settle her life, but to find in the *chance* of her wrong-sidedness neither shame nor restraint, but opportunity. Because of this Dora is able to enjoy her own body, and the bodies of other women too. Maybe one of the meanings of the twins is a rather Laingian[15] one: the idea that one need not be afraid of one's image, but should embrace it, love it instead. Like the autoerotic Dora and Nora, one can 'feast' on oneself. (However, this enlightening idea finds its dark equation on the Hazard side, where the family seal is of an animal devouring itself – a pelican pecking at its own breast. This is because in a value system that is monistic, self-love – as I suggested above in the case of Ranulph and Melchior – inevitably implies incest or its correlative, cannibalism.)

V   FAMILY ROMANCE AND FAMILY SECRETS

'Dread and delight coursed through my veins. I thought what have I done ...' Perhaps part of the reason for Dora's dread and delight, when she momentarily wonders whether, as a young girl, she had fucked her Uncle Perry, has to do with the idea of gaining power not with a man's weapon – his strength; but with a woman's – her sex. One way for Dora, the outsider, to gain access to the power and legitimacy of 'the House of Hazard' is to fuck her way inside, or at least to bring it to its knees by transgressing its laws of order and hierarchy: uncles are not supposed to have sex with their nieces, particularly not when they are only thirteen – Dora's age, it finally transpires, when Peregrine first seduced her.

Wise Children is like the proverbial Freudian nightmare – aided and abetted (as Freud was himself) by Shakespearian example. Dora's family story is crammed with incestuous love and oedipal hatred: there are sexual relationships between parent and child (where this is not technically so, actor-parents marry their theatrical offspring – in two generations of Hazards, Lears marry Cordelias); and between sister and brother (Melchior's children Saskia and Tristram). And there is oepidal hatred between child and parent (Saskia twice tries to poison her father, and she and her twin sister Imogen are guilty either of pushing their mother down a flight of stairs or at least of leaving her there, an invalid, once she has fallen); and between parent and child ('All the same, he [Ranulph] loved his boys. He cast them as princes in the tower as soon as they could toddle').[16]

Nor is Dora's name accidental. In another example of 'writing back', Carter's Dora, unlike her Freudian namesake, suffers very little psychic damage from lusting after her father (she 'fell in love the first time she saw him') or her uncle, or a string of father substitutes (men old enough to be) with whom she has affairs. The fact that it is the female (sisterly) body which seems most erotic to her (the nape of Saskia's neck, Nora's jiggling bottom) is for this Dora a cause for celebration, rather than self-hatred. Her half-sisters, Saskia and Imogen, fare less well in this game of family romance. On hearing that her father, Melchior, is about to marry her best friend (another form of incest), 'Saskia's wails approached hysteria, whereupon Melchior smartly smacked her cheek … She shut up at once.' It is because of this betrayal, and her father's silencing of her anger, that Saskia takes revenge by seducing the couple's son and her half-brother, Tristram.

Ironically, then, it is the legitimate daughters, Saskia and Imogen, who end up emotionally crippled by their family relationships (though this, perhaps, is a reflection of how rotten the family has become). These weird and troubled sisters might have received greater attention in Carter of an earlier vintage, but here Dora asserts: 'I refuse point-blank to play in tragedy.' Perhaps because in dealing with illegitimacy in the past, particularly female illegitimacy, Carter, in her highly wrought and self-conscious work, had sometimes aestheticised pain, even death, now, facing her own, she wanted to face it more squarely or not at all:[17] 'We knew nothing was a matter of life and death except life and death.'

Dora's story-telling is a spilling of all the family secrets, bringing the skeletons out of the closet and exposing them to bright lights. This is a comment in itself: no more family secrets, no more lies, no more illegitimacies, Dora seems to assert, yet there is a powerful and unresolved tension in *Wise Children* between the idea of family secrets and family romance. As the Hazard/Chance family has been shown in the novel to symbolise the broader culture, so too, there is a tension between a desire for openness and equality – a world without secrets or bastards – and the seductive pull of romances from unofficial places, stories from the wrong side of the blanket, from 'the wrong side of the tracks'.

VI HOW SHE WRITES

Mikhail Bakhtin argued that language is inherently dialogic because it implies a listener who must also be another speaker.[18] It's a proposition that Carter, the iconoclast, agreed with and tried to illuminate in her writing: 'A piece of fiction is never static. I purposely try to make what I write open-ended, "user-friendly".'[19] She demonstrates this in *Wise Children* by employing a first-person narrator (a form, she said, that men were afraid to use, because it was too revealing). Carter's mouthpiece, 'I, Dora Chance', speaks to her reader as if she expected him or her to reply: 'There I go again! Can't keep a story going in a straight line, can I?' At the beginning of the book Dora tells us that she is writing her autobiography on a word-processor on the morning of her seventy-fifth birthday, but the vernacular force of her speech is so great that later she magically appears to transcend the written word, becoming, instead, the old bird who's collared you in the local boozer:

> Well, you might have known what you were about to let yourself in for when you let Dora Chance in her ratty old fur and poster paint, her orange (Persian Melon) toenails sticking out of her snakeskin peep-toes, reeking of liquor, accost you in the Coach and Horses[20] and let her tell you a tale.
>
> (p. 227)

Dora's a reader-teaser, endlessly drawing attention to herself by postponing the moment of revelation ('but I don't propose to tell *you*, not now ... ') or prodding her reader into paying attention because 'Something unscripted is about to happen'. She's also a de-mythologiser, keen to let her reader in on the tricks of the trade: a chronicler not just of the Hazard and Chance families but of fashion through the ages – talking about brand names, she says: 'If you get little details like that right, people will believe anything.' As with this last sentence, her gist is always more than surface level, and a huge part of the fun of reading *Wise Children* lies in seeing how far you can unpack the layers of meaning. How far, too, you can unpick the words of others that have been woven into Carter's/Dora's own. There is Shakespeare everywhere, but other writers also: Milton, Sterne, Wordsworth ('If the child is father of the man ... then who is the mother of the woman?'), Dickens, Lewis Carroll making an appearance as a purveyor of 'kiddiporn', Samuel Butler, Shaw, Dostoevsky ('My crime is my punishment'), Henry James and Tennessee Williams ('They lived on room service and the kindness of strangers') are just a random selection.

Like any postmodern novel worth its salt, *Wise Children* not only steals freely from other literary texts but also takes from the texts of other people's lives and uses these too. In Hollywood, Carter has a field day. Armed, I'd say, with the dirt-dishing Kenneth Anger,[21] she has a roster of stars making guest appearances – sometimes as themselves, sometimes in various kinds of drag: featured players are Charlie Chaplin 'hung like a horse', Judy Garland (Ranulph's wife is known as Estella 'A Star Danced' Hazard, and was 'born in a trunk'), Busby Berkeley, Fred Astaire and his wife Adele, Astaire and Ginger Rogers, Ruby Keeler, Jessie Matthews, Josephine Baker, Jack Warner, W. C. Fields, Gloria Swanson, Paul Robeson, Orson Welles ('old buffers in ... vintage port and miniature cigar commercials'), Clark Gable, Howard Hughes, Ivor Novello and Noël Coward (Dora's and Nora's first dancing teacher is called Mrs Worthington). Daisy Duck with her missing back molars (it enhances the cheekbones) is a mixture of Lana Turner and Jean Harlow, ending up like Joan Crawford in TV soaps giving 'good décolleté'. Daisy's 'peel me a prawn' line is Mae West's 'Beulah, peel me a grape' from *I'm No Angel*, and her Puck, with a 'face like an old child', is Mickey Rooney, who starred as Robin Goodfellow in the original Hollywood version of *A Midsummer Night's Dream*. Erich von Stroheim is the model for Genghis Khan, the whip-cracking, jodhpured director with a penchant for cruelty and steak-eating orchids, and Dora's alcoholic, scriptwriting boyfriend Irish is an amalgam of many writers – Scott Fitzgerald, Nathaniel West and William Faulkner – finally succumbing to the abundant alcohol and indifference doled out in equal measures by the studio system. There's a veiled portrait, too, of Brecht in Hollywood, whom Dora employs to teach her German and likes because he's one of the few people she meets out there who aren't terminally optimistic: 'What I say is, fuck the bourgeoisie.'

Wise Children has songs, too: music-hall and patriotic war songs, jazz and pop. And good and bad jokes: as well as Carter's own ('Why are they called Pierrots?' ... 'Because they do their stuff on piers'), she pastiches older camp comedians like Frankie Howerd and Larry Grayson, and picks up on the more recent Thatcherite humour of Harry Enfield's 'Loads a'money', turning it into Tristram's ghastly catchphrase 'Lashings of Lolly'.

If her sources of material are eclectic, so too is her method of writing – Carter trips lightly through many styles and genres: she is an expressionist who paints 'a female city, red-eyed, dressed in black ...'; a magical realist, a student of Hawthorne, Nabokov and Borges, wreathing Perry in magic butterflies; a graffitist scratching 'Melchior slept here' across her page; and a montage Surrealist: 'She was our air-raid shelter; she was our entertainment; she was our breast.' Carter is a conjuror baiting her audience – 'All in good time I shall reveal to you how ...'; a romance novelist who knows where the big bucks are to be found – 'Romantic illegitimacy, always a seller'; a teller of tall tales – 'If you'll believe that ...', and wise old wives' tales. She's a reteller of fairy stores – 'Once upon a time ...'/ 'It had come to pass ...'; an autobiographer and 'inadvertent chronicler', farceur and tragedian, fabulist and 'rival realist' – Sage's[22] phrase for Carter's through-the-looking-glass world.

But just as this is a wise book, knowing about culture, history and politics, it is also a childlike one. The house at 49 Bard Road that Dora and Nora live in all their lives is reminiscent of the kind found in English children's stories. Its large musty rooms and odd-striking grandfather clock, (mysteriously) absent father and mother, and presiding grandmother left to eke out the rent by taking in strange boarders, are all staples of the genre. Orphaned children are free children – free of the sexually proscribing authority of their mum and dad, at least, so perhaps the (Wildean) habit of rather forgetfully losing your parents in these stories (as it patently is in

Wise Children), is strategic: a way of allowing characters a little more space in which to fashion themselves.

Finally, as well as employing all these styles in her own writing, Carter shows us how a familiarity with many ways of seeing is a part of the modern condition: Dora is not only a passive observer of different genres, she also employs them to shape her own world. She does this to heighten experience, but also self-consciously, even paradoxically, to gain a sense of the constructedness of life by turning people into actors. For instance, when Estella leaves for America she imagines herself in a scene from a movie, and when Melchior, at the age of twelve, absconds from the home of his 'dour as hell' puritan aunt, he does so as a character from a children's story, as Dick Whittington.

VII   THE ANXIETY OF PATERNITY

Literal Fathers

The question of paternity arises everywhere in *Wise Children*. Just 'what does a father do?' and 'what is he for?', Dora asks. And well she might, given the example of the Hazard men, all of whom disown their children in one way or another. Ranulph leaves his twin sons Tristram and Gareth, fatherless, abandoning them when he shoots their mother and himself in a lovers' quarrel; Melchior and Peregrine, learning from their father's example, are equally forgetful about their fatherly responsibilities. Melchior forgets to love his children, and when he remembers, it's the chilly, arm's-length affection that the wealthy inadequately bestow on their young. He denies paternity of Dora and Nora altogether, of course – the bastard girls he sired with his landlady one night in Brixton. (Perhaps the reason Grandma creates a romance out of her origins and out of Dora's and Nora's is to protect them from their repudiating father, to allow them the freedom of making themselves up rather than being determined by Melchior's dismissal.) His brother Peregrine, a lavisher of all kinds of love, while watching wistfully after Saskia (and this is ambivalent – are his feelings for her sexual or fatherly?), denies his paternity of both her and her twin sister Imogen.

At the end of this line, Tristram stands no chance as a parent. Not, that is, until his lover, Tiffany, fights back, makes demands upon him, setting down preconditions for his fatherhood. What

Carter hints at here is that it is the absence of practising fathers that causes so much grief and confusion: meaning that fathers, having never properly experienced fatherly feelings, often confuse them with sexual ones – hence the tradition of marrying your daughter, of Lears loving Cordelias, in the Hazard family. In the same way, absent fathers are mysterious fathers, which is why these enigmatic creatures become, for their children, the object of such longing and romance.

However, it is the errant behaviour of fathers that creates, among the Hazards and the Chances, so much opportunity for the breakdown of order, for transgression. It seems that in some way fatherly absence is what creates the carnival. That men are such recalcitrant parents stems from their carnival instincts, a sense of narcissism (Peregrine is far too self-involved to be able to give himself permanently as a parent); selfishness (Melchior is more interested in his work than in his children); and a desire not to be controlled or determined within a family order which limits the patriarch just as it confines women.

The only father who escapes this pattern of paternal abuse is Gareth, Tristram's twin brother, who carries on the evangelical tradition of the Hazard family in the Church rather than the theatre. A disciple of 'liberation theology', Gareth is the only 'non-combatant' father, not engaged in the 'titanic' warfare between parent and child. But he achieves this new stance in the same old Hazard way: by abandoning his children, leaving them with Perry, who passes them on at the birthday finale as a very special gift to Nora, who had always wanted to be a mother.

Literary Fathers

Such fatherly ambivalence, Carter suggests in *Wise Children*, might be rooted not only in carnival selfishness but in the anxiety of paternity: the eternal 'gigantic question mark over the question of their paternity'. It is this forever unresolved uncertainty about their role in biological creativity that has led men to create a mystique around artistic, and especially literary, creativity: as critics like Gilbert and Gubar have shown, the anxiety of paternity is translated into the anxiety of authorship. Here, however, Carter seems to be arguing that women, whose role in biological creativity is not in doubt ('"Father" is a hypothesis but "mother" is a fact'), should now begin to shrug off the male anxiety that they, as writers, have been made to assume, and stop asking questions such as 'Is the pen a

phallus?'[23] Dora does not romanticise or transform sex into something other than it is (which is what men do in their mystifying of
the creative process, to cover their feelings of inadequacy); she
enjoys it for what it is. A straight-thinking woman, Dora would
never mistake a pen for a penis.

VIII   CARNIVAL GIRLS AND CARNIVAL BOYS

As I suggested above, the Bakhtinian idea of carnival is central to
Wise Children. In particular, Carter plays out ideas about sexuality's relationship to the carnivalesque transgression of order – a
transgression that is, according to Bakhtin, at once both sanctioned
and illegitimate. Jane Miller has argued in a collection of essays that
because of the breakdown of all barriers, particularly linguistic and
bodily ones, that carnival entails, women do not appear in
Bakhtin's work as distinct from men: carnival's amassing experience, which collapses laughter with fear, pleasure with nausea,
where the world becomes 'infinitely reversible and remakeable',
ends up denying female difference. The reason Miller tenders for
'the inability of even these writers [Bakhtin, Volosinov and other
Formalists who are interested in power] to make gender difference
and sexual relations central to their work' is that they are limited by
their 'particular history and their own place in it'. What Carter
seems to suggest in *Wise Children*, however, is a prior problem. It is
not just a question of Bakhtin denying difference, denying 'those
pains and leakages that are not common to both sexes',[24] but that
women and carnival might, ultimately, be inimical because female
biology and the fact of motherhood make women an essentially
connecting force, while carnival is essentially the celebration of
transgression and breakdown.

Without entering into the debate about whether transgression can
be revolutionary if it is sanctioned by authority,[25] perhaps it is in
this seeming paradox in Bakhtin's argument – that carnival's transgressions are both allowed and disallowed – that we can see how
well suited a model carnival is to masculinity, and how ill suited it
is to femininity.

Although some women in *Wise Children* possess characteristics
that might be thought of as carnivalesque, it is a man, Peregrine,
who embodies it: he is 'not so much a man, more of a travelling
carnival'. Peregrine is red and rude, a big man and, in the classic

Rabelaisian manner, a boundary-buster, growing bigger all the time. To Dora and Nora he is the proverbial rich American uncle, a sugar daddy whose fortunes dramatically rise and fall but who, when he is in the money, spreads his bounty around with extravagance and enjoyment. He is a big bad wolf of an uncle, too, a randy old devil who seduces the pubescent Dora when she is just thirteen. He is a multiple man, and his multiplicity makes him as elusive as the butterflies he ends up pursuing as a lepidopterist in the Brazilian jungle: to Dora and Nora 'He gave ... all his histories, we could choose which ones we wanted – but they kept on changing, so. That was the trouble.' He is a contradictory presence, a very 'material ghost', in whom Dora sees all her lovers pass by as she and he make love at Melchior's tumultuous birthday party.

If Peregrine's history is unknowable because it is so multiple, Grandma's origins are unknown because she refuses to reveal them: 'our maternal side founders in a wilderness of unknowability'. Grandma arrived in Bard Road at the beginning of the century with no past but enough money to set her going for a year. She is a mystery woman, dateless, nameless, 'She'd invented herself, she was a one-off', just as later she invents her family. And like Perry, she is a woman of contradictions, a naturist who happily reveals her naked body to the world, yet speaks with an elocuted voice, a disguise that sometimes slips as she forgets herself and 'talks up a blue streak'. She and Perry get along famously – they are kindred spirits who joke about the idea of their being married.

Estella, Dora and Nora's 'real' grandmother, also comes close to one of the few descriptions of womanhood in Bakhtin's work ('she represents ... the undoing of pretentiousness, of all that is finished, completed, exhausted'): Estella's 'hair was always coming undone ... tumbling down her back, spraying out hairpins in all directions, her stockings at half-mast, her petticoat would come adrift in the middle of the street, her drawers start drooping. She was a marvel, and she was a mess.' And through her affair with a younger man, Estella is the undoing of Ranulph's old order. But unlike Perry, who is able to skip away from all his sexual transgressions, Estella is destroyed in the *Othello*esque orgy of jealousy and retribution that ensues from her affair.

In the same way, Saskia is a force who wreaks havoc, but like Estella she, too, pays a price. If Saskia's disruptiveness is carnivalesque, there is little of the carnival's laughter in her. Saskia's anger, as it commonly is in women, is directed to the domestic sphere of food and cooking. As a child she'd played a witch in a production of her father's *Macbeth*, 'but she'd shown more interest in the contents of her cauldron than her name in lights'. In later life she continues to be an 'unnatural' witchy woman who, rather than nurturing, seems intent upon poisoning people. From the age of five, when she's seen under a bush devouring the bloody carcass of a swan, to her twenty-first birthday party, when she serves up a duck 'swimming in blood', her conspicuous consumption of meat is perhaps some sort of profane attempt to make herself feel legitimate, to be flesh of her father's flesh. But finally, Melchior's marriage to her best friend forces Saskia to recognise herself as a terminal outsider and, unable to gain the love she needs from her father, she sets about poisoning him instead. (Conversely, the motherly Grandma, who repudiates men, is an avid vegetarian: 'she'd a passion for salads, it went with all that naturism. During her strictest periods, she'd make us a meal of a cabbage, raw in summer, boiled in winter.')

The Lady Atalante Lynde, Melchior's first wife, after falling downstairs (or was she pushed by Saskia and Imogen?), comes to live in Dora and Nora's basement, and is rechristened Wheelchair in honour of her new invalid status. Once at Bard Road she seems to undergo some sort of a transformation: losing her upper-class tightness, she becomes another bawdy, bardy woman: she asks a grocer 'Have you got anything the shape of a cucumber, my good fellow?' But her transformation isn't only psychological. Rather like Flann O'Brien's bicyclists, or one of Bruno Schulz's fabulous creatures, Lynde passes through a 'migration of forms'[26] – the woman becomes her wheelchair, or at least, they become a part of one another. Welded together they now, like twins, contain something of the other's personality. After a breakfast of bacon, Dora describes Wheelchair as 'nicely greased'.

All these women, and Dora too, have elements of carnival in them, but none of them personifies it as Peregrine does. Perhaps this has something to do with carnival's relationship to order. Carter has argued that in the 'real' world, 'to be a woman is to be in drag'.[27] If in the carnival world, by putting on masks and being other than what we are, we transgress the order of the 'real' world, then what does this play-acting mean for women who, in the 'real' world, *already* exist in a duplicitous state of affectation? The idea of carnival seems to presuppose a monistic world: the experience of femininity contradicts this, implying that the 'real' world is itself a place of diversity, of masks and deception.

We can understand better the idea of carnival being both licensed and illicit if we see how masculinity operates within it. In *Wise Children* the anarchic solipsism of carnival allows a forty-year-old man (Peregrine) to seduce/rape a thirteen-year-old girl (Dora). It could be argued that patriarchy relies upon such masculine transgression of order as a reminder and a symbol of the very force which shores it up. This is what Carter seems to be saying in *Wise Children* about the function of war in society: that patriarchy legitimates the violent disorders of war in order to sustain itself. Attractive as carnival's disorder can be to women who have been trapped by patriarchy, when women become the object of this disorder – as they are in war, or in rape, or in 'kiddiporn' – then the idea of carnival becomes much more problematic for them, and their relation to it becomes an inevitably ambivalent one: as with Estella and Saskia, carnival is as likely to defeat women as it is to bring down order.

IX BRINGING THE HOUSE DOWN

Nora and I were well content. We'd finally wormed our way into the heart of the family we'd always wanted to be part of. They'd asked us on the stage and let us join in, legit. at last. There was a house we all had in common and it was called the past, even though we'd lived in different rooms.

(p. 226)

At the end of *Wise Children*, when Dora and Perry are having sex for the last time ('you remember the last time just like you remember the first'), Dora fantasises about what it would be like to bring the house down, to fuck it away in some glorious carnival orgy of destruction. She toys with the idea, sensing the excitement of exerting such eradicating (warlike) power. In the end, though, Dora decides that this is not something she wants to do, because although her historical house has sometimes been a painful place to live in, a place from which people have tried to eject her, it is also where her history, her story, lies. Bastard that Dora is, this is a house that she has built, too. (That the house is a metaphor for the literary canon is quite clear. Should those left outside trash the house of fiction, or try to renovate it?)

For all Dora's carnivalesque enthusiasm, and despite her part in conjuring the fantasy world of illusion, of having lived amidst the 'bruising dew-drops', she's always able to tell the difference between what is real and fake, between what is tragedy (untimely death) and what isn't (a broken heart). In an interview in 1984,[28] Angela Carter said that she was essentially 'an old-fashioned feminist'; her preoccupations were with the material condition of women: 'abortion law, access to further education, equal rights and the position of black women'. On pornography she said: 'I don't think it's nearly as damaging as the effects of the capitalist system.' Dora, too, is of this materialist persuasion:

> wars are facts we cannot fuck away, Perry; nor laugh away either.
> Do you hear me, Perry?
> No.
>
> (p. 221)

Perry cannot hear Dora because at some level the irrational, possibilising, illusion-making carnivaler cannot entertain the ordered, hard 'real world'. But just as Dora would not throw away the historical house of order, she would not banish the chaos of the carnival either. Because it seems to her 'as if fucking itself were the origin of illusion', and in this carnival world of illusion – in fucking, laughter and art – there is the possibility to *conceive* of the world differently, to break down the old. There are 'limits to the power of laughter' – the carnival can't rewrite history, undo the effects of war or alter what is happening on the 'news'. And there is no transcendence possible in life, Carter tells us, from the materiality of the moment, from the facts of oppression and war. But carnival does offer us the tantalising promise of how things might be in a future moment, if we altered the conditions which tie us down. It is only the carnival which can give us such imagined possibilities, which is why the creative things that make it up in life are so precious: laughter, sex and art.

Dora's art reports from both sides of the tracks, chronicling a history of exclusion and opposition, but also of wrong-sided exuberance. She ends her story, and her day, with Gareth's new babies, pocketed deep inside the folds of Perry's greatcoat (carnival bringing newness into the world). As ever in the dialectical Hazard/Chance family, they turn out to be twins, but this time the old sexual divisions are broken, for this latest double-act signals a change of direction – these wise children are 'boy and girl, a new thing in our family'. And who knows where such a strange combination might lead? With this challenge, Angela Carter signed off. Leaving the reader, in the best Bakhtinian fashion, holding the babies. But if we attend, we can hear her out there riding Dora's wind: 'What a wind! Whooping and banging all along the street ... The kind of wind that gets into the blood and drives you wild. Wild.' Listen, wise children, can't you hear her shouting to us: 'What a joy it is to dance and sing!'

From *Flesh and the Mirror: Essays in the Art of Angela Carter*, ed. Lorna Sage (London, 1994), pp. 279–307.

NOTES

[Kate Webb's essay analyses *Wise Children*'s conjugations of class and culture, its questions of cultural domination and British imperialism, capitalism and patriarchy, its challenges to hegemony. (Hegemony is an important term in certain forms of Marxism, denoting the political predominance of one class/race over others, including how one sees the world and social/cultural relationships.) Webb draws on a number of theoretical ideas which are important in cultural analysis: postcolonial theories (the relationship to imperialist culture, the resistance to being made 'other' by that culture, ideas of hybridity, the notion of 'writing back' to the dominant powers); Foucault on the persistence of dualistic power structures and their discourses; and Bakhtin, both for ideas about dialogic relations between text and reader, and, with important reservations in respect of its effect on women, his idea of carnival where popular humour may overturn, albeit temporarily, established hierarchies and the authority of official culture. Ed.]

1. Spring 1993.

2. Angela Carter, *Wise Children* (London, 1992), p. 19.

3. If this seems rather too schematising a response, then I call in my defence Carter herself, who often iterated the idea that she intended her fiction to have direct political meaning: 'My characters always have a tendency to be telling you something' (*Omnibus*, BBC1, 16 September 1992); 'in the end my ambition is rather an eighteenth-century "Enlightenment" one – to write fiction that entertains and, in a sense, instructs' (Lorna Sage, *Contemporary Writers: Angela Carter* [London, 1990]); 'I believe that all myths are products of the human mind and reflect only aspects of material human

practice. I'm in the demythologising business' (Angela Carter, 'Notes from the Front Line', in *On Gender and Writing*, ed. Michelene Wandor [London, 1983], p. 71).

4. Carter, *Omnibus*.

5. 'All art is political and so is mine. I want readers to understand what it is that I mean by my stories' (unpublished interview with Kate Webb, 18 December 1985).

6. Martin Amis, *Other People* (Harmondsworth, 1981).

7. Carter, 'Notes from the Front Line', p. 73.

8. Salman Rushdie, 'Eating the Eggs of Love', in *The Jaguar Smile* (London, 1987).

9. Interview with Mary Harron: 'I'm a Socialist, Damn It! How Can You Expect Me To Be Interested in Fairies?', *Guardian*, 25 September 1984, p. 10.

10. Edward Said, *Culture and Imperialism* (London, 1993).

11. Foucault makes this argument in many of his works. It is a particularly strong theme of *Discipline and Punish: The Birth of the Prison*, trans. Alan Sheridan (Harmondsworth, 1979), and *The History of Sexuality*, vol. 1, trans. Robert Hurley (Harmondsworth, 1979).

12. Carter, *Omnibus*.

13. Sage, *Contemporary Writers*.

14. Carter gets the wheel of fate into the novel by having Tristram spin a wheel (of fortune) on his s/m game show.

15. This is an idea which permeates all of R. D. Laing's work, but is the cornerstone of *The Divided Self: An Existential Study in Sanity and Madness* (Harmondsworth, 1965).

16. It would take another full essay to delineate all the Freudian and Shakespearian connections in *Wise Children*. Here, I am just trying to indicate the extent to which they penetrate the novel.

17. Angela Carter died of cancer on 16 February 1992.

18. Mikhail Bakhtin's work on carnival is to be found in *Rabelais and His World*, trans. H. Iswolsky (Bloomington, IN, 1984); *Problems of Dostoevski's Poetics*, trans. Caryl Emerson (Manchester, 1984); and *The Dialogic Imagination: Four Essays*, ed. Michael Holquist, trans. Caryl Emerson and Michael Holquist (Austin, TX, 1981).

19. Sage, *Contemporary Writers*.

20. There is a pub called the Coach and Horses on Clapham Road, equidistant from where Angela Carter lived in Clapham and the road

where we might suppose that Dora lives in Brixton. Not Bard Road, of course (this is Carter's invention), but Shakespeare Road, which – with Milton Road, Spenser Road and Chaucer Road – runs off Railton Road and parallel to Coldharbour Lane. Coldharbour Lane was the place known traditionally for providing digs to the theatrical profession: it is there that Marilyn Monroe's showgirl lives in the film *The Prince and the Showgirl*. Railton Road was the heart of the area known as the 'Front Line' before the riots of 1981 and 1983, after which Lambeth Council knocked half of it down. When, later in the novel, Dora says that she prefers the heat of Railton Road at half-past twelve on a Saturday night to the freezing country house of Melchior's first wife, she is both making a political statement – choosing the culture of the colonised over that of the empire-builders – and talking about the relative culture of these two groups. At Lady Lynde's house, she is offered lousy food and a cold bed. On a Saturday night on Railton Road, Dora would have found blues parties, booze and many other people who felt 'What a joy it is to dance and sing!'

21. Kenneth Anger, *Hollywood Babylon* (San Francisco, CA, 1975).

22. Sage, *Contemporary Writers*.

23. Sandra M. Gilbert and Susan Gubar, *The Madwoman in the Attic: The Woman Writer and the Nineteenth-Century Literary Imagination* (New Haven, CT, 1979), pp. 3–11.

24. Jane Miller, *Seductions: Studies in Reading and Culture* (London, 1990), pp. 139–50.

25. I'm thinking here in particular of the New Historicist writing on Shakespeare, and of Linda Hutcheon's *A Theory of Parody: The Teachings of Twentieth-Century Art Forms* (London, 1985).

26. Bruno Schulz, *Sanatorium Under the Sign of the Hourglass* (London, 1980).

27. Carter, *Omnibus*.

28. Mary Harron, 'I'm a Socialist'.

Further Reading

Angela Carter's critics certainly don't fit themselves into neat critical boxes – and are arguably the better for this. What follows is an attempt to group some interesting criticism of her work into a few broad categories. These categories do not necessarily indicate that a specific critical approach has been taken by all these commentators; rather, these approaches and theoretical positions are often the subject of inquiry and the commentators may ask questions (either overtly or by implication) about those approaches. Obviously my categories overlap, and a number of items of criticism could be assigned to more than one.

These groupings are preceded, firstly, by a selection of some of the fascinating interviews given by Carter, and secondly, by a list of all full-length critical works entirely devoted to her writings. These are packed with material and wide-ranging in their choice of texts and concerns, and are essential reading. Where appropriate, pieces from the two books of collected essays are also cited in the groupings which then follow.

INTERVIEWS

Scott Bradfield, 'Remembering Angela Carter', *Review of Contemporary Fiction*, 14:3 (1994), 90–3.

Alex R. Falzon, 'Interview: Angela Carter', *European English Messenger*, 3:1 (1994), 18–22.

John Haffenden, *Novelists in Interview* (London: Methuen, 1985), pp. 76–96.

Mary Harron, 'I'm a Socialist, Damn it! How Can You Expect Me To Be Interested in Fairies?', *Guardian*, 25 September 1984, 10.

Kerryn Goldsworthy, 'Interview: Angela Carter', *Meanjin*, 44:1 (1985), 4–13.

Anna Katsavos, 'An Interview with Angela Carter', *Review of Contemporary Fiction*, 14:3 (1994), 11–17.

Lorna Sage, 'The Savage Sideshow', *New Review* 4/39–40 (July 1977), 51–7.

Lorna Sage, 'Angela Carter Interviewed by Lorna Sage', *New Writing*, ed. Malcolm Bradbury and Judith Cooke (London: Minerva Press, 1992), pp. 185–93.

Anne Smith, 'Myths and the Erotic', *Women's Review*, 1 (November 1985), 28–9.

Helen Cagney Watts, 'An Interview with Angela Carter', *Bête Noire* (August, 1985), 161–76.

For a longer list of interviews, profiles and obituaries, see Lorna Sage, *Angela Carter* (Plymouth: Northcote House, 1994), pp. 69–70.

MONOGRAPHS AND COLLECTIONS OF ESSAYS

Joseph Bristow and Trev Lynn Broughton (eds), *The Infernal Desires of Angela Carter: Fiction, Femininity, Feminism* (London: Longman, 1997).
Aidan Day, *Angela Carter: The Rational Glass* (Manchester: Manchester University Press, 1998).
Sarah Gamble, *Angela Carter: Writing from the Front Line* (Edinburgh: Edinburgh University Press, 1997).
Linden Peach, *Angela Carter* (Basingstoke: Macmillan, 1998).
Lorna Sage, *Angela Carter* (Plymouth: Northcote House, 1994).
Lorna Sage (ed.), *Flesh and the Mirror: Essays on the Art of Angela Carter* (London: Virago, 1994).

See also Lorna Sage, *Women in the House of Fiction: Post-War Women Novelists* (Basingstoke: Macmillan, 1992), pp. 168–77.

FEMINIST POLITICS OF (RE)WRITING AND READING

Lucie Armitt, 'The Fragile Frames of *The Bloody Chamber*', in *The Infernal Desires of Angela Carter*, ed. Bristow and Broughton, pp. 88–99.
Nanette Atevers, 'Gender Matters in *The Sadeian Woman*', *Review of Contemporary Fiction*, 14:3 (1994), 18–23.
Sylvia Bryant, 'Re-Constructing Oedipus Through "Beauty and the Beast"', *Criticism*, 31:4 (1989), 439–53.
Robert Clark, 'Angela Carter's Desire Machines', *Women's Studies*, 14 (1987), 146–61.
Patricia Duncker, 'Re-Imagining the Fairy Tales: Angela Carter's Bloody Chambers', *Literature and History*, 10 (1984), 3–14.
Patricia Duncker, 'Queer Gothic: Angela Carter and the Lost Narratives of Sexual Subversion', *Critical Survey*, 8:1 (1996), 58–68.
Elaine Jordan, 'The Dangers of Angela Carter', in *New Feminist Discourses: Critical Essays on Theories and Texts*, ed. Isobel Armstrong (London; Routledge, 1992), pp. 119–31.
Elaine Jordan, 'The Dangerous Edge', in *Flesh and the Mirror*, ed. Sage, pp. 189–215.
Elaine Jordan, 'Enthralment: Angela Carter's Speculative Fictions', in *Plotting Change: Contemporary Women's Fiction*, ed. Linda Anderson (London: Edward Arnold, 1990), pp. 18–40.
Susanne Kappeler, 'Problem 10: Playing in the Literary Sanctuary', *The Pornography of Representation* (London: Polity Press, 1986), pp. 133–47.
Hermione Lee, '"A Room of One's Own, or a Bloody Chamber?": Angela Carter and Political Correctness', in *Flesh and the Mirror*, ed. Sage, pp. 308–20.

Avis Lewellan, 'Wayward Girls but Wicked Women?: Female Sexuality in Angela Carter's *The Bloody Chamber*', in *Perspectives on Pornography: Sexuality in Film and Literature*, ed. Gary Day and Clive Bloom (Basingstoke: Macmillan, 1988), pp. 144–58.

Merja Makinen, 'Sexual and Textual Aggression in *The Sadeian Woman* and *The Passion of New Eve*', in *The Infernal Desires of Angela Carter*, ed. Bristow and Broughton, pp. 149–65.

Paulina Palmer, 'From "Coded Mannequin" to Bird Woman: Angela Carter's Magic Flight', in *Women Reading Women's Writing*, ed. Sue Roe (Brighton: Harvester, 1987), pp. 179–205.

Ellen Cronan Rose, 'Through the Looking Glass: When Women Tell Fairy Tales', in *The Voyage In: Fictions of Female Development*, ed. Elizabeth Abel et al. (Hanover, NH: University Press of New England, 1983), pp. 209–27.

Robin Sheets, 'Pornography, Fairy Tales, and Feminism: Angela Carter's "The Bloody Chamber"', *Journal of the History of Sexuality*, 1:4 (1991), 633–57.

Gina Wisker, 'Revenge of the Living Doll: Angela Carter's Horror Writing', in *The Infernal Desires of Angela Carter*, ed. Bristow and Broughton, pp. 116–31.

For further material, see also the section on Postmodernism below. See also Harriet Kramer Linkin, 'Isn't It Romantic?' (in the Intertextuality section); and Stephen Benson, 'Stories of Love and Death' (in the Formal/Generic Questions section).

INTERTEXTUALITIES AND HISTORICIST STUDIES

Isobel Armstrong, 'Woolf by the Lake, Woolf at the Circus: Carter and Tradition', in *Flesh and the Mirror*, ed. Sage, pp. 279–307.

Kate Chedgzoy, 'The (Pregnant) Prince and the Showgirl: Cultural Legitimacy and the Reproduction of *Hamlet*', in *New Essays on* Hamlet, ed. Mark Thornton Burnett and John Manning (New York: AMS Press, 1994), pp. 249–72.

Peter Christensen, 'The Hoffmann Connection: Demystification in Angela Carter's *The Infernal Desire Machines of Dr Hoffman*', *Review of Contemporary Fiction*, 14:3 (1994), 63–70.

Mary Kaiser, 'Fairy Tale as Sexual Allegory: Intertextuality in Angela Carter's *The Bloody Chamber*', *Review of Contemporary Fiction*, 14:3 (1994), 30–5.

Harriet Kramer Linkin, 'Isn't it Romantic?: Angela Carter's Bloody Revision of the Romantic Aesthetic in "The Erl-King"', *Contemporary Literature*, 35:2 (1994), 305–23.

Marc O'Day, '"Mutability is Having a Field Day": The Sixties Aura of Angela Carter's Bristol Trilogy', in *Flesh and the Mirror*, ed. Sage, pp. 24–59.

Sue Roe, 'The Disorder of *Love*: Angela Carter's Surrealist Collage', in *Flesh and the Mirror*, ed. Sage, pp. 60–97.

Patricia Juliana Smith, 'All You Need Is Love: Angela Carter's Novel of Sixties Sex and Sensibility', *Review of Contemporary Fiction*, 14:3 (1994), 24–9.

Carolyn Steedman, 'New Time: Mignon and Her Meanings', in *Fin de Siècle/Fin du Globe: Fears and Fantasies of the Late Nineteenth Century*, ed. John Stokes (New York: St. Martin's Press, 1992), pp. 102–16.

Susan Rubin Suleiman, 'The Fate of the Surrealist Imagination in the Society of the Spectacle', in *Flesh and the Mirror*, ed. Sage, pp. 98–116.

See also the section on the Politics of (Re)Writing and Reading, in particular Patricia Duncker, 'Queer Gothic'; and Gerardine Meaney, '(Un)Like Subjects' in French Feminisms section.

FORMAL/GENERIC QUESTIONS

Lucie Armitt, 'The Fragile Frames of *The Bloody Chamber*', in *The Infernal Desires of Angela Carter*, ed. Bristow and Broughton, pp. 88–99.

Sarah Bannock, 'Auto/Biographical Souvenirs in *Nights at the Circus*', in *The Infernal Desires of Angela Carter*, ed. Bristow and Broughton, pp. 198–215.

Stephen Benson, 'Stories of Love and Death: Reading and Writing the Fairy Tale Romance', in *Image and Power: Women in Fiction in the Twentieth Century*, ed. Sarah Sceats and Gail Cunningham (London: Longman, 1996), pp. 103–13.

Clare Hanson, 'Each Other: Images of Otherness in the Short Fiction of Doris Lessing, Jean Rhys and Angela Carter', *Journal of the Short Story in English*, 10 (1988), 67–82.

Alison Lee, 'Angela Carter's New Eve(lyn): De/En-Gendering Narrative', in *Ambiguous Discourse: Feminist Narratology and British Women Writers*, ed. Kathy Mezei (Chapel Hill, NC: University of North Carolina Press, 1996), pp. 238–49.

Elisabeth Mahoney, '"But Elsewhere?": The Future of Fantasy in *Heroes and Villains*', in *The Infernal Desires of Angela Carter*, ed. Bristow and Broughton, pp. 73–87.

Colin Manlove, 'In the Demythologising Business: Angela Carter's *The Infernal Desire Machines of Doctor Hoffman* (1972)', in *Twentieth-Century Fantasists: Essays on Culture, Society and Belief in Twentieth-Century Mythopoeic Literature*, ed. Kath Filmer (New York: St. Martin's Press, 1992), pp. 148–60.

David Punter, 'Essential Imaginings: The Novels of Angela Carter and Russel Hoban', in *The British and Irish Novel Since 1960*, ed. James Acheson (Basingstoke: Macmillan, 1991), pp. 142–58.

Marina Warner, 'Angela Carter: Bottle Blonde, Double Drag', in *Flesh and the Mirror*, ed. Sage, pp. 243–56.

See also the section on Postmodernism, and the section on Intertextualities.

FREUDIAN PSYCHOANALYSIS; FILM STUDIES

Maggie Anwell, 'Lolita Meets the Werewolf: *The Company of Wolves*', in *The Female Gaze: Women as Viewers of Popular Culture*, ed. Lorraine Gamman and Margaret Marshment (London: Women's Press, 1988), pp. 76–85.

John Collick, 'Wolves Through the Window: Writing Dreams/Dreaming Films/Filming Dreams', *Critical Survey*, 3:3 (1991), 283–9.

Catherine Lappas, '"Seeing is Believing, But Touching is the Truth": Female Spectatorship and Sexuality in *The Company of Wolves*', *Women's Studies*, 25 (1996), 115–35.

Laura Mulvey, 'Cinema Magic and Old Monsters: Angela Carter's Cinema', in *Flesh and the Mirror*, ed. Sage, pp. 230–42.

Linda Ruth Williams, 'Writing at Play: Fantasy and Identity in Angela Carter', in *Critical Desire: Psychoanalysis and the Literary Subject* (London: Edward Arnold, 1995), pp. 90–124.

FRENCH FEMINISMS

Nicole Ward Jouve, '"Mother is a Figure of Speech"', in *Flesh and the Mirror*, ed. Sage, pp. 136–70.

Gerardine Meaney, '(Un)Like Subjects', *(Un)Like Subjects: Women, Theory, Fiction* (London: Routledge, 1993), pp. 121–60.

Phil Powrie, 'Angela Carter/Chantal Chawaf: Rewriting the Domestic', *New Comparison*, 11(1991), 127–36.

Roberta Rubenstein, 'Intersexions: Gender Metamorphosis in Angela Carter's *The Passion of New Eve* and Lois Gould's *A Sea Change*', *Tulsa Studies in Women's Literature*, 12:1 (1993), 103–18.

See also the section on Poststructuralism.

QUESTIONS ON DECONSTRUCTION, POSTMODERNISM AND POSTSTRUCTURALISM

Beth A. Boehm, 'Feminist Metafiction and Androcentric Reading Strategies: Angela Carter's Reconstructed Reader in *Nights at the Circus*', *Critique*, 37:1 (1995), 35–49.

Michael Hardin, 'The Other Other: Self-Definition Outside Patriarchal Institutions in Angela Carter's *Wise Children*', *Review of Contemporary Fiction*, 14:3 (1994), 77–83.

Elaine Jordan, 'Down the Road, or History Rehearsed', in *Postmodernism and the Re-Reading of Modernity*, ed. Francis Barker et al. (Manchester: Manchester University Press, 1992), pp. 159–79.

Magali Cornier Michael, 'Angela Carter's *Nights at the Circus*: An Engaged Feminism Via Subversive Postmodern Strategies', *Contemporary Literature*, 35:3 (1994), 492–521.

David Punter, 'Angela Carter: Supersessions of the Masculine', in *The Hidden Script: Writing and the Unconscious* (London: Routledge, 1985), pp. 28–42.

Sally Robinson, 'Angela Carter and the Circus of Theory', in *Engendering the Subject: Gender and Self-Representation in Contemporary Women's*

Fiction (Albany: State University of New York Press, 1991), pp. 77–134. [Reprinted only in part in this volume.]

Ricarda Schmidt, 'The Journey of the Subject in Angela Carter's Fiction', *Textual Practice*, 3 (1989), 56–75.

Susan Squier, 'Representing the Reproductive Body', *Meridian* 12:1 (1993), 29–45.

Robert Rawdon Wilson, 'SLIP PAGE: Angela Carter, In/Out/In the Post-Modern Nexus', in *Past the Last Post: Theorizing Post-Colonialism and Post-Modernism*, ed. Ian Adam and Helen Tiffin (Hemel Hempstead: Harvester, 1991), pp. 109–24.

ON GENDER AS PERFORMANCE; TRANSGRESSIVE SEXUALITIES

Clare Hanson, '"The Red Dawn Breaking Over Clapham": Carter and the Limits of Artifice', in *The Infernal Desires of Angela Carter*, ed. Bristow and Broughton, pp. 59–72.

Heather Johnson, 'Unexpected Geometries: Transgressive Symbolism and the Transsexual Subject in Angela Carter's *The Passion of New Eve*', in *The Infernal Desires of Angela Carter*, ed. Bristow and Broughton, pp. 166–84.

Paul Magrs, 'Boys Keep Swinging: Angela Carter and the Subject of Men', in *The Infernal Desires of Angela Carter*, ed. Bristow and Broughton, pp. 184–97.

Paulina Palmer, 'Gender as Performance in the Fiction of Angela Carter and Margaret Atwood', in *The Infernal Desires of Angela Carter*, ed. Bristow and Broughton, pp. 24–42.

CARNIVAL, SPECTACLE AND POWER: BAKHTIN, FOUCAULT, BATAILLE, BAUDRILLARD

Lucie Armitt, 'Changing the Narrative Subject: Carroll's *Alices* and Carter's *The Passion of New Eve*', in her *Theorising the Fantastic* (London: Edward Arnold, 1996), pp. 150–82.

Joanne M. Gass, 'Panopticism in *Nights at the Circus*', *Review of Contemporary Fiction*, 14:3 (1994), 71–6.

Clare Hanson, '"The Red Dawn Breaking Over Clapham": Carter and the Limits of Artifice', in *The Infernal Desires of Angela Carter*, ed. Bristow and Broughton, pp. 59–72.

Sarah Sceats, 'Eating the Evidence: Women, Power and Food', in *Image and Power: Women in Fiction in the Twentieth* Century, ed. Sarah Sceats and Gail Cunningham (London: Longman, 1996), pp. 117–27.

Sarah Sceats, 'The Infernal Appetites of Angela Carter', in *The Infernal Desires of Angela Carter*, ed. Bristow and Broughton, pp. 100–15.

See also Paulina Palmer, 'From "Coded Mannequin" to Bird Woman' in the Feminist Politics of (Re)Writing section; and Susan Rubin Suleiman, 'The Fate of the Surrealist Imagination in the Society of the Spectacle', in the Intertextualities section.

Notes on Contributors

Christina Britzolakis is Lecturer in English and American literature at the University of Warwick. She is author of *Sylvia Plath and the Theatre of Mourning* (1999), and has published articles on modernist poetry and fiction.

Heather Johnson is currently completing a book-length study of gothic iconography in contemporary women's writing, and is co-editor of a collection on the 'posthuman' in twentieth-century literature. She has written on Carter, Plath, and female Surrealist painters. Having been a tutor at the University of Edinburgh for several years, she is now teaching courses on modern literature in Dublin.

Sally Keenan is Lecturer in English at the University of Southampton New College. Her research interests include contemporary women's writing, and feminist and post-colonial theory. She has published essays on Toni Morrison and Angela Carter.

Merja Makinen is Principal Lecturer in English Literary Studies at Middlesex University. She is author of *Joyce Cary: A Descriptive Bibliography* (1989) and co-author, with Lorraine Gamman, of *Female Fetishism: A New Look* (1994). She has published a number of chapters on Angela Carter, and latterly on gender issues in detective fiction. She is currently working on a book examining feminist attempts to re-appropriate a range of popular fiction genres.

Jill Matus is Associate Professor of English at the University of Toronto. She is author of *Unstable Bodies: Victorian Representations of Sexuality and Maternity* (1995) and *Toni Morrison* (1998). She has also published essays on literary theory, Victorian travel writing, George Eliot, sensation fiction, and contemporary writers such as Angela Carter and Gloria Naylor.

Gerardine Meaney is author of *(Un)Like Subjects: Women, Theory, Fiction* (1993) which examines the shared preoccupations of contemporary feminist theory and contemporary fiction by women. She has also written extensively on gender and culture in Ireland. She is currently Director of the Centre for Film Studies at University College Dublin.

Sally Robinson is Assistant Professor of English and Women's Studies at the University of Michigan, Ann Arbor. In addition to *Engendering the Reader*, from which the Casebook essay is drawn, she has pubished articles on fiction, feminist theory, and film and is currently completing a book on representations of wounded white men in post-liberationist American culture.

Mary Russo is Dean of the School of Humanities, Arts and Cultural Studies and Professor of literature and cultural theory at Hampshire College. She has published widely in the fields of European culture, semiotics, cultural studies and feminist studies. In addition to her book, *The Female Grotesque: Risk, Excess, and Modernity* (1994), she has co-edited *Nationalism and Sexualities* (1992) and *Revisioning Italy: National Identity and Global Culture* (1997).

Kate Webb lectures part-time in English Literature at the University of East Anglia. She is finishing a PhD on *I'm Dying Laughing*, Christina Stead's novel about Hollywood Communist renegades. Angela Carter was a family friend.

Jean Wyatt is Professor of English at Occidental College, Los Angeles. She is author of *Reconstructing Desire: The Role of the Unconscious in Women's Reading and Writing* (1990). Most recently she has published essays on Toni Morrison, Sandra Cisneros, and Margaret Atwood. She is working on a book on identification in contemporary novels by English and American women.

Index